Making the Financial System Sustainable

The EU Action Plan on Financing Sustainable Growth is the most advanced and comprehensive policy agenda on sustainability in the world. But is it going in the right direction? Acting as a bridge between policy and academia, this up-to-date contribution to the global policy debate brings together some of the leading experts from the European Commission's High-Level Expert Group on Sustainable Finance, to discuss how the financial system needs to be reformed to promote sustainability. Finance has long been criticised for being short-term focused and concerned with maximising returns to intermediaries, rather than with the interests of savers and borrowers. The financial system must now take into account environmental, social and governance considerations to support a sustainable economy and this volume offers new insights on the way forward. Essential reading for anyone working on financial sector policy and sustainability.

PAUL G. FISHER is a Fellow at the Cambridge Institute for Sustainability Leadership.

Making the Financial System Sustainable

Edited by

PAUL G. FISHER

University of Cambridge Institute for Sustainability Leadership.

CAMBRIDGE
UNIVERSITY PRESS

CAMBRIDGE
UNIVERSITY PRESS

University Printing House, Cambridge CB2 8BS, United Kingdom

One Liberty Plaza, 20th Floor, New York, NY 10006, USA

477 Williamstown Road, Port Melbourne, VIC 3207, Australia

314–321, 3rd Floor, Plot 3, Splendor Forum, Jasola District Centre, New Delhi – 110025, India

79 Anson Road, #06-04/06, Singapore 079906

Cambridge University Press is part of the University of Cambridge.

It furthers the University's mission by disseminating knowledge in the pursuit of education, learning, and research at the highest international levels of excellence.

www.cambridge.org
Information on this title: www.cambridge.org/9781108842297
DOI: 10.1017/9781108908269

© Cambridge University Press 2021

First published 2021

A catalogue record for this publication is available from the British Library.

Library of Congress Cataloging-in-Publication Data
Names: Fisher, Paul G. (Paul Gregory), editor.
Title: Making the financial system sustainable / edited by Paul G. Fisher.
Description: Cambridge, United Kingdom ; New York, NY : Cambridge University Press, 2020.
| Includes bibliographical references and index. | Summary: The EU Action Plan on Financing Sustainable Growth is the most advanced and comprehensive policy agenda on sustainability in the world. But is it going in the right direction? Acting as a bridge between policy and academia, this up-to-date contribution to the global policy debate brings together some of the leading experts from the European Commission's High-Level Expert Group on Sustainable Finance, to discuss how the financial system needs to be reformed to promote sustainability. Finance has long been criticized for being short-term focused and concerned with maximizing returns to intermediaries, rather than with the interests of savers and borrowers. The financial system must now take into account environmental, social and governance considerations to support a sustainable economy and this volume offers new insights on the way forward. A must-read for anyone working on financial sector policy and sustainability.
Identifiers: LCCN 2020013359 (print) | LCCN 2020013360 (ebook) | ISBN 9781108842297 (hardback) | ISBN 9781108827560 (paperback) | ISBN 9781108908269 (epub)
Subjects: LCSH: Finance–Environmental aspects. | Capitalism–Environmental aspects. | Economic development–Environmental aspects. | Sustainable development.
Classification: LCC HG101 .M35 2020 (print) | LCC HG101 (ebook) | DDC 332–dc23
LC record available at https://lccn.loc.gov/2020013359
LC ebook record available at https://lccn.loc.gov/2020013360

ISBN 978-1-108-84229-7 Hardback

Contents

List of Figures   *page* vii

List of Tables   ix

List of Boxes   x

List of Contributors   xi

Foreword   xx
CHRISTIAN THIMANN

Preface   xxix

Introduction   1
KAJETAN CZYŻ AND PAUL G. FISHER

1 Capitalism Meets Multilateralism   13
PADDY ARBER AND STEVE WAYGOOD

2 Public Meets Private: Sustainable Finance for
   a Sustainable Economy   26
INGRID HOLMES

3 Central Banking and Climate Change   49
KERN ALEXANDER AND PAUL G. FISHER

4 Sustainable Finance and Prudential Regulation of
   Financial Institutions   75
ESKO KIVISAARI

5 Transparency and Accountability Standards for
   Sustainable and Responsible Investments   104
FLAVIA MICILOTTA

v

6 Environmental Risk Analysis by Financial Institutions   122
NINA SEEGA AND ANDREW VOYSEY

7 Sustainable Governance and Leadership   145
CLAUDIA KRUSE AND MICHAEL SCHMIDT

8 ESG Risks and Opportunities: A Fiduciary Duty
Perspective   168
WILL MARTINDALE, ELODIE FELLER AND RORY SULLIVAN

9 Active and Responsible: A Cost-Efficient Model for
Integrating Sustainability   196
MAGNUS BILLING AND CARINA SILBERG

10 Passive-Aggressive or Just Engaged: New Active
Ownership Approaches through Benchmarks   214
DAVID E. HARRIS

11 Financing a Just Transition: How to Connect the
Environmental and Social Dimensions of Structural
Change   237
NICK ROBINS

12 Sustainable Finance for Citizens   258
ANNE-CATHERINE HUSSON-TRAORE

13 Individual Impact Investors: The Silenced Majority   276
STAN DUPRé

14 Strengthening Green Finance by Better Integrating
the Social Dimensions in the European Union's
Sustainable Finance Laws   299
MYRIAM VANDER STICHELE

Index   327

Figures

6.1 An analytical framework for understanding
environmental sources of financial risks   *page* 126

6.2 The focus of the illustrative case studies featured
in this study   132

8.1 The growth in responsible investment regulation
and policy   176

11.1 Reasons for investor action on the just transition   248

11.2 Priorities for investor action on the just transition   250

13.1 The preferences of French and German retail
investors: consulting clients and AGM resolutions   283

13.1a Should end clients be consulted on voting
preferences on climate? Should the preferences be
binding for intermediaries?   283

13.1b Preferred categories of climate resolution for retail
investors   283

13.2 Investment impact   284

13.3 Frequency of investors' environmental impact
claims by sustainable investment products
manufacturers   289

13.4 Compliance of investors' environmental impact
claims made by sustainable investment products
manufacturers   290

13.4a Frequency of problematic claims per MDEC criteria
(in per cent of funds)   290

13.4b Funds categorised based on how deceptive the claims
are (by per cent of funds)   290

13.5 Interpretation of investor impact claims by German
and French consumers   291

13.5a Interpretation of a false claim (green equity fund)   291

13.5b Interpretation of an accurate but ambiguous claim
       (thematic equity fund)   291
13.6   Sustainability investment preferences of French and
       German consumers   292
13.7   French and German consumers for taking action
       on their equity investment   293

Tables

6.1 Illustrative case studies of climate risk
     assessment   *page* 130

8.1 Examples of policy instruments promoting
     sustainable investment by pension funds   177

11.1 Employment implications of the transition: key
      findings   243

11.2 Setting the scope of the just transition: initial
      illustrations   245

12.1 Screening choices   263

12.2 Funds with particular ESG labels   266

Boxes

8.1 Common and civil law   *page* 170
8.2 The traditional fiduciary duties   172
8.3 EU regulation on sustainability-related disclosures in the
    financial services sector   181
8.4 Examples of integrated finance and sustainability policy   184
8.5 Modern fiduciary duty   190
8.6 A legal framework for impact   193
10.1 ESG data types   224
10.2 How ESG data is applied in the index design   227
10.3 Index regulation   228
10.4 Smart sustainability case study   231

Contributors

Kern Alexander holds the Chair in Law and Finance at the University of Zurich, and Director of Studies, Queen's College, University of Cambridge. Publications include *Principles of Banking Regulation* (Cambridge University Press, 2019) and *Brexit and Financial Services* (coauthored with Moloney et al., 2018). Since 2009 he has served as a regulatory and policy adviser to the European Parliament, the G20, and the United Nations Environment Programme. His report, 'Stability and Sustainability in Banking Reform: Are Environmental Risks Missing in Basel III?' (Cambridge, 2014) was the first study of the interrelationship between banking regulation and environmental sustainability. He is the founder of the Research Network for Sustainable Finance.

Paddy Arber is Head of International Government Engagement at Aviva, the United Kingdom's largest insurer and a significant global investor. He leads work across Aviva's insurance and investment arms to develop and advocate policy for market reform that will help build a more sustainable global financial system. His recent work includes contributions to the EU High Level Expert Group on Sustainable Finance and UN Global Investors for Sustainable Development Alliance. Before joining Aviva, Arber worked for the UK Government on international negotiations, including EU finances and the Paris climate change agreement.

Magnus Billing^{**} is the CEO of Alecta and represents Alecta on nomination committees of Swedish A-list companies. Billing was previously the CEO of Nasdaq Nordic and Baltic Markets. Within Nasdaq, he held such positions as Chief Legal Counsel and Senior Vice President. He was a member of the Nasdaq Listing Committee, chair of the Nasdaq Nordic Foundation and served as a member of the Board of Directors of Federation of European Securities Exchanges, Swedish House of Finance and as an alternate director of the Swedish Corporate Governance Code Board of Directors. He is chairman of the Advisory Board at the Stockholm Sustainable Finance Centre.

Kajetan Czyż is a Senior Income G&S Specialist at Baillie Gifford where he leads on sustainability across the income strategies. Previously as Programme Director, Sustainable Finance at the Cambridge Institute for Sustainability Leadership (CISL), he led private sector research and engagement across banking, insurance and investment. A contributor to EU High Level Expert Group, UK Green Finance Task Force and ISO sustainable finance standards. Before CISL, he headed work on securitisation with the UN, developed green bond markets in India and Brazil, and led on green infrastructure at the Climate Bonds Initiative. From 2013 at BMO GAM he worked on the energy transition and represented the EU investment industry at the Paris Climate Summit.

Stan Dupré[**] is founder and CEO of the 2° Investing Initiative, a leading think tank on sustainable finance globally. It is particularly known for having introduced portfolio climate scenario analysis into financial regulation and supervisory practices, as well as into banking and investors voluntary practices. Dupré teaches at Paris Dauphine University. He has authored multiple papers on sustainable finance, including *All Swans Are Black in the Dark, Non-Financial Message in a Bottle* and *Connecting the Dots between Climate Goals, Portfolio Allocation and Financial Regulation*. Before creating 2° Investing Initiative, Dupré was Managing Director of the strategic planning consultancy *Utopies*.

Elodie Feller[*] is the Investment Programme Lead at the UN Environment Programme Finance Initiative (UNEP FI). UNEP FI's activities include research, advocacy, awareness raising, capacity building and the development of guidelines and tools for financial institutions to align investment practices with the Paris Agreement and the Sustainable Development agenda. She leads the Fiduciary Duty in the 21st Century programme, the Task Force on Climate-Related Financial Disclosures Investor Pilot and the Legal Impact Framework project. Feller is a member of the EU Technical Expert Group on Sustainable Finance developing the EU Taxonomy. Previously she worked at Lombard Odier Investment Managers as product specialist and ESG analyst.

Paul G. Fisher[**] (Editor) is a fellow of the Cambridge Institute for Sustainability Leadership. After ten years as an academic at the University of Warwick, he served at the Bank of England for twenty-six years, in a number of senior management positions. He was a member of the Monetary Policy Committee (MPC) and the interim Financial Policy Committee (FPC) (serving as Executive Director for Markets on both) and as the Deputy Head of the Board of the Prudential Regulation Authority (PRA). His current portfolio includes serving as Chair of the London Bullion Market Association; Non-executive Director at the UK Debt Management Office; Visiting Professor at the London Institute of Banking and Finance and at Richmond University, London; and Senior Research Fellow at King's College Business School, London.

David Harris[**] is Head of Sustainable Business, London Stock Exchange Group, where he is responsible for sustainability and green finance integration into service. Harris also leads sustainable investment engagement at FTSE Russell where he led the development of FTSE Russell's sustainable investment index capabilities. He has held a variety of industry positions including Vice Chair of the UK Sustainable Investment and Finance Association (UKSIF) and chaired the UN Sustainable Stock Exchange's Working Group developing Model ESG Reporting Guidance.

Ingrid Holmes is a director at Hermes Investment Management, leading on Hermes Policy and Advocacy. She has more than fifteen years of experience working on environmental policy and sustainable finance issues – with a long-standing interest in climate change. Prior to joining Hermes, Holmes was a director at a sustainable development think tank, had worked in asset management and had been an adviser in the UK Parliament and Government. Holmes has also held several Government advisory roles including as Sherpa to the Green Investment Bank Commission (2010/2011), member of the UK Green Finance Initiative (2016/2018) and running the Secretariat for the Green Finance Taskforce (2017/2018).

Anne-Catherine Husson-Traore is a CEO and cofounder of Novethic, the sustainable transformation accelerator of the Caisse des Dépôts Group. Originally a journalist in the television sector, she became passionate about sustainable finance in 2001 and has since then focused on how to accelerate the transformation of the financial sector and companies towards greater social and environmental responsibility. She participates in many initiatives, speaks at numerous conferences, teaches business school students and continues with journalism. Husson-Traore invests all her energy to enhance, connect and activate the catalysts of sustainable and inclusive performance.

Esko Kivisaari is the Deputy Managing Director of Finance Finland. He was also Immediate Past Chairperson (2019–2020) of the Actuarial Association of Europe (Chairperson 2018–2019), member of the Executive Committee of Insurance Europe, member of the EFRAG European Lab Steering Group and member of the Consultative Expert Group on Digital Ethics in Insurance of the European Insurance and Occupational Pensions Authority (EIOPA). Kivisaari's publications include *Vakuutusoppi* (in Finnish, translated: *Insurance Handbook*) and *Vakuutustalous* (in Finnish, translated: *Insurance Economics*).

Claudia Kruse** is Managing Director Global Responsible Investment & Governance at APG, a fiduciary manager for Dutch pension funds with € 505 bn of assets under management (April 2019). She is part of the management team of the Chief Investment Officer. Kruse is also a board member of the International Corporate Governance Network (ICGN) and co-chair of the Advisory Committee on the UN Sustainable Development Goals of the Principles for Responsible Investment. Before joining APG in April 2009, Kruse worked in London for almost a decade in the investment industry on the buy- and sell-side (JPMorgan).

Will Martindale* is Director of Policy and Research at PRI. Martindale leads PRI's global regulatory affairs and public policy programme, the flagship fiduciary duty project jointly with UNEP FI and the implementation of PRI's sustainable financial system activities in national policy reform. Martindale has a background in banking, joining JPMorgan's graduate programme in June 2004. In September 2010, he joined BNP Paribas, as a business manager for it's credit trading desk.

Flavia Micilotta** leads the sustainability practice of Deloitte in Luxembourg and was previously Director at the Luxembourg Green Exchange, the key stock exchange for listing of green bonds and in that capacity was a member of the EC Technical Expert Group focussed on an EU green bond standard. She is a member of EFRAG's EU Corporate Reporting Lab and of the EIOPA Occupational Pension Stakeholder Group. Micilotta has also been an Executive Director of Eurosif. Previously a sustainability consultant and qualified environmental auditor, she assisted companies to embed sustainability in their business models and go beyond the remits of social and environmental compliance. She was a founding member of the UN Global Compact in Belgium.

Nick Robins* is Professor in Practice for Sustainable Finance at the Grantham Research Institute at the London School of Economics. Previously, Robins was codirector of UNEP's Inquiry into a Sustainable Financial System. Before that, he was Head of the Climate Change Centre of Excellence at HSBC and earlier Head of socially responsible investment funds at Henderson Global Investors. Robins is a cofounder of Carbon Tracker and Planet Tracker and has published widely on business, finance and sustainability, including *The Corporation that Changed the World: How the East India Company Shaped the Modern Multinational* and *Sustainable Investing: The Art of Long-Term Performance.*

Michael Schmidt** is a member of the management board and the Chief Investment Officer of Lloyd Fonds AG. Schmidt is also a board member of DVFA – the German Society of Investment Professionals – and heads its Commission on Corporate Governance & Stewardship. He is a member of the Sustainable Finance Committee of the German Federal Government and a member of the Sustainability Advisory Council at Deutsche Post DHL. In previous roles, Schmidt served on the management boards of Deka Investment and Union Investment for three and six years, respectively. Prior to that, he worked for fourteen years in the asset management division of Deutsche Bank.

Nina Seega is Research Strategy Director, Centre for Sustainable Finance, University of Cambridge Institute for Sustainability Leadership. Seega is an Academic Visitor at the Bank of England and in 2016–2017 she co-led the CISL team serving as Knowledge Partner for the risk analysis track of the G20 Green Finance Study Group. She sits on the Strategic Advisory Board for Sustainable Finance at the British Standards Institute and Advisory Board of the Hughes Hall Climate Change Engagement Centre. Previously,

Seega was the Head of the London Traded Products Desk for Dresdner Kleinwort, responsible for credit risk management of traded products.

Carina Silberg is the Head of Sustainability at Alecta and is responsible for overseeing and advancing Alecta's sustainability work. Silberg represents Alecta in a number of initiatives including Swedish Investors for Sustainable Development (SISD), facilitated by the Swedish International Development Cooperation Agency (Sida). She was previously a member of the Executive Management team at corporate communications advisory firm Hallvarsson & Halvarsson, heading its CSR and sustainability practice with multinational corporate clients. Her other experiences include the role as Senior ESG analyst and Head of Engagement at GES Investment Services (today part of Sustainalytics).

Rory Sullivan is CEO of Chronos Sustainability, Visiting Professor in Practice at the Grantham Research Institute at the London School of Economics, Strategic Advisor to the Principles for Responsible Investment and Chief Technical Advisor to the Transition Pathway Initiative. He is an internationally recognised expert on responsible investment and climate change, with more than thirty years of experience in these and related areas. Previously, he was Head of ESG Research and Standards for FTSE Russell and Head of Responsible Investment at Insight Investment. His publications include *Valuing Corporate Responsibility: How Investors Really Use Corporate Responsibility Information* (Greenleaf, 2011) and *Responsible Investment* (Greenleaf, 2006).

Christian Thimann*** (Foreword) has been the Chair of the EU High-Level Expert Group on Sustainable Finance, while acting as the Head of Strategy and member of the Executive Committee of the AXA Group. He has subsequently advised the European Commission in the area of financial regulation. Prior to that, he worked in executive positions at the European Central Bank, most recently in the role of Director General.

Myriam Vander Stichele˙˙ is a senior researcher at the Centre for Research on Multinational Corporations. Since 1999, she has been researching and publishing about the financial sector from a sustainability and public interest perspective and its integration in trade and investment agreements. She focuses on the EU regulatory process since the 2008 financial crisis Vander Stichele and her publications include *The Missing Dimension – How European Financial Reforms Ignore Developing Countries and Sustainability (2011) and Mobilising the Financial Sector for a Sustainable Future (2015).* supports civil society around the world to promote a sustainable and stable financial sector.

Andrew Voysey is responsible for Strategy and Business Development at Soil Capital, a farm management and independent agronomy firm committed to scaling regenerative agriculture through market solutions via its activities across Europe, Latin America and beyond. Over the previous decade, Voysey built and led the sustainable finance team at the University of Cambridge Institute for Sustainability Leadership, where he retains a senior associate position. He was also an academic visitor at the Bank of England, advising on climate change.

Steve Waygood˙˙ is a member of the CIO Investment Committee at Aviva investors and chairs the ESG Senior Management Team. He founded Aviva Investor's Sustainable Finance Centre for Excellence and also co-founded the Corporate Human Rights Benchmark, the World Benchmarking Alliance and the UN Sustainable Stock Exchange Initiative. Waygood has advised the UK Government, the European Commission, the Financial Stability Board and the UN on the creation of sustainable capital markets. He is Honorary Senior

Visiting Fellow at City University Business School and Senior
Associate at the Cambridge Institute for Sustainability Leadership and
has received awards from Brummell, the Chamber of Commerce, the
City of London, the United Nations Foundation, Yale and Harvard.

*** Chair, EU High-Level Expert Group on Sustainable Finance
** Member, EU High-Level Experts Group on Sustainable Finance
* Observer/observer organisation, EU High-Level Experts Group on
Sustainable Finance

Foreword

Sustainable Finance and the Need for a 'New and Sustainable Globalisation'

by Christian Thimann[1]

Rarely has a topic gained global prominence as fast as has 'Sustainable Finance': the integration of long-term sustainability goals, including climate, into financial decision-making. The aim is to support the economy on a path that maintains employment and welfare in a way that is sustainable in the long-term.

The Paris Agreement, reached at the Conference of the Parties 21 (COP21) on climate change in late 2015, laid the basis for the sustainable finance agenda. For the first time in twenty years of this annual conference, the financial sector was mentioned as playing a role to help bring more investment into decarbonisation. In 2016, a majority of the signatories ratified the agreement at national level and the threshold for global implementation was passed. In 2017, the European Commission launched a High-Level Expert Group on Sustainable Finance, which I had the privilege to chair and whose membership included many contributors to this book, including the editor.

The group presented its report in early 2018, and the European Commission built its Action Plan on Sustainable Finance only a few months later, largely inspired by the group's work. Implementation started whilst the group continued to meet, based on a broad-based recognition of the issue among the financial sector at large as well as the supervisory, and ultimately the central banking community. By the start of 2020, one can safely say that sustainability issues, regarding climate change and other long-term objectives, had been

---

[1] Chair of the EU High-Level Expert Group on Sustainable Finance and Vice-Chair of the FSB Task Force on Climate-related Financial Disclosures (TCFD). Views expressed are personal.

'mainstreamed' in the financial system. From niche to mainstream in less than five years—a remarkable achievement.

The second remarkable aspect about sustainable finance is that it is ultimately science-based, at least when relating to climate change. It is the natural sciences that have measured global warming and sea level rise, qualified and quantified greenhouse gas emissions and developed a metric for the trend in total emissions to keep climate change in check. There are not many instances where the work of the natural sciences has fed into financial regulation as rigorously as for climate change.

With great prominence comes great responsibility. It is a huge task to finance the transformation of the global economy towards lower emissions and generally a much more environmentally responsible functioning. The implications go far beyond the energy and even the transportation sectors; a far-reaching decline in global CO_2 emissions will only be possible if there is change along the entire process in which goods are produced, transported, consumed and disposed of in the global economy.

We will soon realise that the biggest 'climate killer' is not coal, as is sometimes postulated, but the way in which globalisation has been pursued. The globalisation that we have witnessed over the past three decades has incurred a shift of production towards geographical areas with weaker environmental and social standards; it has also pushed to the extreme the focus on maximising the profits from consumption through low production costs with disregard to all areas of sustainability; and it has led to an astronomic rise in global transportation of all sorts: people, raw materials, unfinished goods and finished goods, creating massive emissions, pollution and environmental damage.

The environmental damage is most visible in the emerging economies where a large share of the production destined for final consumption in developed markets has been located; this has been a high price to pay for the income rise in these economies. And western Europe has witnessed the social damage of this globalisation in terms of structural unemployment and desertification of entire regions – think of Southern Italy, many regions of France, Northern England or Eastern Germany, to name just a few.

At the same time, however, this globalisation has boosted economic development in emerging markets in a speed and breadth never seen before. This is the positive side of globalisation, and this is also why the solution cannot consist of backtracking on globalisation as such. The solution cannot be protectionism or autarky; the solution is a *different globalisation* as suggested below.

To correct some of these trends and arrive at a sustainable manner of global production and consumption will be a herculean task, for European policy makers and others alike. Europe has much to gain from taking sustainability seriously but could also lose on both environmental and other economic grounds if the process is not well handled. The following paragraphs explain the reasoning.

* * *

Sustainable finance is, first of all, a call on the financial sector itself to change its functioning away from a short-term focus towards a long-term orientation. Financial speculation, short-term profit extraction, betting on (and hence forcing) corporate distress by way of short-selling, must be brought in check much more resolutely than has been the case so far. There are too many pockets in the financial system that are on a monthly, quarterly or annual performance cycle and push the real economy towards similar performance cycles. We cannot build a long-term future while focusing on swings in quarterly earnings. And none of the new ESG-disclosures demanded from the real economy will help if the financial sector is unable to process them properly.

The changes towards sustainability and long-term orientation are necessary in particular for the structure and functioning of financial markets; specifically, the stock market and corporate bond market. There is far too much short-term profit seeking in trading of stocks and long-term bonds. The market economy does not need stock prices changing by the minute or by the nano-second. It may even be seen as unethical to trade people's jobs by the minute and pretend that the value of a corporation with tens of thousands of employees should be re-priced several hundred times per day. In economic terms, such price fluctuations are meaningless, and for sustainability they are poisonous. In contrast, much less change is necessary as regards banking, insurance or pension funds as these institutions in Europe are already today strongly focused on the real economy and on long-term welfare generation.

* * *

For the European economy, three issues must be kept in mind.

First, global CO_2-emission targets are science-based, but national targets are not, and neither is the European Union (EU) target. National targets and the EU target are the outcome of negotiations that took place in Paris. Here, the EU and its Member States promised a much deeper decline in emissions – namely of 40% over a few decades – than other developed economies (for example, the US promised only a 10-15% cut before stepping out of the Paris agreement altogether). China will continue to increase CO_2 emissions until at least 2030. The EU must remember that great ambition comes with great risks, because such an emissions reduction is not possible with today's technologies other than through a massive cut in European economic activity, which would have huge and possibly unsustainable consequences. The EU emissions reduction path is only economically and socially sustainable if it remains open to new technologies, while keeping jobs and production in Europe.

Second, the easy answer for the EU would be to lay on top of the European financial and real economy industry yet another layer of rules and regulations that would be so strict that it would severely constrain economic activity on the continent. Already today, the European economy is the most tightly regulated economy in the world. This is not just true for banking and insurance, but also for agriculture, telecommunications and many other sectors. Sustainable finance must not simply create an additional layer of regulation but should lead to a *change* in regulation – or even just a change in how it is applied – to promote sustainable outcomes. Ideally, it would lead to far less complex regulation, as the single overarching objective of sustainable economic development is unambiguously clear.

Europe is one of the continents with the cleanest, most environmentally friendly industrial production processes. Therefore, if Europe were to raise standards unilaterally and further regulation were to lead to the delocalisation of industrial activity outside of Europe, this might seemingly help towards Europe's extremely ambitious CO_2 emissions targets. But actually, it would be net negative for the global climate to the extent that production is just moved to more polluting locations and it would diminish Europe's remaining industrial base, which carries millions of jobs and the European welfare system. Such a strategy would have economic costs for the EU and environmental costs for the planet.

The experience of the delocalisation of the European steel industry to other continents is a case in point: when steel factories in France, Germany and other countries were dismantled and rebuilt in the far East, the desulphurisation facilities were often left behind. The global environmental impact was severely negative. Therefore, sustainability should lead to a *re-localisation* of part of the activity that was lost. Such re-localisation to Europe would improve environmentally friendly productions, reduce transportation and lower global emissions. Europe should *favour* economic activity *in its own regions* and focus on local, sustainable production rather than global, unsustainable production. 'New and sustainable globalisation' would favour local production wherever possible, and imports from far around the globe would be the exception and not the rule. 'Sustainable Finance' should therefore have a spatial dimension. Vicinity matters, and proximity is preferable.

It is simply against common sense that Europe has its shoes, textiles, household goods, household appliances, stationery, basic machinery and tools and a rising share of food imported from locations thousands of kilometres away. What has led to this outcome? Economics and non-sustainable finance have played a key role in driving this process by focusing on short-term monetary returns at the expense of social and environmental costs in both the production country and the European Union.

A key concept is the one of 'comparative advantage' postulating that differing relative costs of production within a country favour specialisation by each country and international trade. While conceptually appealing, the argument has two shortcomings.

The concept of comparative advantage overlooks transportation costs including environmental costs, and it overlooks size differences and market power. It is best to illustrate the latter point with the economic development in the country of origin of the inventor of 'comparative advantage', David Ricardo. Ricardo's family was originally from Portugal and emigrated to England. His father became wealthy as a stockbroker in London, and David Ricardo developed theories on international trade.

English officials made heavy use of his argument of 'comparative advantage' in the second half of the 19th century to convince Portugal to open its domestic market on a large scale through advantageous tariffs to English industrial goods. England was seeking market access for its booming industrialisation. In exchange, Portugal would export Port wine, as the theory had famously suggested.

What was the result? The Portuguese economy was provided with cheap industrial goods from much larger England, practically wiping out any existing and nascent industrial activity in Portugal. The economic impact was devastating: before this opening occurred, around 1860, Portuguese per capita GDP was 75% of that of France and supported by industrial activity in textiles in particular. By 1910, this share had fallen to 13% and industry was virtually absent in Portugal. There is little doubt for economic historians, that this broad opening to trade with a much larger economy was the main reason for

late economic development in Portugal, famously called 'le retard
Portugais'.

Replace England with China and Portugal with selected EU
regions, say in France or Italy, respectively, and the economic
consequences become visible again. Consumers in these regions are
flooded with cheap industrial goods from China and other Asian
emerging economies, but domestic industry and employment have
been massively diminished. The only difference to the historical
example is that these regions do not export Port wine, but tourism
services to a fast-growing number of tourists from China and other
emerging markets.

This is why the EU's Sustainable Finance should focus in
particular on fostering local and regional activity within Europe, for
the economic and social benefit of the EU and for the environmental
benefit of the planet. In this way, it would support the 'new and
sustainable globalisation'. The benefits of such new and sustainable
globalisation for emerging markets would remain: they would still
have access to all technological progress available, but not so as to
destroy their own environment in favour of mass production for
developed countries.

Third, getting the pacing right on implementing sustainable
finance, and climate polices more broadly, is critical. Regulatory
changes can steer industry but must not be so fast that European
industry does not have the time to adjust. It would not be the first
time that abrupt policy changes had wiped out entire European
industry sectors: it happened to the photovoltaic industry after the EU
opened abruptly to massive imports; it happened to the lighting
industry after the EU set up lightbulb regulations and demanded a
quick shift towards halogen and then LEDs that now almost
exclusively come from China. As a result, Europe lost jobs and
product prices rose sharply. These may seem very specific sectoral
examples, but developments in the energy, car manufacturing,
machinery, technology and digital sectors are also worrying.

Implementing sustainable finance must happen with resolve, but with protection of Europe's economic interests and standards. Bliss would be to rediscover and revive many of Europe's regions that lost out in merciless globalisation and see manufacturing activity, which once made these regions powerful and proud, come back and recover.

This is where this book comes into play. It is a collection of very pertinent essays on the topic of sustainable finance. Each chapter represents personal views on a relevant policy topic from authors who are recognised experts in their fields They truly help us to advance our thinking on this issue, which is not only important for our planet and the future but also for our economy today and tomorrow.

I commend the authors for all their work and Paul Fisher as the editor of this volume and wish the readers the same enjoyment and enlightening that I felt when reading the final manuscript.

Preface

Towards the end of 2016, the European Commission set up the High-Level Expert Group on Sustainable Finance (the HLEG) with '20 policy leaders from civil society, the finance sector and academia'.[1] They were joined by nine observers from industry associations and other stakeholders, and were supported by a Secretariat from DG FISMA. This group was originally tasked with 'making recommendations for a comprehensive EU strategy on sustainable finance as part of the Capital Markets Union'. Privately, the group was told that it would help if it could come up with a handful of practical recommendations that the Commission could implement as part of the work of developing the Capital Markets Union. By the end, the group's mission had become to 'develop an overarching and comprehensive EU road map on sustainable finance'. As a method of compiling input to EU policy, the approach of using an expert group was not new – but the outcome went way beyond any previous experience.

During 2017, the HLEG broke new ground: the first such group to launch a public consultation and to have a huge, open conference in Brussels to discuss its Interim Report.[2]

The HLEG met regularly for around twelve months, publishing its Final Report[3] on 30 January 2018 – thanks to some outstanding chairpersonship and secretarial support. Rather than a handful, there were more than a hundred specific recommendations (in truth, no one has ever counted, exactly!). The Commission published its Action

[1] https://ec.europa.eu/commission/presscorner/detail/en/IP_16_4502
[2] https://ec.europa.eu/info/publications/170713-sustainable-finance-report_en
[3] https://ec.europa.eu/info/publications/180131-sustainable-finance-report_en

Plan[4] in response just six weeks later (accompanied by another Brussels conference) and published draft legislation[5] in May the same year. For the public sector, such speed was remarkable. But the urgency was warranted, and not just by the proximity of European Parliament elections. Progress globally on reducing greenhouse gas emissions (both flow and stock) is still not fast enough to avoid the high probability of climate-related catastrophe. Indeed, there are already events around the world leading to death and destruction – and financial loss – which are being amplified by global warming.

One of the successes of the HLEG was its use as a model for other countries. Canada, Australia and New Zealand all set up similar policy fora. It matters that similar action plans are instituted everywhere: climate change – reflected in global warming, sea-level rise and more extreme natural disasters – does not recognise the artificial national and other political boundaries that humans create.

For this new book – playing my nominated role as the 'academic' in the group – I asked the various members of the group and its observers if they would like to write some new material, each on a topic of their choice, outlining their views on some of the important ongoing debates on how to make the financial system sustainable. Many from the original group and several of the organisations involved volunteered. However, this is not an authorised official report, nor a group project in which one inevitably has to seek compromise and consensus in order to produce recommendations that would be agreed upon and then accepted. Here, we have asked authors to give their own personal views on – and criticisms of – policy on sustainable finance. These views are intended to maintain the momentum for change and to help drive constructive progress.

---

[4] https://eur-lex.europa.eu/legal-content/EN/TXT/PDF/?uri=CELEX:52018DC0097& from=EN

[5] https://ec.europa.eu/info/publications/180524-proposal-sustainable-finance_cs

The purpose of finance can be said to be to help allocate scarce resources between competing ends for the benefit of society as a whole, now and in the future. It may be true that financial sector policy cannot solve all the challenges of economic sustainability on its own: none of the various challenges will be met without input from governments, corporations and individuals alike. But it is also likely that none of those challenges will be met successfully without the contribution of a supportive financial sector.

Introduction

Kajetan Czyż and Paul G. Fisher

1.1 UNSUSTAINABLE ECONOMICS

The aim of sustainable finance has been to introduce into the financial practitioners' world view the awareness of two fundamental concepts which are notably absent from applications of traditional economic theory.[1] First, the value of a balanced and productive ecosystem, which forms the foundation of any society, and second, the societal values and norms which in turn form the basis of societal aspirations and goals.

Fundamental economics nearly always begins with the concept of 'utility' – which should mean the welfare of the individual in a very broad and personal sense. In contrast, the application of economic theory generally makes simplifying assumptions that have significant consequences. Economic models often use aggregate output (goods and services, including leisure time) as a proxy for societal utility.[2] The usual outcome of economic analysis is seemingly focussed solely on the hard-headed business of allocating resources optimally, so as to maximise output, having as little 'values interference' as possible. Concern for environmental damage in some political debates has been branded as ideological rather than taken as empirical fact and as such has been dismissed as potentially obstructing the economic system from achieving its optimally efficient allocation of resources.

Macroeconomics developed over time to focus on short-term resource allocation, in particular to smoothing out the boom and bust

---

[1] We distinguish between the tools of economic theory and the uses to which they have generally been put.

[2] Accepting that at the macro level value-added output equals total income equals final expenditure.

of the business cycle so as to get closer to the frontier of production possibilities. In such analysis, the potential growth rate is often treated as a fundamental which cannot be affected much by policy, as it depends on the combination of population growth and technological progress[3]. That has led to a model of growth which implicitly assumes the possibility of ever-increasing material and energy throughput ad infinitum. The consequences of such an economic system operating on a finite planet will lead to a depletion of resources and a distortion of the environment beyond that which nature is able to rebalance (Jackson, 2009).

Economics also assumes a time discount factor to reflect the assumption that people care less about future utility than they do about current utility. The chosen size of the discount factor is empirically important as small differences can shorten or extend the time horizon for policy quite markedly and makes accounting for long-term costs a challenge. For example, a social planner who cares about individuals not yet born would have a much lower discount factor than the average economic model.

The subsequent chapters of this book will discuss these and related issues. For this introduction it suffices to say that empirical facts about the state of our biosphere and natural resources are just that – well-documented facts,[4] and if the design of a system which aims to efficiently allocate scarce resources is incapable of incorporating empirical facts that have the potential to undermine the long-term viability of the system as a whole, then such a design needs updating.

I.2   THE RISE OF SUSTAINABLE FINANCE

The financial sector has long embraced a free-market economic world view built on classical assumptions. The Great Financial Crisis (GFC)

---

[3] More sophisticated analysis does, of course, make these endogenous, but seldom involving natural capital.

[4] See the many works of the International Panel on Climate Change cited throughout this volume.

of 2007–2009 undermined somewhat the confidence and belief in efficient financial markets which were supposed to operate in everyone's best interests. This book is primarily about how to challenge the underlying assumptions in the existing model, so as to refashion the financial system to be sustainable (i.e. viable in the long-term). Broadly, the financial system should embrace a wider view of societal utility which we take to be represented by the seventeen United Nations Sustainable Development Goals.[5] Particular attention is paid to the threat to the planetary system from climate change. Upgrading current financial models and regulatory approaches has been the focus of sustainable finance efforts to date – it remains to be seen whether this is feasible to a sufficient extent in the time we have left.

Sustainable finance professionals have primarily focussed thus far on improving quantified methods of risk analysis related to environmental, social and governance (ESG) issues, as this proved to have the greatest uptake with mainstream financial companies and their regulators. These efforts succeeded where concepts around 'ethical' finance had failed, because it was speaking the language of finance about a new emerging risk, which if properly understood, could be a source of competitive advantage and improved resilience. Within the climate theme, forecasts relating to future costs of compliance with climate regulations (e.g. emission trading schemes), transition risk frameworks and stranded assets identification were all work programmes within this vein. The primary objective was to increase the financial system's appreciation and integration of these risks, so as to ultimately improve its resilience and protect assets. To a lesser degree, efforts have been made to create financial products to direct capital towards ESG-related opportunities or solution providers, most notably green bonds and impact funds. Indeed, these two goals (ESG risk management and new channels of investment towards

---

[5] See United Nations website: www.un.org/sustainabledevelopment/sustainable-development-goals.

sustainable solutions) are a common definition of sustainable finance (European Commission, 2018).

From a systemic perspective, what has ultimately happened within the world of sustainable finance is an improved ability not to lose money due to ESG issues, hitherto known as 'non-financial'. This does not mean that all the risks can be hedged (Cambridge Institute for Sustainability Leadership, 2015). What it does mean is that, as of today, no financial company can justifiably claim that (a) they did not know ESG issues were a source of financial risk or (b) that they did not know how to integrate them into financial decision making – since much of the work in this area has been built by the third sector and is freely available. What then about the ability of the finance sector to 'finance' the transformation of the economy towards long-term viability? At present, the financial system's contribution to this goal has been somewhere between marginal and negligible as its flagship programme – the green bond market – still constitutes less than 1 per cent of all bonds outstanding (Climate Bonds Initiative, 2019).

Why is this? First, a practical reason: financiers rarely pro-actively create new assets – they typically provide finance to those that demand it or that are brought before them by the private or public sector and meet certain typological and qualitative criteria. These assets in turn are, or are not as the case may be, financially viable based on the policy environment in which the project is due to be executed (including the state subsidy and tax context). Although the finance sector lobbyists (sustainable finance lobbyists included) do have some sway over what policies get adopted, ultimately it is the policymakers and regulators that determine them. As of the recent past, with a few exceptions, policies have continued to effectively favour the incumbent vested interests of our high-carbon infrastructure configuration.

Second, there remains an open question as to who has the mandate to implement structural changes to the economy and indeed to society as a whole. Sustainable finance has been trying to demonstrate the higher risk profile of unsustainable enterprises, thus aiming to increase their costs of financing and to some extent promote financial products channelling capital towards solutions. In doing so, however, it can be argued that they have to take on the role of the policymakers. It is the various democratically elected and other authorities who actually hold the societal mandate to plan and determine which modes of production and sectors are allowed to flourish and which should be pruned. Sustainable finance professionals are trying to make it easier for policymakers to make the difficult decisions around transitioning their economies, but they do not have the authority to make the decisions for them.

Today, the question seems to remain unanswered as to who should be leading in this dance towards change – policymakers, financiers, their regulators, the public or perhaps corporates who directly manage physical assets? Great care must be taken when approaching this question and one must be mindful where power sits – the economy is a great servant but a poor master (Schumacher, 1973). Should we be educating the economic system or strengthening the institutions and social systems that were supposed to guide it? Convincing the servant of the master's perspective may be a futile exercise.

I.3   THE CONTEXT FOR SUSTAINABLE FINANCE

When trying to answer questions about possible futures, it is valuable to understand where the field of sustainable finance grew. Early 'ethical funds' in the 1980s, and the first dedicated ESG data providers[6] which were established to service them, were typically aligned with ethical, moral or religious concerns and mostly followed a negative screening model with exclusion lists of 'sin stocks'. The market profoundly changed with the development of carbon accounting standards and the first emission trading schemes in the early 2000s which effectively gave the market a way of putting a value on

---

[6] Vigeo-Eiris (2020).

the cost of carbon. For example the cost of emitting one tonne of carbon is around €24 per tCO_2e[7] at the beginning of 2020.

This ability to precisely quantify and price the climate externality allowed for the development of the concept of the carbon bubble in the early 2010s and with it the concept of stranded assets (McKibben, 2012). Simply put, there is a finite amount of greenhouse gases we can emit if we wish to keep global warming to a certain level, for example 1.5°C above preindustrial times.[8] That finite 'budget' is (much) lower than the emissions which would result from burning all the fossil fuel assets which are accounted for on the balance sheets of listed fossil fuel companies. We cannot burn all the coal, oil and gas that form the basis of stock valuations of fossil fuel companies and not go over the 'safe' warming threshold of 1.5°C or even 2°C. The planet must choose. As of 12 December 2015, in Paris (United Nations, 2015), world governments have explicitly committed to stopping global warming at 'safe' levels, which implies that fossil fuel producing companies' stock prices are overvalued since the assets forming the basis of those prices cannot be utilised in full.

The two concepts mentioned above-carbon accounting and the carbon bubble-together gave rise to climate risk factors which have a very concrete financial dimension. There are other ESG aspects outside of climate change which also have a distinct financial impact (positive or negative). This ability to translate ESG factors into financial terms has led to a clear distinction between responsible investment, as it pertains to 'ethical values' and those that have a financial dimension, that is 'ESG risks'. The distinction may be subtle; however, it is of critical importance because, if indeed ESG factors can have material financial impacts, then a prudent fiduciary or indeed any financier, should have assessed them through their normal due diligence process and if they have not, then this constitutes a breach

[7] Sandbag (2020).
[8] The Paris Agreement (2015) reference point is the change from the average global temperature from 1850 to 1900.

of fiduciary duty (Principles for Responsible Investment, 2015). If the whole market is guilty of this omission of practice, then this constitutes a market failure and requires regulatory involvement which is exactly what we are observing at the moment.

The wheels of regulation typically move slowly; however, as of 2020 they are in full swing. Momentum has been gathering since the 2015 report of the Prudential Regulation Authority of the Bank of England (Prudential Regulation Authority, 2015) which highlighted the insurance sector's exposure to climate change risk. Subsequently the Bank's governor, Mark Carney, who coincidently was also the chairperson of the Financial Stability Board (FSB), established the Task Force of Climate-Related Financial Disclosures (TCFD). Since then a number of other intergovernmental organisations, for example the World Bank, the Bank for International Settlements (BIS), the European Insurance and Occupational Pensions Authority (EIOPA) and the European Central Bank (ECB) have become engaged. In fact, so many regulators are now working on developing climate regulation that there are now multiple member organisations established for the sole purpose of helping to coordinate and share best practice between them. Of note are the Network for Greening the Financial System[9] (NGFS) and the UN Sustainable Insurance Forum (SIF).

The above efforts are moving in the same direction as other initiatives aimed at aligning the *structure* of the financial system with sustainability objectives such as the UN Sustainable Stock Exchanges Initiative (SSE) and the Financial Centres for Sustainability network (FC4S). The momentum over the past few years generated between multilateral organisations, the private sector and regulators has been truly inspiring and has given policymakers the confidence that the finance sector will support them and be open to finance efforts to decarbonise the economy and align it with the UN's Sustainable Development Goals (SDG).

---

[9] Fifty-four members representing central banks and regulators globally, at the start of 2020.

I.4   CONVERGENCE

Many think that, at the start of 2020, we are at a tipping point of several trends relating to sustainability which are converging and amplifying one another. There is an upswell of activity from a wide range of sources currently supporting this momentum. In addition to the broad financial sector increasingly seeing sustainability as a source of competitive advantage and regulators moving to set down basic compliance standards, the world at large is also moving. From increased pressure from civil society groups (Extinction Rebellion) to religious leaders (Pope Francis) and shifting consumer preferences and societal attitudes (e.g. 93 per cent of Europeans now believe climate to be a serious problem (European Commission, 2019[10])), through an increasing number of court cases against corporate negligence, the increasing costs of physical damage to infrastructure (e.g. California and Australian wildfires) to rapidly falling costs of technological solutions (e.g. renewables, electric vehicles and batteries) and availability of information, society at large does indeed seem to be at an intersection of trends which have the potential to create great change.

All of this is encouraging and bodes well for future action; however, this is the end of the beginning only and as such puts us about three decades behind schedule, if not more. The 2019 greenhouse gas emissions were at business-as-usual levels as estimated in 2009 (UNEP, 2019), that makes it clear that despite momentum building, and some countries making progress, little has been achieved in the global economy as a whole. After several decades of sustainable finance work, one can only say that the finance sector is ready to withstand *some* of the shocks coming from climate change and/or society's response to it. Unfortunately, the sector is only beginning to create and scale financing towards solutions that match the scale of the problems. This may be caused to a large extent by the finance sector being a 'policy-taker' rather than a 'policymaker' and

[10] European Commission (2019).

because of sluggish policymaking by governments to stimulate innovation by companies, too few opportunities in the green space have been forthcoming for financiers to finance. Indeed, one could argue that all this effort from the responsible investment industry has been a desperate, and often impotent, effort to do politicians' jobs for them. Ultimately if politicians could simply agree to set a universally applicable carbon price, most of the uncertainty surrounding the economic impact of climate adaptation or mitigation efforts would simply disappear and we could get on with solving the problem.

At the beginning of the Anthropocene, it is perhaps important to remind ourselves of a few basic truths. First, for better or worse, we are not going back to the Holocene. Since that is the case, we as a community of interdependent societies need to take on the responsibilities of shaping this next epoch. As of now, it is very likely to be worse than the previous one. That does not necessarily have to be the case. We could decide to work together, take the knowledge and ingenuity we have developed to enhance nature, rather than exploit it; care for one another rather than use each other. Second, the rules of economic conduct and economics as a field of inquiry are not immutable natural laws. They are a set of tools which generate a shared, imagined mental construct which changes over time, and indeed can be changed if we so please. Third, adjustments to economic activity and its associated financing need to focus as much on reducing and restricting the negative externalities as enhancing and growing the positive ones. Without a sufficiently large pipeline of opportunities, little will change in aggregate. Fourth, at this stage of technology the true costs of averting climate change are close to zero – an assessment for the whole of the United Kingdom indicates costs of 1–2 per cent of GDP in 2050 (much less than the measurement error in GDP itself) to achieve carbon neutrality (Committee on Climate Change, 2019). Similarly, as far back as 2014, the International Energy Agency (IEA) indicated that transitioning the global energy sector would be a positive investment if energy efficiency savings are fully taken into account (IEA, 2014). Furthermore, retooling the global energy, building, agriculture and transport sectors may possibly be the largest growth opportunity humanity has ever had, worth some US$26trn (New Climate Economy, 2018). Solving climate change seems like a good investment.

Ultimately, any change requires only two ingredients: decision and action. It seems that we have as a society, with minor exceptions, decided to act and it is quite clear the direction and scale of what that action has to be. What is left now is only to not be afraid of our own courage and add the final ingredient: action.

We hope that the chapters of this book will not only spell out the need for action but also detail practical ways forward for the financial sector.

I.5   THIS BOOK

The chapters in this book each stand by themselves but form a natural sequence. The first chapters, by Arber and Waygood, and Holmes, further the discussion of how the financial system as a whole needs to change in its broad aspect. The regulatory meat of the book is in the ensuing three chapters by Alexander and Fisher, Kivisaari, and Micilotta (and later by Dupré). Thereafter there are five chapters relating to the actions and behaviour of financial firms and investors: Seega and Voysey consider financial risk analysis; Kruse and Schmidt tackle governance; Martindale, Elodie and Sullivan consider fiduciary duty; Billing and Silberg discuss how an active pension fund can practically implement sustainable principles, and Harris looks at the development of benchmark indexes. Last but not least, we have four chapters which widen out to consider the people aspects: Robins considers the Just Transition whilst Husson-Traore and Vander Stichele look at how citizens and the social dimension could be better recognised in current policy. Dupré looks at the non-engagement of, and new regulations governing, personal financial advice.

REFERENCES

Cambridge Institute for Sustainability Leadership (2015), 'Unhedgeable Risk: How Climate Change Sentiment Impacts Investment', Investment Leaders Group. www.cisl.cam.ac.uk/resources/sustainable-finance-publications/unhedgeable-risk.

Climate Bonds Initiative (2019), 'Green Bonds: The State of the Market 2018'. www .climatebonds.net/resources/reports/green-bonds-state-market-2018.

Committee on Climate Change (2019), 'Phase Out Greenhouse Gas Emissions by 2050 to End UK Contribution to Global Warming'. www.theccc.org.uk/2019/05/02/phase-out-greenhouse-gas-emissions-by-2050-to-end-uk-contribution-to-global-warming/.

European Commission (2018), 'Final Report of the High-Level Expert Group on Sustainable Finance'. https://ec.europa.eu/info/publications/180131-sustainable-finance-report_en.

European Commission (2019), 'A European Green Deal, Striving to Be the First Climate-Neutral Continent' [online]. https://ec.europa.eu/info/strategy/priorities-2019-2024/european-green-deal_en.

International Energy Agency (2014), 'WOE2014, Special Report, World Energy Investment Outlook', Paris. https://webstore.iea.org/weo-2014-special-report-world-energy-investment-outlook.

Jackson, T. (2009), *Prosperity without Growth: Economics for a Finite Planet*, London: Earthscan. https://content.taylorfrancis.com/books/download?dac=C2016–0-25003-3&isbn=9781136546785&format=googlePreviewPdf.

McKibben, B. (2012), 'Global Warming's Terrifying New Math', *Rolling Stone*, August. www.rollingstone.com/politics/politics-news/global-warmings-terrifying-new-math-188550.

The New Climate Economy (2018), 'Unlocking the Inclusive Growth Story of the 21st Century', The Global Commission on the Economy and Climate. https://newclimateeconomy.report/2018/wp-content/uploads/sites/6/2018/09/NCE_2018_FULL-REPORT.pdf.

Principles for Responsible Investment (2015), 'Fiduciary Duty in the 21st Century'. www.unpri.org/fiduciary-duty/fiduciary-duty-in-the-21st-century/244.article.

Prudential Regulation Authority (2015), 'The Impact of Climate Change on the UK Insurance Sector, a Climate Change Adaption Report by the Prudential Regulation Authority', September. www.bankofengland.co.uk/prudential-regulation/publication/2015/the-impact-of-climate-change-on-the-uk-insurance-sector.

Sandbag (2020), 'EUA Price'. https://sandbag.org.uk/carbon-price-viewer.

Schumacher, E. F. (1973), *Small Is Beautiful: A Study of Economics As If People Mattered*, London: Blond & Briggs. www.daastol.com/books/Schumacher (1973) Small is Beautiful.pdf.

United Nations Environment Programme (2019), 'Production Gap Report'. www .unenvironment.org/resources/report/production-gap-report-2019.

United Nations Framework Convention on Climate Change (2015), 'Adoption of the Paris Agreement, 21st Conference of the Parties', Paris: United Nations. https://unfccc.int/resource/docs/2015/cop21/eng/l09r01.pdf.

Vigeo-Eiris (2020), 'About Us, History'. http://vigeo-eiris.com/about-us/history.

1 Capitalism Meets Multilateralism

Paddy Arber and Steve Waygood

1.1 INTRODUCTION: THE THREE FAILURES OF CAPITALISM

The idea at the heart of capitalism is deceptively simple: prices signal which goods or services are to be produced, ensuring that supply and demand are matched. In Adam Smith's famous image, the 'invisible hand' of the market allocates resources efficiently between corporations and individuals.

Today, capital markets are failing to deliver on this promise in three related ways: they are failing the investors and corporations they exist to bring together, by forcing them to focus on short-term profit at the expense of long-term growth; they are failing to preserve the health of our planet, upon which we all rely; and they are ultimately failing the people of the world, by both destroying the resources upon which we also rely and assuming that the people who make up markets have no ethics. The invisible hand is choking the planet.

The evidence for these market failures is widespread, compelling and well-known. But some figures are so stark that they bear repeating: over a third of the world's agricultural land is now seriously degraded (see e.g. United Nations, 2017). Over 90 per cent of the world's marine fish stocks are now 'fully exploited, overexploited or depleted'.[1] An estimated half of the world's coral has been lost since the 1980s (Hughes et al., 2018). And we are on track for an average temperature rise of almost 4°C by 2100,[2] threatening drought and weather conditions that humanity has never before witnessed.

---

[1] According to the United Nations: https://unctad.org/en/pages/newsdetails.aspx?OriginalVersionID=1812.

[2] World Meteorological Organization (2019).

Globally, one person in nine does not have enough to eat. Two billion people live on less than US$3 per day and over 70 million people are unable to find work. Yet, the world's richest 1 per cent now own more wealth than all the other 99 per cent put together,[3] with just the eight richest people in the world owning the same as 50 per cent of the world's population.

Increasingly, economists, investors and regulators are recognising that these issues, previously perceived in largely environmental and social terms, will also have severe financial and economic consequences if left unchecked. Unsustainable economic growth will harm people's pensions, savings and investments. Many sustainability issues, notably climate change, will harm long-term economic growth and create financial instability, as the chapters in this book set out.

This damage is not inevitable, however. The world does not lack the capital required to deliver the UN Sustainable Development Goals.[4] We lack imagination, compassion and equality of opportunity. And we lack capital markets that factor in people and planet, while making a profit.

Markets are built, operated and regulated by people. They respond to price signals that are a function of government policy and to regulations that are determined by domestic and regional supervisory bodies, and global standard setters. Policymakers and regulators therefore have levers at their disposal to alter market behaviour and deliver a more sustainable future.

We need to restore compassion to the heart of capitalism, by reconnecting the capitalists with their capital. Markets are amoral. People are not.

In this chapter, we examine the reasons behind capital markets' contribution to an unsustainable future, considering the distinction between market inefficiencies and market failures, and suggest five steps for policymakers and regulators to consider.

---

[3] See, e.g. Credit Suisse (2019).
[4] See: www.un.org/sustainabledevelopment/sustainable-development-goals.

1.2 CORPORATE VALUE AND SUSTAINABILITY: MARKET INEFFICIENCY AND MARKET FAILURE

The valuation of every company helps it to compete: a higher market price means a lower cost of capital, which is a competitive advantage. In capital markets that functioned for the long term, sustainable companies should be able to raise capital more cheaply than unsustainable ones. The key sustainable development problem with the existing capital markets is that the cost of capital for companies is not sufficiently influenced by how sustainable the company is.

In other words, sustainability issues do not matter enough to ensure that the performance is sustainable.

We believe that this is for two related reasons: market inefficiency and market failure. Both create substantial barriers to a sustainable financial system and wider economy.

1.2.1 Market Inefficiency

Market efficiency is a central concept in fund management. Markets are often hypothesised to work well in transmitting produce-relevant information. It is true that some markets are efficient, but many are not. Market inefficiency is what active fund managers attempt to exploit when seeking to outperform their financial benchmark. From a sustainability perspective, market inefficiency is the situation where it pays companies to do the right thing and be sustainable, but markets neither recognise nor reward this behaviour until the company delivers the results within their accounts. In other words, while companies plan to be sustainable, investors do not proactively see the business case, and their ensuing investment decisions do not contribute towards lowering a company's short-term cost of capital, until the benefits are obvious to all. This time lag can punish more sustainable companies via a higher cost of capital until, that is, the benefits of their behaviour become clear when they appear in the company's accounts.

As the market inefficiency argument cuts against the efficient market hypothesis (e.g. Malkiel, 1989), it is worth dwelling on the practical sources of some of these market inefficiencies. There are a number of reasons: a lack of complete and comparable market data on environmental, social and governance (ESG) factors and a lack of expertise on ESG analysis within institutional investors, or the syllabus of the chartered financial analyst qualifications. But arguably one of the main sources of market inefficiency is the incentives within the system that lead to an excessively short-term view among the market participants who are more concerned about short-term costs or benefits of an initiative than the long-term costs or benefits arising from it. The short-termism argument rests on capital markets being too near-sighted in the way that they evaluate companies.

One root cause is that fund management organisations are evaluated by their clients – for example pension funds – based on criteria that are themselves too short term. Such evaluation motivates short-term investment behaviour on the part of fund managers that is more akin to speculation than to genuine ownership. Fund managers are subject to a legal fiduciary duty to obtain the best risk-adjusted financial returns for their clients; and this is often evaluated on the basis of very short-term, even daily results. In an ideal world, their interest would be in the long-term, but the structure of the market pushes them into maximising short-term returns.

This maximisation of short-term results is a long-term problem for the economy as a whole: if the capital market does not sufficiently factor in long-term capital investment returns, then it undermines long-term investment decision-making by company directors and leads them to allocate insufficient capital to investing in the long-term health of companies overall. While a lack of focus on the long-term financial health of a company is a general problem, short-termism is also a particular problem for sustainable development: it systematically erodes incentives for company directors to invest in a sustainable business.

One of the most significant sources of market inefficiency here is the business model of the investment banks. The remuneration of brokers is directly linked to trading volumes. As a result, they have a powerful incentive to encourage market activity. Even when sell-side analysts are aware of corporate governance or sustainability concerns, these analysts do not report this in their reports to buy-side analysts for fear of losing access to those boards. The pressures and commercial conflicts they are under are leading them to produce research that looks to enhance the profitability of investment banks at the expense of an efficient and properly functioning capital market.

In 2017, Aviva Investors collaborated with Tomorrow's Company and Extel on a study into this market inefficiency. Entitled 'Investment Research: Time for a Brave New World?', we anonymously surveyed the personal views of 342 sell-side analysts across the world. Our findings indicated that 90 per cent of mainstream analysts would at least undertake some additional caution when writing on topics sensitive to the bank. Over a third of mainstream respondents readily acknowledged that they should avoid damaging investment banking relationships if they are to have a successful career (Aviva Investors, 2018).

These commercial conflicts are well known and derive from the function of investment banks, which intermediate between issuers and investors in capital markets. The information produced by an analyst who works in the research department can be of use to the bank's investment bankers. To disparage a client or potential client of the investment bank would not, therefore, be beneficial for the bank or for the analyst's career.

This has consequences for the efficient functioning of markets. Significantly, 42 per cent of analysts agree that sell-side research has a detrimental short-term focus, and only 35 per cent agree that sell-side research tackles controversial topics and offers negative assessments of companies where appropriate. We also find that a mere 12 per cent of mainstream sell-side analysts' time is spent researching companies' prospects beyond a 12-month horizon.

This suggests that responsible investors with a long-term view need to ensure that the research payment accounts under the Second Markets in Financial Instruments Directive (MiFID II) reward the right kind of investment research. Furthermore, policymakers should look carefully at these commercial conflicts on the sell side if they want capital markets to focus on the long term and allocate capital sustainably.

1.2.2 Market Failure

In contrast to market inefficiency, market failure refers to the situation where it pays companies in the long term to do the wrong thing and be unsustainable. In other words, a market failure is where the externalities associated with unsustainable business practices do not hit the company's profit and loss (P&L) statement at all. This is largely because global governments have not taken corrective action to internalise the costs onto corporate balance sheets through, for example measures to price the externalities correctly.

The difference between capital market inefficiency and capital market failure is that the former is a failure of the predictive power of investors, whereas in the latter case, it is a failure of the governments to create a market price mechanism that ensures that companies have to pay the cost of their externalities.

The reason why this distinction matters to us as institutional investors (e.g. pension funds, insurance companies), is that we need to be strategically very clear about where our own spheres of responsibility begin and end. We have a fiduciary duty to attempt to capitalise on market *inefficiencies* in the pursuit of excess returns from our investment decisions. We also have a duty to behave as good owners – or stewards – of the businesses we own. But we cannot correct market *failures* by ourselves. Ensuring that the price mechanism works effectively and, for example, properly values environmental and social goods and services, is the role of governments, not investors. That said, investors can advise governments on the most effective way to achieve this – as we attempt to do later in this chapter.

If the economy is to be moved onto a truly sustainable basis, then we would expect to see governments taking action to correct the many distortions in the pricing systems on fisheries, fresh water, climate change and natural resource depletion. This is how sustainability issues become relevant to the corporate valuation work that informs most investment decisions, and how ultimately capital would be put to work in the right places. This requires, for example setting standards, creating fiscal measures such as carbon taxes or setting up market mechanisms such as carbon trading schemes that price the externalities and ensure that the negative externalities are corrected.

Arguably, the biggest contemporary market failure is climate change. As well as an environmental and social challenge, climate risk has become an exceptionally urgent and important economic and financial problem. In 2015, Aviva worked with the Economist Intelligence Unit (EIU, 2015) to calibrate the value-at-risk to climate change. We found that 6°C of warming by the end of the century could lead to a present value loss of US$13.8trn of manageable financial assets, roughly 10 per cent of the global total. These values are based on the discount rate of a private investor, a reasonable baseline, as the affected losses mentioned earlier will be on the privately held pool of global assets. However, as climate change is also a systemic problem, with issues of wider societal concern, it is often appropriate to apply a lower discount rate, consistent with public sector actors that have longer time horizons than individuals. When the expected losses are considered from a government's point of view, employing the same discount rates as the Stern Review (Stern, 2006), they rise dramatically. From the public sector perspective, the expected value of a future with 6°C of warming represents present value losses worth US$43trn – 30 per cent of the entire stock of manageable assets. The consequences for long-term economic growth would be catastrophic (EIU, 2015).

In the presence of market failure, integration of ESG into investment analysis can motivate the wrong behaviours, and engagement with companies is doomed to fail as one is essentially asking the company to go against the market incentives and lose money.

I.3   FIVE POLICY STEPS TO BUILD FINANCIAL MARKETS THAT ARE FIT FOR THE FUTURE

In 2015, landmark agreements on climate change, financing for development and sustainable development goals were reached in the United Nations (UN).

Our financial services system should help deliver these global agreements: all three agreements reference the importance of private sector financial flows. Yet, in practice, as we have seen earlier, market failures and inefficiencies prevent finance from being directed where it will make the most positive impact.

It is the role of policymakers and regulators, guided by civil society, to shape financial markets to deliver the positive outcomes of the agreements to which the world has signed up. Yet few policymakers, politicians or civil society representatives understand how the many different financial services institutions work together to finance the world we live in today and will retire into tomorrow, and even fewer have considered systematically how to reform the financial system to promote sustainable outcomes. In the absence of appropriate oversight, society and the real economy currently serve financial interests, rather than the other way around.

There is an increasing number of examples of positive policy actions, however, to shape sustainable financial markets around the world. We have drawn on these to develop the following recommendations, which look at how policymakers and regulators at the national, regional and global level can develop more sustainable financial systems.

i. *Establish and strengthen international and national frameworks for sustainable finance*
   - The UN, IMF and World Bank should work together to create a Global Climate Capital Raising Plan: this plan could inform national Capital Raising Plans, which include a view on the infrastructure required, the capital involved and the financing that can be raised via infrastructure investment, project finance, corporate debt, foreign direct investment,

equity investment as well as sovereign and MDB debt. The UN's Addis Agenda notes that 'integrated national financing frameworks that support nationally owned sustainable development strategies' will be at the heart of countries' efforts, supported by an enabling international economic environment and international cooperation. At the High-Level Political Forum (HLPF) in New York in July 2019, however, only a quarter of the Voluntary National Reviews presented an investment strategy at all.

- Governments should establish an International Panel on Climate Finance (IPCF): this would be a capital market-focussed equivalent to the Intergovernmental Panel on Climate Change (IPCC), which focuses on the science base around climate change. Rather than look at the science base, an IPCF could support an assessment of article 2.1.c of the Paris Agreement – that is the 'consistency of finance flows with a pathway towards low greenhouse gas emissions and climate resilient development'. It would conduct an assessment of market-based analysis on the impact of climate policy. Observations would be secured from the various market disclosures by companies and investment analysts from various sectors and regions. The report would serve as a market test of policy effectiveness. Such a report would be provided to policymakers at each Conference of Parties (COP) and inform them about the view of capital market participants in relation to the likelihood of the delivery of the Paris agreement. The IPCF could also coordinate and assist on the creation of national Capital Raising Plans.

ii. *Ensure a greater share of all public sector financial flows are sustainable*

Many governments in the world have started the journey towards using public spending to support green and sustainable initiatives. But the scale and speed of this spending need to increase exponentially if we are to meet the challenge of the UN's Sustainable Development Goals (SDGs).

Public bodies should therefore look to 'green' a significant share of all public sector financial flows, including not only standard spending but also:

- Ensuring a proportion of all funded public sector pensions is invested in sustainable assets – for example if just an additional 5 per cent of US-funded state pension schemes were invested sustainably, this would amount to over US$300bn.

- Looking at how central banks can use their balance sheets to support sustainable investment, for example by tilting asset purchases towards sustainable investments. For example, the European Central Bank's asset purchase scheme since the financial crisis has seen it purchase over €180bn in corporate bonds.

- Ensuring Sovereign Wealth Funds (SWF) invest a proportion of their investments sustainably. Again, if an additional 5 per cent of SWF assets were invested sustainably, this would amount to almost US$400bn.

iii. *Shift private sector financial flows by adjusting pricing and other incentives*

Public bodies also influence sustainable finance by creating the incentives in which market forces operate. Much more needs to be done to shift these incentives towards sustainable investments.

- Carbon pricing is fundamental to internalising the externalities of climate change. All governments must work together to agree and implement a meaningful cost of carbon. But we cannot wait for everyone to agree before individual countries act. Where countries move ahead of others in pricing carbon, they should also consider carbon border adjustments to ensure a level playing field. At the same time countries must transition away from fossil fuel subsidies that prop up polluters while damaging citizens' long-term future.

- A major factor in institutional investors' decisions about what to invest in is based on the amount of capital they must hold against each investment. If regulators set capital levels to reflect the long-term risks of assets to financial stability, thereby incentivising more investment in green assets and a transition away from polluting assets, the largest investors in the world would move money in a more sustainable direction without costing governments a penny.

- Governments could also look to support measures to ensure that the polluter pays to clean up the pollution they have created, thereby making them far less attractive investments – the EU's Producer Responsibility Directive, for example, could be extended to ensure that fossil fuel extractors and utilities are required to pay for the cost of carbon capture and storage.

- Governments also need to remove damaging fossil fuel subsidies that create perverse incentives to fund emissions. Yet fossil fuel subsidies in 2018 actually increased by a third, to more than $400bn globally.[5]

---

[5] See: https://energypost.eu/400bn-in-global-fossil-fuel-consumption-subsidies-twice-that-for-renewables.

iv. *Improve market information to make the sustainability risks and rewards of financial assets clearer*

- Currently, not only are market incentives misaligned, but there is very little consistent information on environmental issues available in financial markets.
- Central banks could help support the production of sector-specific reference climate risk scenarios for corporate boards – particularly banks, insurers and investors – to see as input and base their own scenario plans upon (Bank of England, 2019). This would significantly help the process of scenario planning within financial institutions and assist the comparability of the scenario plan outputs, which are currently based upon disparate assumptions.
- Global regulators and standard setters should also look to make the analysis and disclosure of climate risk mandatory for all companies. The International Organization of Securities Commissions (IOSCO) could begin by recommending that all stock market regulators make listed companies adopt the governance and strategy recommendations of the Task Force for Climate-related Financial Disclosures (TCFD, 2017).

v. *Educate people about the connection between their personal finances and sustainability*

Most people that own capital through their pensions and investments have no idea how the financial system works, or how their money impacts the world for good or ill. More can be done to correct this.

- Governments should provide strong backing for civil society campaigns that would look to mobilise their supporters. Actions that government and non-governmental organisations (NGOs) could jointly take include NGO sustainable finance education initiatives that teach people about the climate impacts of their investments and encourage them to think about how it impacts everyone on the planet and shapes all our futures. Teaching the owners of capital how to care about the climate impact of their assets would change the nature of the supply of capital overall as well as what concerns are raised via investment.
- Governments should back at scale public league tables ranking the actual climate disclosure reports, sector by sector. For Aviva's part, we have also helped to set up and then finance the World Benchmarking Alliance to work with a group of allies including the Carbon Disclosure Project to build climate change benchmarks. The benchmarks will use

the new disclosures created by the TCFD as the underpinning framework. When they start to come out towards the end of 2020, the youth movement and mainstream investors alike will be able to use these benchmarks to hold companies to account for their climate impacts on the most climate impactful sectors. However, it needs many more allies from across the spectrum if it is to be successful.

- NGOs should also look to move the considerable influence within finance, so that it focusses on this area more. For example, they could build a Global Youth Movement of shareholder activists within the youth community inspired by Greta Thunberg's strong action on climate change, working with financial institutions that run their parents' pensions to attend company AGMs and call on the boards to take strong action aligned with the Paris agreement.

I.4 CONCLUSION

If incentives are aligned, capital markets have the potential to substantially aid the transition to a more sustainable global economy. However, despite some notable exceptions, current legislation and regulation actively exacerbates unsustainable investment behaviour.

Policymakers and regulators around the world must therefore massively accelerate the shift towards innovative, forward-leaning regulatory approaches to correct market failures and expose market inefficiency. Only with bold action can the world be set on a sustainable course in time to avoid the worst ecological, financial and human damage to which we are exposed. We now need to add a guiding mind that considers the sustainability of people and planet to Adam Smith's 'invisible hand'.

REFERENCES

Aviva Investors (2018), 'Investment Research: Time for a Brave New World'. https://integratedreporting.org/wp-content/uploads/2017/10/research-brave-new-world.pdf.

Bank of England (2019), 'The 2021 Biennial Exploratory Scenario on the Financial Risks from Climate Change'. www.bankofengland.co.uk/news/2019/december/boe-consults-on-proposals-for-stress-testing-the-financial-stabilit y-implications-of-climate-change.

Credit Suisse (2019), 'Global Wealth Report 2019'. www.credit-suisse.com/about-us/en/reports-research/global-wealth-revport.html.

Economist Intelligence Unit (2015), 'The Cost of Inaction: Recognising the Value at Risk from Climate Change'. https://eiuperspectives.economist.com/sites/default/files/The%20cost%20of%20inaction_0.pdf.

Hughes, T. P., Kerry, J. T., Baird, A. H. et al. (2018), 'Global warming transforms coral reef assemblages', *Nature* 556, 492–496. www.nature.com/articles/s41586-018-0041-2.

Malkiel, B. G. (1989), 'Efficient Market Hypothesis'. In: Eatwell, J., Milgate, M. and Newman, P. (eds.), *Finance. The New Palgrave*. Palgrave Macmillan, London. https://link.springer.com/chapter/10.1007/978-1-349-20213-3_13#citeas.

Stern, N. (2006), 'The Economics of Climate Change: The Stern Review'. https://webarchive.nationalarchives.gov.uk/20100407172811/http://www.hm-treasury.gov.uk/stern_review_report.htm.

Task Force for Climate-related Financial Disclosures (2017), 'Final Report: Recommendations of the Task Force on Climate-related Financial Disclosures (June 2017)'. www.fsb-tcfd.org/publications/final-recommendations-report.

United Nations (2017), 'Global Land Outlook'. https://knowledge.unccd.int/publication/full-report.

World Meteorological Organization (2019), 'WMO Statement on the State of the Global Climate in 2018'. https://library.wmo.int/doc_num.php?explnum_id=5789.

2 Public Meets Private

Sustainable Finance for a Sustainable Economy

Ingrid Holmes

2.1 INTRODUCTION

Mobilising capital for a sustainable economy requires action on two fronts. First, current capital allocation must be shifted from an unsustainable pathway to a sustainable one. Second, the investment gap must be filled to ensure that sustainable economy objectives are achieved. This includes the provision of long-term finance to achieve the goals articulated by both the Paris Agreement on climate change and the broader Sustainable Development Goals (SDGs). This also involves the creation of a more resource-efficient, resilient and net zero carbon economy in 2050 and the achievement of social objectives such as creating jobs for young people, improving education, providing adequate pension and tackling inequality.

This chapter will focus on the issue of filling the investment gap. Primarily, it will focus on the example of tackling the climate change challenge, although these ideas can be applied to the wider environmental and social agendas too.

2.1.1 *Understanding and Articulating Investment Needs*

Significant amounts of work have been done by international bodies and global think tanks to estimate the investment required to meet the goals of the Paris Agreement on climate change and the SDGs; for example, New Climate Economy estimated that until 2030 an average investment of US$6.27trn per year will be needed globally to deliver the low carbon infrastructure required to fulfil the goals of the Paris

Agreement on climate change (The New Climate Economy, 2014[1]). The United Nations (UN) estimates a financing gap of US$2–3trn per year to achieve the SDGs in developing countries; but, at the same time, it estimates that this investment could unlock US$12trn in market opportunities (United Nations Secretary General, 2019).

These global estimates are useful as they give a sense of the overall scale of the investment opportunity. The estimates will be of interest to private sector investors because they represent the opportunity to generate financial returns through the development of new products, technologies and business models. They will also be of interest to progressive public policymakers not only because the deployment of such investment would help achieve the goals of the Paris Agreement and SDGs but also because the investment itself would present an opportunity to create new jobs, create new markets and, of course, generate new tax income.

In order to maximise the chances of achieving a sustainable economy, the first task should be to set out the investment needs – disaggregated to the same level at which responsibility for implementation can be reasonably delegated/expected. Neglecting to do this makes it much harder to develop the interventions required to galvanise private sector investment at the scale needed, because the investment target being aimed for is uncertain. Articulating the investment target also helps policymakers focus on those that are responsible for ensuring the targets are delivered and on how the goals will be achieved.

In the European Union (EU), for example, while there is a high-level aspiration to deliver a resource-efficient economy, data on how much investment is already happening is patchy and lacks comparability. In addition, there is no official top-line figure for what amount of investment might be needed overall. The Ellen MacArthur Foundation (2017) estimates that the EU needs to invest around

---

[1] Of this, US$6trn is expected to be business-as-usual investment and US$270bn the uplift cost to make investment climate-compatible.

€320bn by 2025, but the foundation's definition goes well beyond the EU's definition of what this would encompass and could therefore be an overestimate.

There are, however, also examples of good practice. At the European Commission (EC), the Directorate General in charge of energy in the EU (DG ENER) undertook analysis to understand the investment levels required to meet the EU 2030 climate and energy goals. These comprised at least 40 per cent greenhouse gas (GHG) emission cuts from 1990 levels, at least a 32 per cent share of renewable energy and at least a 32.5 per cent increase in energy efficiency. This was found to be around €11.7trn in total, with a projected annual investment gap of €177bn between 2021 and 2030. The analysis went on to identify that the biggest gaps are expected to be in relation to energy efficiency in buildings and transport and, geographically, in central and eastern Europe. This gap analysis, as well as concerns over the size of the investment shortfall, was one of the drivers for the findings and final report of the High-Level Expert Group on Sustainable Finance (European Commission, 2018) being quickly transformed into a ten-point Action Plan on Financing Sustainable Growth that included legislative proposals.

In developed economies, such as the EU, analysis is usually undertaken through the use of combined in-house and third-party providers. Where resources and capacity are relatively scarce, in emerging economies for example, this is a function that multilateral development banks (MDBs) can usefully undertake and then use to inform client country investment strategies through the provision of technical assistance. Indeed, announcements made by the MDBs and international development finance corporations in 2017 envisage this type of support, as is discussed later in this chapter.

Having these investment needs set out in detail acts as a device for policymakers to understand what private investment is already going into a sector and what further interventions may (or indeed may not) be justified to ensure that investment is delivered to scale and over the time frame needed.

In 2010, for example, the UK energy regulator, the Office of Gas and Electricity Markets (Ofgem), set up Project Discovery – a year-long study of whether the current arrangements in the United Kingdom are adequate for delivering secure and sustainable electricity and gas supplies over the next ten to fifteen years, including meeting the UK's 2020 renewable energy targets (Ofgem, 2010). The study found that unprecedented levels of investment were required to meet these targets and that existing policy measures would be insufficient in delivering the outcomes needed. The analysis catalysed a review, the Electricity Market Reform process, and the eventual revision of current UK market arrangements to focus on a new capacity market and the introduction of a policy instrument to create revenue certainty for renewable energy providers: 'contracts for difference' (CfDs). A contract form used in many other financial markets, these CfDs incentivise investment in renewable energy by providing developers of projects with high upfront costs and long lifetimes with direct protection from volatile wholesale prices, and they also protect consumers from paying increased support costs when electricity prices are high (BEIS, 2019).

2.2   ADAPTING MARKET ARRANGEMENTS USING POLICY TO ENCOURAGE INVESTMENT

In their interim reports, the EU HLEG (European Commission, 2017b) and the Commission's European Political Strategy Centre (European Commission, 2017a) had both suggested that detailed national capital raising plans be developed by EU member states to set out how a combination of policy frameworks and public and private investment could be deployed in order to deliver 2030 climate and energy goals. Similar suggestions were made for the United Kingdom by the Green Finance Taskforce (2018) to meet the UK climate and energy goals. To date, such overarching strategies have not been forthcoming, probably because most economies are not run in this centralised way. Instead there has been a tendency to look sector by sector at what needs to be achieved. Some examples of how this can and has been approached are discussed subsequently.

Once investment goals are articulated, there may be a number of challenges to then overcome before investment is forthcoming. For different sectors and their infrastructure and technologies, these challenges might include:

a. Lack of clarity on business models, some of which may be based on public–private structures, or on the source of returns for new and unregulated assets.
b. Unproven demand making upfront infrastructure investment difficult to justify.
c. The 'valley of death' funding gap – a gap in the market for important but unproven technologies with a required high 'capex' (capital expenditure) for demonstration.

Well-designed public policy frameworks can help overcome these types of challenge and facilitate private investment to support delivering of the goals by generating demand for new products or by incentivising supply to develop new markets. Success requires a clarity of purpose – and a laser-like focus on overcoming market failures, either through addressing risk or through creating opportunity. Poorly designed frameworks, on the other hand, have the opposite effect, with the resulting uncertainty created having a significant effect on access to and cost of capital. This is especially the case for the type of newer high-capital cost, low or zero carbon infrastructure needed to address the climate change challenge, but is equally as important when considering social infrastructure such as schools and hospitals and the delivery of long-term social change programmes to address inequality or achieve meaningful new job creation.

The need for certainty is the reason why a coherent and long-term focussed policy strategy is an important tool to translate sustainable economy goals into investment opportunities. Among some policy circles, this type of coherent and long-term focussed policy strategy is referred to as being 'investible' – also referred to 'long, loud and legal' or 'investment-grade' policy.

Investible policy has the following general characteristics:[2]

a. Clear and **transparent policy objectives** underpinned by a public value case. The public value case is important for securing the long-term political consensus that any market intervention is appropriate and worthwhile.

b. A set of clear **time-bound targets** setting out overall investment goals that are of suitable duration. A clear legally binding framework set over a sufficiently long period can help build confidence in the underlying policies and goals.

c. Objectives and targets should be underpinned by **new regulation** or **by financial incentives or public procurement programmes** that create sufficiently attractive returns on investment to offset risks taken. They should be easy to comprehend and avoid retroactive adjustment. In the case of regulation, this could provide a requirement to build all new buildings to a specific level of energy or water efficiency from a certain date. For financial incentives this could constitute a feed-in tariff (FiT), a payment linked to renewable energy power generation for example, that enables the project developer to overcome the financial disincentive of deploying a potentially higher-cost renewable energy technology compared to a lower-cost fossil fuel–based option. Alternatively, it might be a guaranteed long-term power offtake price, which a renewable energy provider might bid to secure in a capacity auction – the aforementioned 'contract for difference' approach.

d. **Coherency and efficiency**: Where possible, targets and incentives should not be undermined by targets and goals giving conflicting signals. Capital will generally flow to the easiest-to-finance investments with the most attractive risk-adjusted returns, and conflicting signals may well undermine the efficacy of policy signals; for example, in the climate and energy space, fossil fuel subsidies will undermine the signals created by renewable energy targets and feed-in tariffs by sending conflicting messages about the future of the energy system. They may also cause the taxpayer/consumer to pay more than needed due to the effect of one system of subsidy, meaning a second system must be set at a higher price to overcome the first subsidy's effect on market prices. Similarly, incentivising renewable energy investment, while not enabling projects to

---

[2] Adapted from Department of Energy and Climate Change (2012).

connect to the electricity grid and so generate a return, underpins investor confidence and market growth; for example, in China, the percentage of unconnected wind power was at its peak in 2008 at 31 per cent, prompting a mass build out of grid infrastructure (Zhao, 2015).

e. **Avoiding retroactive adjustment** of policy. Once the policy is made it should be fixed and any payment commitments made under existing contracts honoured. The instances where retroactive adjustments have been applied (e.g. in Spain in 2010 with solar photovoltaic energy[3]) had a very significant chilling effect on investor sentiment.

The development of an investible policy approach that addresses the above-mentioned barriers to deploying sustainable infrastructure and technology could be achieved in the following ways:

Lack of clarity on business models: Going beyond simple technology regulation, in 2018 the UK introduced new rules making it illegal to rent out a property with an energy performance certificate rating of below 'E'. This is expected to stimulate the market for whole-home energy efficiency retrofits through creating new demand. A similar lack of clarity on business models faces the mass deployment of electric vehicle charging structures. Demand is likely to be forthcoming, but questions remain as to the scale and pace of that demand growth and how, when and by whom upfront investment will be repaid in the interim, which creates uncertainty for the investors in charging infrastructure. In London the issue is being tackled through a joint public–private initiative led by London's mayor. As well as providing ultra-rapid charging points at London petrol stations and new multi-car charging hubs, it includes demand indication initiatives such as a 'one-stop shop' for Londoners to request new charging infrastructure from local authorities in areas of high demand.

---

[3] The government introduced attractive FiTs in 1994, then revised them upwards in 1997, which led to a boom in solar PV in particular so that by 2008-end the 2010 targets for PV had been exceeded eightfold with ~4 GW installed compared to a target of 500 MW. In November 2010 the government introduced a royal decree that reduced the solar PV tariff for existing assets by 45 per cent for ground-mounted projects, 25 per cent for 21 kW–100 kW medium-sized roof installations and 5 per cent for smaller household-sized installations.

Unproven demand: In order to boost demand for energy efficiency products and services, the UK government made it a requirement in 2007 that all new gas boilers installed be condensing boilers, which are 20–30 per cent more efficient than standard ones. To boost demand for more energy-efficient vehicles, in 2008 the French government introduced a bonus-malus 'feebate' scheme, linking carbon dioxide (CO_2) emissions from vehicles to levels of road tax levies. The car buyer would either pay a fee (malus) for vehicle CO_2 emissions above certain levels (as officially determined by the EU vehicle-type approval procedure) or receive a rebate (bonus) if the vehicle's CO_2 emissions were below certain limits. Both of these measures incentivised businesses to invest in the development of more efficient products.

The 'valley of death' funding gap: Early support for strategically important sectors is critically important to overcome the 'valley of death' phenomenon; for example, in Denmark, decisions were made in the 1970s to pioneer the development of commercial wind power through a close collaboration between publicly financed research and industry players, in key areas which included research and development, certification, testing and the preparation of standards to roll the technology out at scale. In 2019, Denmark topped the world in renewable power generation at 51 per cent (REN21, 2019) In the United Kingdom, a similar strategic commitment was to offshore wind. Originally deemed too expensive to deploy at scale, it was nonetheless supported by the UK Treasury with subsidies worth £150/MWh (or £167/MWh in current money). Less than ten years later, costs had fallen dramatically to £44/MWh (in current money) (CarbonBrief, 2019).

In summary, policy measures should act to address identified market barriers, both on the demand and supply side, in order to deliver the market disruptions required to achieve public policy goals.

2.3   THE ROLE OF PUBLIC FINANCE IN CROWDING-IN PRIVATE FINANCE

Throughout the examples given in this chapter, there has been either an explicit or implicit mention of the important role that public-sourced funding plays in facilitating the transition to a sustainable economy, crowding in sustainable finance as it goes.

The approach to date – particularly in relation to climate change – has generally been to use policy to create revenue streams that incentivise new market creation. The examples provided show how FiTs have been used to encourage private sector investment into renewables, with great success. Renewable energy now makes up one-third of global capacity, with FiTs in 111 countries (see REN21, 2019). Such approaches can also be used for social programmes. One example is the GAVI vaccination programme. This was developed in response to concerns that by the late 1990s there were still 30 million children living in poor countries who were not fully immunised. As a unique public–private partnership, the GAVI initiative worked with governments to pool demand for vaccines in the world's poorest countries, creating markets as it did so. The upfront cost of vaccination is covered through issuing vaccine bonds – this provides long-term funding that is underwritten and also repaid from pledges by donor governments.[4] By 2019-end, more than US$6bn has been raised and more than 700 million children have been vaccinated.

To move markets at scale to deliver public policy goals, however, there needs to be a focus on both creating incentives to deliver returns and managing downside risks to encourage private sector investment. Public finance can be used as an especially useful tool to achieve this.

2.4   INNOVATIVE PUBLIC FINANCE SOLUTIONS

2.4.1   The Role of Public Banks in Attracting Private Investment

To date, governments have generally deployed public finance instruments on an ad hoc basis, oftentimes delivered by government departments rather than by public banks. Yet the challenge of delivering a sustainable economy is a long-term multifaceted and dynamic challenge. Increasingly there is an understanding that, on the public sector

---

[4] See https://iffim.org/investor-centre/vaccine-bonds.

side, there is a need for institutional innovation for public finance institutions globally to play a more activist role. More innovative and systematic approaches are needed, as is captured well in the following quote.

> Some argue that good government policies and waiting for the
> financial market to return to 'normal' after the credit crunch will be
> enough to deliver the necessary investment [to decarbonise the
> economy]. We disagree. Even a return to the 'old normal', which is
> not likely, would not accommodate the unprecedented scale,
> urgency and nature of the challenge. The only sensible plan given
> the conclusion of the Stern Review is to act now to facilitate the
> required investment needed to safeguard our future.
>
> *(Green Investment Bank Commission, 2010)*

Public banks have, historically, often played a role in the transformation of economies. For example, the *Sparkassen* (public savings banks) in Germany helped bankroll the Industrial Revolution and *Caisse des Dépôts et Consignations* in France was founded to reorganise the French financial system after the fall of Napoleon. Their financial expertise and public interest mandate can act as another check and balance in the system to ensure that member state governments effectively target scarce public money to maximise the leveraging of private capital. They can also help build confidence – by ensuring governments have 'skin in the game'.

As a result, it is clear that public banks are and will continue to be important players during the process of transition from the old to the new, more sustainable ways to running the global economy. They have an important role to play in reducing costs through managing risks and accelerating the scale up of private sector investment by building confidence through co-investment that clearly aligns the financial interests of the public and private sectors.

Public banks are also usually better able to adapt and remove financial interventions based on the changing realities of markets, rather than support mechanisms directly controlled by government officials. They can also drive innovation in the market, as the following examples showcase.

To scale up energy efficiency investment in the EU, the Private Finance for Energy Efficiency Initiative (PF4EE) – the latest evolution of the European Investment Bank's (EIB) energy efficiency finance offering – aims to address the limited access to adequate and affordable commercial financing for energy efficiency investments. Launched in 2017, the PF4EE instrument's two core objectives are:

- to make energy efficiency lending a more sustainable activity within European financial institutions, considering the energy efficiency sector as a distinct market segment.
- to increase the availability of debt financing to eligible energy efficiency investments.

The PF4EE instrument provides:

1. a portfolio-based credit risk protection provided by means of cash collateral (risk sharing facility), together with
2. long-term financing from the EIB (EIB Loan for Energy Efficiency) and
3. expert support services for the Financial Intermediaries (Expert Support Facility)

The instrument targets projects that support the implementation of National Energy Efficiency Action Plans or other energy efficiency programmes of EU member states.[5] To date the programme has financed investment programmes based in nine European countries and is deemed a success, with a second requests for proposals now issued.

To connect more institutional investment to infrastructure projects, the EIB has also developed instruments at the other end of the spectrum. Dating back to 2012, and still operational today, the Project Bond Credit Enhancement (PBCE) is a subordinated

[5] See the EIB website: www.eib.org/en/products/blending/pf4ee/index.htm.

instrument – either a loan or a contingent facility – targeted to support senior project bonds issued by a project company for infrastructure projects. As a subordinated instrument, PBCE is designed to increase the credit rating of the senior bonds, not to extend the EIB's AAA credit rating to the project. PBCE can disburse a subordinated tranche in one of two ways:

- Funded PBCE: A loan provided to the project company from the outset.
- Unfunded PBCE: A contingent credit line that can be drawn if the cash flows generated by the project are not sufficient to ensure senior bond debt service or to cover construction cost overruns.

The instrument targets infrastructure-related projects in transport, energy and ICT (information communications technology) (Asian Development Bank, 2019).

A similar initiative – launched in 2019 by the Asian Infrastructure Investment Bank's (AIIB) Board of Directors – approved US$500mn for a managed credit portfolio that aims to develop infrastructure as an asset class, develop debt capital markets for infrastructure and promote the integration of environmental, social and governance (ESG) principles in fixed income investments in emerging Asia. Focussed on infrastructure-related bonds as an asset class, the AIIB Asia ESG Enhanced Credit-Managed Portfolio will be comprised of corporate bonds issued by infrastructure-related issuers, including quasi-sovereign bonds and green bonds, where proceeds are directed to sustainable infrastructure and other productive sectors (Asian Development Bank, 2019).

In the United Kingdom, the Green Investment Bank, when still under public ownership, established the world's first listed renewables energy infrastructure fund, the purpose of which was to enable more equity to be available to be deployed into UK offshore wind investment. Through buying out equity stakes in operational offshore wind projects and aggregating them into the listed fund, offshore wind developers – typically large utilities – were able to refinance part of their investments in operating assets to reinvest in new developments.[6]

Also, in the United Kingdom there is a strong argument to make that the private finance initiative (PFI), where private firms are contracted to complete and manage social infrastructure projects, would have delivered much better value for money for taxpayers if public banks instead of government had been the counterparty. The PFI approach has been beneficial in many ways – it fits the 'long, loud and legal' criteria – in that it clarifies the level of demand for investment to the private sector, by setting up investment programmes and guaranteeing revenue streams that will come from them. It also borrows from the future to pay for assets that are needed now, bringing many short-term benefits. The approach can increase both the accountability and efficiency of public spending investment. This assumes, however, that risk and cost are apportioned appropriately between the public and private sectors. It is on this last count that the PFI has fallen down, arguably something that is less likely to have happened if government project financiers – a public infrastructure bank – had been involved. The London Underground public–private partnership saw the bankruptcy of private company Metronet, tasked with a £17bn upgrade of the tube network. The government was forced to step in and bring the underground upgrade back into public hands at a cost of £2bn to the public purse.

2.4.2   Technical Assistance

Public banks also have a critically important role to play in the provision of technical assistance for project development. Lack of project development capacity to meet investment targets was one of the key gaps identified by the HLEG, which noted that there is a need for a 'match making' facility between infrastructure developers and infrastructure investors. In particular, where responsibility for delivering environmental or social goals is devolved to subnational-level

---

[6] www.bloomberg.com/quote/PE11831:LN.

jurisdictions, there can be a lack of capacity on the part of the public authority to understand how to structure, develop and bring onstream infrastructure projects in a way that is attractive to investors.

The EIB has established the European Investment Advisory Hub, which provides targeted support to identify, prepare and develop investment projects across the EU. Services via the Hub include project development support throughout all project stages, as well as upstream or policy advice. Financial advice is also provided to enhance companies' ability to access adequate sources of financing. Sectors covered include those with high environmental or social value including:

- Research, development and innovation.
- Development of the energy sector (renewables, energy efficiency and grid investment).
- Development of transport infrastructures, equipment and innovative technologies for transport.
- Financial support for SMEs and small mid-cap companies.
- Development and deployment of information and communication technologies.
- Environment and resource efficiency.
- Human capital, culture and health.

The Hub is designed to act as a single access point to various types of advisory and technical assistance services. It supports the identification, preparation and development of investment projects across the EU. The Hub's advisers work directly with project sponsors to prepare a bespoke advisory package that turns the project from an idea into an investible proposition.[7]

In Europe, another example is the European Bank for Reconstruction and Development (EBRD), which has established the Green Economy Financing Facility (GEFF) that supports businesses and homeowners wishing to invest in green technologies. The GEFF programme operates through a network of more than 130 local

---

[7] See https://eiah.eib.org/about/index.

financial institutions across 24 countries supported by almost €4bn of EBRD finance. GEFF goes beyond providing simple lines of finance. An experienced EBRD team of bankers and technical programme managers ensures consistent quality and innovation in the GEFF product and service delivery. In addition, advisory services are available to help participating financial institutions and their clients enhance their market practices.[8]

2.4.3   *Where Next for the Public Bank Sector?*

Public banks have focussed historically purely on social and economic agendas. It is only relatively recently (in the last two decades) that they have switched their focus to addressing environmental and, in particular, climate change-related investment issues. One of the challenges they have faced institutionally is having misaligned investment priorities – that is a mandate to support continued investment into unsustainable infrastructure (airports, fossil-based power generation, gas pipelines) at the same time as sustainable infrastructure (ground-based public transport, renewable energy and energy efficiency), which could in fact shorten the economic life and returns from the unsustainable infrastructure. During the period 2014–2018, for example, the national and regional development banks of the International Development Finance Club (IDFC[9]) reported on average close to US$150bn yearly of climate finance, representing only around 20 per cent of their total financial commitments.

After years of campaigning by civil society actors, public banks including those in the IDFC and the MDBs[10] are now publicly recognising this disconnect. A major milestone was reached in 2017 at the One Planet Summit in Paris, where the IDFC and MDBs committed

---

[8] See https://ebrdgeff.com/about-seff.

[9] This includes banks such as the African Development Bank, Asian Development Bank, European Investment Bank and World Bank Group.

[10] This includes banks such as KfW, CDP and so on. The full list provided in www.idfc .org/members.

to increase their financing for climate change-related activities, agreeing to:

- Further embed climate change considerations within their strategies and activities and promote the mainstreaming of climate action throughout the financial community.
- Redirect financial flows in support of transitions towards low carbon and climate-resilient sustainable development.
- Catalyse investments to address new economic, social and environmental challenges and opportunities related to climate change, in particular by using capital to mobilise additional private capital and to blend public financing most effectively with other sources to drive climate action and results.
- Pursue the development of processes, tools, methodologies and institutional arrangements that make it possible to design and implement climate action at the required scale. This includes reinforcing the collaborative effort between development finance institutions (DFIs) to improve the quality, robustness and consistency of climate finance tracking and reporting through the sharing of best practices and knowledge and by increasing the transparency and accessibility of their climate finance data.
- Collaborate with national and subnational governments to promote the reduction of greenhouse gas emissions, including the development of sustainable alternatives to fossil fuel investments, based on national circumstances and contexts, and prioritising the financing of these alternatives.
- Support the development of enabling policy and regulatory environments, at both national and subnational levels, in conjunction with the private sector and civil society. Importantly they stated IDFC members and MDBs will continue to deepen this work and increase country-level coordination between institutions. As per their respective mandates, IDFC members and MDBs will continue to contribute to policy dialogues, develop technical capacities of clients and strengthen institutions to enable the translation of national development plans (in relation to climate change) into policies, investment plans and financeable programs and projects, as well as into incentives for the business community.
- Provide further support to countries and partners to accelerate climate action and ambition by 2020, including the development of long-term

2050 decarbonisation pathways and strategies to reach zero net emissions and promote shorter-term actions that provide the building blocks for achieving these longer-term development pathways.[11]

These commitments were notable; in particular the efforts made by the MDBs and IDFC to work with governments to deliver, in effect, national capital raising plans and support their delivery with investment grade policy.

Further, important commitments have been made more recently, by the IDFC in particular. In short, their member organisations have committed to mainstream climate considerations into their investment decisions and work with others to play an increasingly proactive role in actively facilitating the transition to a sustainable economy.

In September 2019, the IDFC issued a communique[12] that acknowledged that national and regional MDBs have huge potential to support the implementation of the Paris Agreement on Climate Change and to generate green and climate – public and private – finance at scale to address the specific needs of their national economies, societies and environments. They noted that current efforts are not sufficient and that public banks must do much more to mainstream climate change considerations into all their investment and advisory activities. Further, the IDFC committed to contribute to this qualitative agenda by promoting the mainstreaming of climate considerations throughout the international and national financial communities and forcefully engaging, along with all interested partners, on the alignment of all financial flows with the Paris Agreement through:

- Committing US$1trn to climate finance by 2025.
- Sharing knowledge for climate finance and action.

---

[11] The full statement can be found here: www.afdb.org/fr/news-and-events/one-planet-summit-joint-idfc-mdb-statement-together-major-development-finance-institutions-align-financial-flows-with-the-paris-agreement-17685.

[12] www.idfc.org/wp-content/uploads/2019/09/official-idfc-communique-vdef21-09-2019-22h50-cet.pdf.

- Integrating climate considerations within financial institutions.
- Supporting capacity building activities and facilitating access to finance to achieve this.
- Outreach and awareness raising.

Since then further progress has been made by the EIB. In November 2019, it agreed an updated energy lending policy. Commitments include an end to fossil fuel financing from the end of 2021 and in the meantime a commitment to align all financing activities with the goals of the Paris Agreement from the end of 2020.

The EIB's commitments to end fossil fuel investment are notable. It includes a moratorium on support for upstream oil or gas production, coal mining, infrastructure dedicated to coal, oil and natural gas, and power generation or heat production from fossil fuel sources – effectively becoming the first non-dedicated green public bank to do so. It also reaffirms a commitment to supporting energy efficiency, renewables, innovation and energy infrastructure, including through the establishment of a new European Initiative for Building Renovation (EIB-R) to support new ways to attract finance for building rehabilitation, including models of mortgage-based lending.[13] The proposal has been given further momentum by the new European Commission President Ursula von der Leyen's promise of a Green Deal for Europe, part of which means transforming part of the EIB into Europe's Climate Bank, with at least 50 per cent of the Bank's financing to be dedicated to double action projects (double what it was in 2019).

2.4.4 Green Investment Banks

The issues set out above indicate some of the challenges faced by mainstream public banks trying to support the development of economics according to the old (high carbon) and the new (low carbon and resource-efficient) mantras. It was, in part, these competing objectives

---

[13] www.eib.org/attachments/draft-energy-lending-policy-26-07-19-en.pdf.

that led to the setting up of the UK's Green Investment Bank, the Australian Clean Finance Corporation and a whole host of dedicated institutions including the Japan Green Fund, Malaysia Green Technology Corporation, Connecticut Green Bank, NY Green Banks – institutions operating from a smaller capital base than their mainstream public bank partners but working solely to promote a low carbon economy.

These institutions will continue to play an important and focussed role in catalysing the transition to a resilient and net zero global economy.

2.5   ENSURING IMPACT

In their 2017 commitments at the One Planet summit, members of the IDFC and MDBs agreed to continue to lead on the transparent tracking and reporting of climate finance flows and impacts, stepping into a breach left by policy makers at national level. Official data on the current ability of the financial system (public and private) to deliver global and local climate and sustainability goals is sorely lacking. This makes efforts to close investment gaps less precise and effective than they should be. It also hinders the relevant authorities from making assessments of whether public policy and public finance interventions are being effective in closing any targeted investment gaps. Improved tracking of the sustainable investment and progress in closing investment gaps is therefore urgently needed. In the context of the EU, the HLEG proposed the formation of an EU Observatory on Sustainable Finance to help track sustainable investment from public and private sources and inform evidence-based policy making on sustainable finance. It suggested that, given the urgency of addressing climate change, the initial focus of the Observatory should be on tracking investment and capital formation towards the EU's 2030 climate and energy targets and its commitments under the Paris Agreement. It was also suggested that the focus could later be extended to include other sustainable development priorities and the tracking of sustainable and responsible investment trends in Europe, thus supporting other existing institutions working to assess how private flows actually contribute to sustainability.

It was felt that the significant public value created by such an Observatory would offset the costs of collecting and making the data publicly available in two ways. First the Observatory would connect the dots between multiple aggregated and disaggregated public and private data sources and publish in one repository. This in turn would generate system-wide cost savings for the public and private sector users of such data. It would also create a level playing field in terms of access to data across all member states. Second, the governance of the Observatory, which would be established jointly by key European environmental and financial regulators along with input from member states, would confer official status on the data, enabling government and EU institutions to use it to inform public policy making in relation to delivering climate change and, in due course, wider sustainability goals. It was proposed that the Observatory should therefore provide four core functions:

- Supporting decision making by both national governments and European institutions.
- Supporting member states in their efforts to develop and employ specific methodologies and tools that can track investment needs and match policy plans with a supply of capital.
- Reporting annually on progress towards meeting sustainable infrastructure and other capital formation needs in the EU.
- Supporting the development and monitoring of green and sustainable taxonomies as well as track the expansion of sustainable and responsible private investment in Europe.

The Observatory has not be taken forward as originally envisaged, but the EU has committed to setting up a 'platform on sustainable finance': one of its tasks will be to take on responsibility for further developing the EU's new taxonomy – which is a tool to help investors understand whether an economic activity is environmentally sustainable or not (a further recommendation of the HLEG).

The lack of usable data remains a significant and enduring gap, which is only partially being filled through ad hoc NGO and public bank-led efforts.

2.6 CONCLUSIONS

Meeting the challenges of the SDGs and Paris Agreement on Climate Change will require the public and private sectors to work together. The greater scrutiny of investors that will be brought about by the new EU Sustainability-related Financial Disclosures Regulation in relation to ESG issues, due to come into force in 2021, and the ramping up of regulators' expectations on investor disclosure in line with the recommendations of the G20 Financial Stability Board's Task Force on Climate-Related Financial Disclosures (TCFD) are welcome.[14] Such disclosures should make investors more engaged with and aware of the risks and opportunities around the transition to a climate-resilient and sustainable economy. After awareness and a sense of responsibility are created, proactive actions will – one hopes – follow. After all, objective of disclosures is not, in the end, just the provision of information on a tick box basis, it is to drive operational and strategic change within business.

On this basis, one would hope that the disclosures, along with low carbon benchmarks and a sustainable taxonomy, will increasingly drive private sector actors to seek out and create more sustainable investment opportunities – either through engagement with investee companies, thereby directly influencing capex decisions, or through direct private investment, including with public banks, into sustainable assets and projects. The creation of investible opportunities at scale will remain key. Thus, greater capacity in the public policy space to create investible policy – supported by the MDBs and IDFCs – will also help accelerate actions, and announcements to support policy makers in this way are welcome.

---

[14] Information about the Taskforce can be found at www.fsb-tcfd.org/about. The latest status report can be found at www.fsb-tcfd.org/publications/tcfd-2019-status-report.

Finally, people must not be forgotten. The growing focus on social factors within the responsible investment agenda is important for delivering the just and inclusive transition that is required. This facet is key to securing the buy-in needed from citizens to ensure the transition to a sustainable economy can proceed at the pace needed to achieve the goals of the Paris Agreement.

REFERENCES

Asian Development Bank (2019), 'AIIB to Develop Infrastructure as an Asset Class and Catalyze ESG Investing Principles in Emerging Asia'. www.aiib.org/en/news-events/news/2019/20190109_001.html.

BEIS – Department for Business, Education and Skills (2019), 'Contracts for Difference', Policy Paper, updated January. www.gov.uk/government/publications/contracts-for-difference/contract-for-difference.

CarbonBrief (2019), 'Analysis: Record Low Price for UK Offshore Wind Cheaper Than Existing Gas Plants by 2023'. www.carbonbrief.org/analysis-record-low-uk-offshore-wind-cheaper-than-existing-gas-plants-by-2023.

Department for Energy and Climate Change (2012), 'Principles for Investment Grade Policy and Projects', Corporate Report, June. www.gov.uk/government/publications/principles-for-investment-grade-policy-and-projects.

Ellen MacArthur Foundation (2017), 'Achieving "Growth Within"'. www.ellenmacarthurfoundation.org/assets/downloads/publications/Achieving-Growth-Within-20-01-17.pdf.

European Commission (2017a), 'Financing Sustainability: Triggering Investments for the Clean Economy', European Political Strategy Centre, Policy Note, June. www.ec.europa.eu/epsc/sites/epsc/files/strategic_note_issue_25.pdf.

European Commission (2017b), 'Interim Report of the High-Level Expert Group on Sustainable Finance'. www.ec.europa.eu/info/publications/170713-sustainable-finance-report_en.

European Commission (2018a), 'Final Report of the High-Level Expert Group on Sustainable Finance', Brussels, January. https://ec.europa.eu/info/publications/180308-action-plan-sustainable-growth_en.

Green Finance Taskforce (2018), 'Accelerating Green Finance', HMG website, March. https://assets.publishing.service.gov.uk/government/uploads/system/uploads/attachment_data/file/703816/green-finance-taskforce-accelerating-green-finance-report.pdf.

(The) Green Investment Bank Commission (2010), 'Unlocking Investment to Deliver Britain's Low Carbon Future'. www.e3g.org/docs/Unlocking_investment_to_deliver_

Britains_low_carbon_future_-_Green_Investment_Bank_Commission_Report_June_2010.pdf.

(The) New Climate Economy (2014), 'Better Growth, Better Climate: The Synthesis Report', The Global Commission on the Economy and Climate, Washington. https://newclimateeconomy.report/2016/wp-content/uploads/sites/2/2014/08/BetterGrowth-BetterClimate_NCE_Synthesis-Report_web.pdf.

Ofgem (2010), 'Project Discovery: Options for Delivering Secure and Sustainable Energy Supplies'. www.ofgem.gov.uk/ofgem-publications/40354/projectdiscoveryfebcondocfinalpdf.

REN21 (2019), 'Renewables Global Status Report'. www.ren21.net/gsr-2019.

United Nations Secretary General (2019), 'Roadmap for Financing the 2030 Agenda for Sustainable Development 2019–2021', United Nations, Washington. www.un.org/sustainabledevelopment/wp-content/uploads/2019/07/UN-SG-Roadmap-Financing-the-SDGs-July-2019.pdf.

Zhao, F. (2015), 'China's Great Unconnected Wind Reserve', Energy World, December, pp. 24–25. www.fticonsulting.com/~/media/Files/us-files/intelligence/intelligence-events/energy-world–fti-article.pdf.

3   Central Banking and Climate Change

Kern Alexander and Paul G. Fisher

3.1   INTRODUCTION

The role of the financial system in the economy is to facilitate the
necessary financing for human activity to thrive – not only today, but
also for future generations. Central banks and financial regulators play
an important role in controlling the risks that imperil the stability and
sustainability of the financial system and hence the economy.
Following the Great Financial Crisis of 2007–2009 (the GFC), central
bank mandates have come under increasing scrutiny by policymakers
and, in some cases, are being reviewed to consider how they can be
interpreted to support broader financial regulatory reforms that aim to
generate strong, sustainable and balanced growth.

This chapter considers how central banks can play an important
role in mitigating the risks from environmentally unsustainable economic activity, particularly that which contributes to climate change.
We argue that the potential consequences of climate change – for the
economy and especially the financial sector – mean that it falls
squarely within the existing mandates of central banks and their
primary objectives. Beyond that, many central banks have secondary
objectives to support wider governmental policies which enable them
to go further, without compromising their primary objectives.

As fiscal and political authorities, governments are uniquely
situated to take the lead in mitigating climate change risks, for they
control legislation, taxation and expenditure programmes, and have
overall responsibility for regulatory frameworks and direct economic
interventions. However, the main agents for implementing governmental policies are in the private sector – which generate most of the
risks and have the greatest potential for managing them.

49

Notwithstanding those roles of government and the private sector, we argue that central banks must take climate change into account to the extent that it is part of their core mandates in delivering monetary and financial stability, and in discharging their supervisory responsibilities – as well as their broader balance sheet and other institutional responsibilities.

3.2 ENVIRONMENTAL RISKS AND CENTRAL BANKING

3.2.1 Historical Overview

Economic historians have demonstrated relationships between weather, agricultural markets and financial markets to show that there are linkages between natural disasters (e.g. drought) and financial market instability.[1] The United States suffered from dust bowls in the farm belt states in the 1880s and 1890s and again in the 1930s, because of soil erosion that occurred from unsustainable farming methods (Hornbeck, 2012). Some of the banking sector distresses experienced in the farm belt states can be attributed to the dustbowl phenomenon (Hornbeck, 2012, pp. 1481–1483).

More recently, increased hurricane activity in the Caribbean and south-eastern United States caused huge losses to businesses and individuals. Hurricane Andrew caused US$24bn in damages to the South Florida economy in 1992, while Rita, Wilma and Katrina each caused widespread and extensive damage in the region. Katrina ranks as one of the costliest natural disasters in US history (Lambert et al., 2017, p. 3). The damages led to high loan losses and provisioning for banks that were based in the impacted areas. Those losses led US regulators to review the adequacy of bank risk models regarding credit risk and hurricane damage.

Furthermore, the International Panel on Climate Change (IPCC) has documented the scientific evidence in support of the proposition

---

[1] For a review of the literature, see Landon-Lane et al. (2011), pp. 73–84.

that carbon-intensive activities lead in the longer-term to global warming, rising sea levels and ocean acidification, while in the shorter term they can lead to increasingly volatile weather patterns, including extreme temperatures and intensified flooding of coastal and low-lying areas, water shortages and the health costs arising out of pollution.[2] The linkages between environmental sustainability and economic and financial stability raise the fundamental question of whether, and if so how, central banks should respond to the risks associated with environmentally unsustainable activity.

The scale of the economic impact of such risks and of the economic transformation required to address them is significant. A study by the UN estimates that the annual cost to the global economy of maintaining the current scale of unsustainable economic activity will reach nearly US$28trn by 2050, equivalent to 18 per cent of global GDP (UNEP FI and PRI, 2011, p. 20). Meanwhile, estimates indicate that around US$1trn of additional investment is needed annually through to 2030, for new green infrastructure in energy, transport, buildings and industry (World Economic Forum, 2013).

Some believe that these externalities will be controlled and even mitigated through adaptations in the economy, such as alternative production processes and redirecting transport routes to avoid flooded coastlines (Nordhaus, 2013). According to this view, investors, aware of the scientific evidence supporting the risks from climate change, should discount the value of high carbon assets and increase the value of low carbon assets, resulting in investment shifting over time to low carbon assets. Nevertheless, the history of financial crises demonstrates that financial markets suffer from serious over- and underestimation of risks because of asymmetric information and moral hazard, resulting in large externalities for the economy and society (Eichengreen, 1999, pp. 80–82; Aliber and Kindleberger, 2015).

The risks from climate change are undoubtedly amongst the most important and urgent facing the world today – in 2019, the

[2] See IPCC (2018).

annual World Economic Forum Global Risks Report was once again dominated by climate and environmental factors amongst the top ten risks. But what is it that central banks can reasonably do to limit or mitigate the risks from climate change?

3.2.2   Modern Central Bank Responsibilities

Central banks have developed into a successful class of public institutions, largely since the 1990s when many were given independent authority to set monetary policy to achieve anti-inflationary objectives. This model is now recognised as best practice globally across a wide range of developed and developing countries, around thirty years since New Zealand adopted the first inflation target in 1990. By 2018, over forty central banks had an explicit inflation target framework and over twenty had a price stability objective operationalised in much the same way (International Monetary Fund, 2019).

Other core responsibilities of central banks include the issuance of domestic currency in the form of bank notes, providing clearing and settlement accounts for the banking system and responsibility for payments systems. All of these core responsibilities relate to the broad concept of 'sound money' or 'monetary stability' and its role in supporting economic welfare over the medium term.

Most central banks also have an actual or implied remit to preserve financial stability, either as a primary or as a secondary objective. This focus has grown as a result of the global financial crisis and can now be treated as a principal objective in most countries (Mersch, 2019).

Some central banks (e.g. European Central Bank (ECB), Bank of England) have broader authority, including the regulation and supervision of banks and other financial institutions (e.g. insurers, pension funds). In this chapter, we take the broadest view of central bank objectives regardless of national differences. These immensely important responsibilities are allocated to 'independent' central banks – whose leaders are unelected and are largely technocratic organisations that operate within their legal remits. On what basis could we expect central banks to play a role in climate change policy? This is a question which is being increasingly raised, not just by campaigners, but by the central banks themselves (Cœuré, 2018; PRA, 2018a; Debelle, 2019; Lagarde, 2019). The role of central banks has become even more important during the COVID-19 crisis, which provides a vivid example of the challenges that confront central banks in dealing with unforeseen sustainability risks of such magnitudes (Draghi, 2020).

3.3 MONETARY STABILITY

Monetary stability is perhaps the prime responsibility of a modern central bank. In developed countries, it usually involves targeting price stability directly, although many countries (e.g. Hong Kong, Saudi Arabia) remain focussed on their exchange rate (International Monetary Fund, 2019).

The primary tools of monetary policy are market operations – involving the purchase and sale (or repurchase) of bank assets and government debt – to guide short-term market interest rates and the supply of the narrow money base.[3] In recent years, with interest rates close to zero, the focus in many larger countries (the United States, Euro area, Japan, the United Kingdom) has been on expanding the supply of money through quantitative easing (QE) to prevent deflation.

Central banks use these tools to influence intermediate targets such as the balance between real aggregate demand and supply and to influence inflation expectations. Although there can be a short-term positive correlation between inflation and output in response to demand shocks, that relationship does not hold in the medium-term, and if consistently exploited, will lead to ever higher inflation. This tempts politicians to overstimulate the economy for political gain in the short-term. Committing to keep inflation low and stable is a prerequisite for maintaining sustainable growth and is in the broader public interest.[4]

---

[3] The narrow money supply, or base money, defined as bank notes in circulation plus private sector deposits held at the central bank in domestic currency.

[4] See H M Treasury (2018).

Similar medium-term considerations apply to both financial stability and micro-prudential supervision: seeking to steer a medium-term, resilient path for the economy rather than maximising (or allowing financial firms to maximise) short-run gains which lead to subsequent, costly crashes.

In the context of climate change, the imperative is to take a longer-term view of sustainability than just the five-to-seven years of the business cycle or the somewhat longer credit cycle. Sustainability needs to be considered across generations if the right policy choices are to be made (Stern Review, 2006). Carney (2015) described this as the 'Tragedy of the Horizons', in which the costs of preventing or mitigating the effects of climate change are lower, the sooner action is taken. But since the benefits largely accrue to later generations, current generations may not be willing to bear the costs. The likely consequence is that future generations will have to take much more costly actions later.

We might also identify market failures – that there are external-ities to current decisions, which are not priced properly. The market-based solution would be for governments to apply carbon taxes to correct the externalities directly – but such taxes are unpopular polit-ically and lack effective international co-ordination.

The risks associated with climate change are directly relevant to central banks because of their impact on monetary policy and in particular on price stability. As global temperatures rise, and so do sea levels, the impact of physical climate events such as droughts, storms, floods and wildfires could cause large relative price shocks: especially for food and other agricultural-related produce. There will also be price shocks arising from the transition to a lower carbon economy or to a higher temperature economy (possibly both) caused by changes in economic structure affecting the demand and supply of goods and services, for instance, the demand for air conditioning will likely rise. Longer-term impacts could include the re-location of large popula-tions from flooded or drought-stricken sites. There may also be struc-tural changes resulting directly from policy action, such as the banning of petroleum-driven vehicles from city centres.

These are supply side shocks, and the likely impact on inflation will be at varying frequencies: both relatively slow-moving trend changes in price differentials and sudden volatility in relation to climate or policy shocks. In all cases, there could be a rise(fall) in the retail price level that shows as a temporary upwards(downwards) movement in recorded inflation – possibly for some years – but not as a permanent change unless inflation expectations also rise(fall) and policy is accommodative. In the past, such effects have been evident in the case of oil price shocks and, to a lesser extent, food prices and tax changes.

Monetary policy is simplest to set for demand shocks – if output and (expected) inflation rise together, then the obvious policy is to tighten (and vice versa for negative shocks). But supply shocks drive inflation and output in opposite directions and policy is then less clear. Tightening to bring down inflation after a supply shock could worsen the fall in output – an unnecessary cost if the inflation movement is temporary. Policy should be adjusted only if there is a significant risk of inflation expectations becoming de-anchored, threatening a more general inflationary (deflationary) outcome.

The appropriate monetary policy response to a supply shock could be confined to communications aimed at anchoring expectations. But the more frequently such shocks occur, the more likely it is that temporary inflation movements lead to expectations changing.

3.3.1 What Can Monetary Policy Do to Mitigate the Threats from Climate Change?

First, we observe from previous crisis episodes, that when monetary or financial stability is lost, the resources of governments and central banks alike become devoted to short-term crisis management. That is probably the easiest way to lose sight and control of any longer-term sustainability agenda. Indeed, one of the main motivations for low and stable inflation is precisely that it enables economic agents to concentrate on matters related to real outcomes and long-term planning without being distracted by the costs of inflation or short-term volatility in the economic cycle. Central banks must not compromise on their core objective of monetary stability. Sound monetary and financial control is a prerequisite for a long-term sustainable economy.

Second, central banks need to refocus their analytical abilities more to the supply side, including better data collection. In the history of inflation targeting, it was widely assumed that changes in potential growth were too slow moving to be relevant for monetary policy, whilst supply shocks were isolated and transient. It was only labour markets that were of interest on the supply side, as they had long been seen as a source of inflationary expectations manifesting themselves via wage increases.

Third, central banks have monetary tools that involve adjusting the size of their own balance sheets to change the level of base money supply. These tools could affect the supply of credit or liquidity for banks and the financial system to support lending and investment in environmentally sustainable sectors of the economy. Between 2009 and 2014, the Bank of England followed a 'Funding for Lending' (FLS) scheme that involved the central bank providing liquidity at low interest rates to banks, secured largely on illiquid assets, in order to reduce the pressure on bank funding that had been driving up the interest rates paid on deposits (Fisher, 2013).

The FLS and similar schemes in the United Kingdom and in the Euro area have raised the question of whether central banks should routinely make funding available to banks or other credit providers in order to promote increased lending to environmentally sustainable economic activity. Other central bank monetary actions could involve, for example, favourable treatment of collateral in routine liquidity-providing operations.

Collateral policy is a relatively narrow, technical issue. Normally central banks will prefer liquid, safe assets as collateral in lending operations. That may or may not include 'green' or 'brown' assets. Markets are generally more liquid where the assets are eligible as collateral at the central bank and that could suggest a more positive stance towards sustainable assets. Meanwhile, the risk stays with the collateral provider unless there is a default, when central banks may become the asset owners. It would be appropriate for central banks to review their collateral policies on both market liquidity and the riskiness of their counterparties. For example, the People's Bank of China (PBOC, 2015) utilises more proactive measures to provide additional liquidity support to Chinese banks, such as the acceptance of 'green asset-backed securities' as collateral (Peng et al., 2018).

3.3.2 Bank Notes

An area of monetary stability that is directly relevant to carbon emissions is the issuance of bank notes. Although the actual process of printing banking notes is largely industrial and often outsourced, central banks retain the policy responsibility and, in some cases, they operate the actual printing presses.

Traditionally, banknotes were made from cotton-based paper. But polymer bank notes have been in circulation in some countries for decades (Australia since 1988) and introduced in others more recently (Canada in 2011; the United Kingdom in 2016). To meet government commitments to limit global warming, it should be expected that all manufacturing processes for bank notes will come under pressure to be more energy efficient and less polluting.

Polymer bank notes are more durable than paper-based notes and, perhaps surprisingly, easier to recycle, but they cost more to produce. A conservative estimate by the Bank of England is that they would last 2.5 times longer than a paper-based equivalent. Based on that, a life cycle analysis commissioned from an independent consultant concluded that polymer had less environmental impact than paper (Bank of England, 2013). A report commissioned from The Carbon Trust (Bank of England, 2017) certified that over their full life cycle, the carbon footprint of a £5 polymer banknote is 16 per cent lower than the previous £5 paper banknote, while that of a £10 polymer banknote is 8 per cent lower. The economic and sustainability case for polymer bank notes seems clear, although it was notably rejected by the ECB (Reuters, 2014).

3.4   CENTRAL BANK BALANCE SHEETS

3.4.1   *Quantitative Easing*

Central bank balance sheets are primarily used to implement monetary policy. Whether there is an exchange rate target or an inflation target, the policy instruments of interest rates and/or the narrow money supply can be adjusted accordingly. Foreign exchange reserves may also be part of the central bank balance sheet and used for monetary policy purposes. Occasionally, central bank balance sheets are used to support financial stability, in part by being lender of last resort (LoLR) to the banking system.

The central banks of most of the world's large developed economies began QE during the GFC, undertaken as a combination of both their monetary and financial stability responsibilities. After interest rates were cut to near zero, QE involved buying large quantities of financial assets. That automatically injected historically large amounts of base money and hence liquidity into the system, reducing interest rates and spreads at all maturities.

One of the main motivations for QE was to counter the risk of falling prices at the same time as stagnation in output, a combination which could have been very difficult to escape otherwise. QE was generally successful in pushing inflation back up towards target. Arguably it was most effective during the periods in which financial markets were dysfunctional – during 2008–2009 and then the Greek sovereign debt crisis in 2012. Despite popular misconceptions to the contrary, expanding the money supply cannot (much) affect the medium-term growth rate and is not a cause of, nor a cure for, poor productivity growth.

Central banks have expanded their balance sheets again in response to the COVID-19 health and economic crisis in order to support governments in stopping a cascade of debt defaults that could topple healthy businesses and exacerbate job losses across countries. Moreover, Fisher and Hughes Hallett (2018) suggest that it is likely that central bank balance sheets will remain much larger than before the GFC, since banks require many more liquid assets to meet their new Basel minimum liquidity requirements. Expanded central bank balance sheets have highlighted several questions including how large they could be and what assets they should hold? In particular, some politicians and campaigners have argued that central banks could invest in social or green assets ('People's QE' or 'Green QE'). The question has become acutely political for the ECB which bought large quantities of corporate bonds, and some members of the European Parliament have demanded to know what the carbon footprint of these assets is and why climate change risks were not taken into account when selecting bonds for purchase (ECB, 2018).

We note that QE operations are intended by central banks to be market neutral, that is, not to allocate capital between competing borrowers. And whatever is purchased, all asset prices tend to rise together, and hence green and brown assets are both automatically supported by any form of monetary expansion.

Purchasing particular assets in large scale using cash can also be used to change the liquidity properties of financial markets: (a) buying less liquid assets reduces total market liquidity risk; (b) buying long-dated assets shortens total market-held duration risk; (c) buying credit-risky assets reduces credit spreads. By reducing risks and hence spreads, all of these factors can then force some investors to seek out higher returns. And if a market for a particular asset is dysfunctional for some reason, then central bank buying of those assets can improve market functioning (e.g. the US Federal Reserve policy of buying housing-backed assets and ECB purchases of corporate bonds). This can be termed 'credit easing' rather than QE.

Should QE be used to purchase green assets? At the start of 2020, there is no shortage of demand for green assets – if anything there is insufficient supply. Green bond issues are regularly increased in size during the issuance process, without any detrimental effect on price. Given that, there is currently no obvious policy case for central banks buying green assets. It would simply crowd out private sector purchases by removing those bonds from the tradeable market at a time when the investor base is still growing rapidly. That is more likely to disrupt market growth, rather than add to it. Meanwhile, existing QE will have been indirectly supporting private sector demand for all assets. The balance of demand and supply may change in future, but for now the purchase of green assets by the central bank in large scale would likely be counterproductive.

There are also other concerns. Central bank balance sheets need to be able to both expand and contract quickly – whatever assets are purchased for monetary purposes may be sold quickly if policy needs to tighten. And if central banks want to buy assets on ESG grounds they would first need to be able to identify them – that would currently be difficult given the lack of defined asset classes.

Overall, there are good reasons why central banks might prefer to remain neutral in their asset purchases. But a counter case can be made. First, central banks are exposed to climate risks in their asset holdings, just like any other financial institution. These risks should be recognised in their own risk management frameworks. Second, central bank balance sheets will likely stay enlarged. If so, there will be a large portion of their asset base which will not need to be sold in future and, risk considerations aside, there is no clear policy reason for holding, or not, any particular type of asset. Some portion of the expanded balance sheet could be allocated to hold an investment tranche of long-term assets other than government bonds.

Central banks could also become more transparent in their balance sheet operations. As discussed subsequently, the recommendations of the Task Force on Climate-Related Financial Disclosures (TCFD, 2017) were not designed for central banks, but they could be adapted to allow the public to know, at least generically, what assets are being held by public sector institutions (e.g. central banks) and what their carbon footprint is.

3.4.2 *Foreign Exchange Reserves and Sovereign Wealth Management*

Central banks often hold large quantities of foreign exchange reserves on balance sheet or manage them on behalf of governments. Currency reserves may be held for policy purposes such as potential intervention in foreign exchange markets or as a store of national wealth. Where the latter is large, it can be held by a Sovereign Wealth Fund (SWF) which can be an active manager. Governance varies from the central bank owning the SWF (e.g. Botswana) to managing it (Norway), to having partial responsibility (China), to having none (Singapore). Leaving aside the tranche of funds that are invested for policy purposes, sovereign wealth funds can be very large and potentially internationally significant: China has US$3trn of reserves, and the largest single SWF is the Norwegian Government Pension Fund Global with over US$1trn.

The considerations for managing such funds are very similar to large private sector asset managers, except for the fact that sovereign investors have more political/social mandates and they might be expected to take rather more externalities into account. These funds are for national saving and should be used to generate sustainable returns for future generations. We should therefore expect SWFs to demonstrate best practice in managing their investments sustainably. For example, that may mean avoiding the obvious downside tail risks from investing in the coal industry, as Norway has announced. Such decisions by the larger SWFs could influence other asset managers.

3.5 FINANCIAL STABILITY

Systemic crises usually occur when risks have accumulated unseen or been underestimated and then suddenly crystallise leading to market price 'jumps'. Financial market prices do not always adjust smoothly. They are forward-looking, which means that particular pieces of news are extrapolated across time and sectors to take account of broader implications. This can cause asset re-pricing to be exacerbated, potentially to large jumps for whole asset classes.

Although regulators would aim to mitigate such shocks, history suggests that severe shocks are recurring. As financial stability policy is oriented towards making the system resilient, the regulatory objectives for the banking system should include ensuing that the interconnections between institutions does not lead to a single firm's failure bringing down the financial system. Institutions should hold enough capital to absorb severe but plausible losses under a stress scenario, whilst continuing to provide financial services to their customers. Co-ordinated stress tests are now undertaken in many jurisdictions to help achieve this objective.

The main financial stability risk from climate change is that there could be a sufficiently large and widespread fall in financial asset prices, possibly from stranded fossil fuel assets, to cause system-wide effects that disrupt financial services. To address this, the United Kingdom has made its first proposals for climate stress tests (Bank of England, 2019).

Market price jumps could occur as a result of transition risks crystallising, via sudden government policy changes – especially if global in impact. These would be regarded as extreme tail risks, but preserving financial stability generally requires being robust to tail events. Changes in energy policy have already led in whole, or in part, to significant changes in the prices of individual energy company stocks.

One can also imagine financial market dislocations arising from physical events, should they be sufficiently severe or simultaneous. An extreme example would be if there were floods in London, severe hurricanes in New York and an earthquake in Tokyo by random chance at the same time. Not only would markets be disrupted by those events, but also by changing assessments of the likelihood of future disruptions.

One policy response to the risks of climate change, which would make the system more resilient, is to have more public information on climate-related exposures of corporate entities. Such information can be used to price the risks that firms face (including the credit risk in loans) and to re-price should an event change perceptions of the future. That should mean that jumps in asset prices are smaller and occur less frequently.

A major benefit of disclosure is that the firm disclosing must first evaluate the risks that it is exposed to and that alone may prompt changes in behaviour. One disincentive to disclosure is the risk of a negative market reaction and so the worst carbon emitters are least likely to disclose voluntarily. That argues for making such disclosures mandatory.

The private sector-led TCFD has provided the main policy initiative on disclosure. The TCFD report of July 2017 (TCFD, 2017) recommended that firms should disclose, in their main financial filings, how they are managing climate-related risks in four areas: governance, strategy, risk management, and targets and metrics. Although the 2017 report is not a blueprint for all firm disclosures, it recommends that firms should use scenario analysis to assess climate-related risks. A number of countries have endorsed the TCFD recommendations, including the EU and the United Kingdom, and hundreds of large companies internationally are seeking to implement them (TCFD, 2018, 2019). In the longer-term, once the methods for disclosure have become settled, it is probably inevitable that such disclosures will become required reporting requirements.

3.6 PRUDENTIAL SUPERVISION

Not all central banks undertake prudential regulation and supervision, but they are usually a key stakeholder and policy contributor through their interest in financial stability. Broadly speaking we can describe regulation as setting and enforcing rules, and supervision as a more investigative and intrusive oversight. Both have a role to play. In this section, we outline the nature of the risks in insurance and banking and then consider how regulators might intervene.

3.6.1 Insurance Supervision

In 2015, the Bank of England's Prudential Regulation Authority (PRA) published an influential paper on the risks to the UK insurance industry (PRA, 2015). This has been followed with an assessment of risks to the UK banking sector (PRA, 2018a). Insurance firms are in the front line for climate risks, as it affects both their underwriting and asset management functions. The market has broadly three categories of insurer, each facing different risks: general, life and re-insurance.

General insurers are those who write insurance policies for retail and businesses relating to day-to-day risks such as accidental damage, loss, theft and so forth. These policies cover general business and consumer disruption, including climate-related events such as floods, storms and droughts and even catastrophes. Their modelling has to reflect the trends and so-called tail risks (high impact, but low probability). These policies can usually be re-priced every year, thereby allowing the general insurance industry – providing it stays alert and extrapolates reasonably – to protect itself. Indeed, it has a key part to play in climate risk adaptation – helping to spread the costs from global warming over time, space and people.

In much of the world, especially in poorer countries, insurance coverage is weak. And particular risks may become uninsurable even in developed countries. For example, as sea levels rise or rainfall increases in certain areas, flood insurance may no longer be available. In the United Kingdom, this has led to the government and industry jointly creating Flood-Re – a re-insurance company that helps insurance companies to pass on their more extreme risks.

Climate losses can also be large and unpredictable. A report by Lloyd's of London (Lloyd's, 2014) into Superstorm Sandy in New York in 2012 estimated that the losses from the groundwater upsurge were increased by some 30 per cent (cUS$6bn) because of the rise in sea level at the Battery, of some 20 cm since the 1950s.

Life insurance companies (or superannuation funds) face additional risks on the asset side. These insurers need to match their longer-term liabilities with similarly long-term assets. These assets, especially property, are subject to physical and transition risks.

Re-insurance can reduce the capital requirements of the industry by diversifying underwriting risks – if uncorrelated enough they shouldn't all crystallise at the same time, so capital can do 'double duty'. There is a risk from climate change, however, that correlations may be changing, for example climate events appear to be becoming more directly interdependent, in which case the diversification benefits may be overestimated – an example of 'wrong-way' risk.

3.6.2 Banking

The risks for banks are more nuanced because their assets tend to be shorter-term, and they take security against loans. But banks lend to some activities which will become unsustainable – such as the coal industry. Over time, the associated credit risks will increase and could crystallise suddenly: Peabody Energy, the world's largest private coal producer eventually filed for chapter 11 protection in the United States, after a US Government shift in policy in favour of gas. And short-term lending is not always less risky than long-term – the original maturity date of a loan is not relevant if default happens suddenly.

The availability of collateral to take as security can also be a false comfort. That security is often in the form of property (e.g. for a mortgage) or plant (for a firm). Physical climate events could cause the borrower to default and simultaneously wipe out the physical asset. Hence it is a 'wrong-way' risk. The collateral may be protected by insurance. But banks do not typically keep records of whether their borrowers have maintained the relevant insurance. So, they do not know how much security they would really have in the event of extreme climate events.

3.6.3 The Role of Regulators

The role of financial regulation is to ensure that the financial system remains stable, not to protect the shareholders or management of individual companies. Even if a financial firm needs to be publicly supported so it can continue to provide necessary services, the shareholders should be wiped out and senior management fired. But climate risks are systemic and will most likely affect the whole financial system at the same time.

Alexander (2014) argues that the Basel system of capital requirements has all the elements that are necessary to protect the banking system in the context of climate change. Basel regulations comprise three pillars. Pillar I is the system of minimum capital requirements that apply to all firms. Pillar II is additional capital that is required to cover risks not captured by Pillar I. Normally, these will be idiosyncratic to the firm: capital 'add-ons' can be imposed using supervisory judgement. Pillar III is market discipline through disclosure.

Climate change represents a material financial risk and, regardless of the minimum calculations specified, the rules require that banks hold capital against all material risks that they themselves have identified. Supervisors should then examine banks to see whether climate-related risks are being properly identified and managed and that they are holding adequate capital. If not, then capital add-ons can be either threatened or imposed to incentivise banks to decrease their exposure to environmentally unsustainable financial risks.

This process is hindered by the lack of definitions of what assets are, or are not, sustainable. The EU is developing a taxonomy of green assets to remedy that, as part of its Action Plan on Financing Sustainable Growth (EC, 2018b). But, at the current time, supervisory action needs to be justified on broad grounds of risk management, rather than related to specific assets.

There have been propositions in favour of reducing Pillar I risk weights to incentivise green lending. In particular the so-called Green Supporting Factor (EBF, 2018) which was proposed by some European banks to be an ad hoc cut of 25 per cent in risk weights for 'green' lending. Alexander and Fisher (2019) argue that this would be a mistake on a number of grounds.

Financial stability is a prerequisite for a sustainable economy and, consistent with that, the Basel capital weights system is risk-based. It would be a mistake to jeopardise financial stability, and hence sustainable growth, by making non-risk-based adjustments to capital requirements.

Pillar I capital weights are both approximate and complicated. There are not yet any green asset classes defined to which differential capital weights could apply and there is no evidence yet that the risk-based weights in the Basel system are inappropriate for green lending. It is much more likely that lending to unsustainable activities could justify increased weights. Producing evidence to support changes in risk weights would be a lengthy and difficult process, however. In contrast, Pillar II is immediately available and can be used by supervisors now to directly increase capital requirements where banks do not have adequate risk management. That is the path on which leading supervisors are embarked (PRA, 2018b), although until there are more specific definitions, it will be up to the banks to both identify their risks and take appropriate action.

Similar arguments apply to the insurance industry. One difference is that the use of internal models to assess risk and capital is more advanced for an insurer which needs to link its assets to its liabilities, whereas a bank typically judges its capital needs solely by its assets. In both sectors, internal models should eventually capture any risk benefits of green lending and any costs from brown, but these risks will not be in the data underlying their models yet, since climate change is ongoing. Ideally one needs to use forward-looking scenario analysis to judge the extent of the risks and this may well be easier to do in the approach of insurance modelling where balance sheets are simulated tens of thousands of times, using different parametric assumptions.

Finally, one of the key supervisory issues is governance. The United Kingdom has shown a lead here by making the responsibility for managing climate risks a designated function under its Senior Managers Regime. All authorised firms are now required to have a named person with that function, who can be held personally responsible for any failures (PRA, 2018b).

3.7   MARKET REGULATORS: CONDUCT, CONSUMER PROTECTION AND MARKET EFFICIENCY

In many smaller countries such as Ireland and Singapore, the central bank has responsibility for regulating most areas of financial market activity, including oversight of capital markets and related areas of market misconduct. The UK Financial Conduct Authority is one of the first conduct regulators to take climate risks seriously, and it only published its first paper on the topic in October 2018 (FCA, 2018).

As conduct regulation involves effectively meeting the needs of financial customers, the growing demand for investment in green assets by retail investors has not been met with adequate access to information or suitable products. A particular issue is that Independent Financial Advisors do not appear to be routinely asking their customers about their sustainability preferences and thus do not end up recommending funds dedicated to sustainable outcomes – despite many opinion surveys revealing a latent demand. This is not simply a question of whether customers are willing to trade off some returns for the comfort of investing sustainably.

Moreover, there is growing evidence that companies with high ESG ratings produce higher returns over the medium term. Following a recommendation from the Commission's High-Level Experts Group on Sustainable Finance (HLEG) (EC, 2018a), the EU countries are adapting the Markets in Financial Instruments Directive (MIFID) rules to make it a requirement for investment advisors to ask their clients about their sustainability preferences (EC, 2018b).

Given the demand by investors, both retail and professional, there is also an incentive to advertise investment products as 'green' when they are not. This so-called green washing is clearly a conduct issue. In addition, many working practices of asset managers have been challenged for not being aligned to sustainable capital. This may include excessive churn of securities, excessive focus on very short-term returns and a misunderstanding of fiduciary duty.

Conduct regulation should also address the definition of the board's fiduciary duties, which has been interpreted at times to mean maximising the short-term returns for shareholders. In fact, fiduciary duty relates to the interests of the corporate entity as a whole, which is measured only in part by the short-term economic returns for shareholders. Of primary concern is the performance of the company (including its profitability) over the medium to long term and whether it is fulfilling its stated purpose as a company and its treatment of employees and other stakeholders. Hutley and Hartford-Davies (2016) argue that because climate change represents a clear and material financial risk, fiduciary duty requires boards to assess the risks and take them into account. Failure to do so will leave directors liable in the event of climate-related losses.

3.8 SUMMING UP AND CONCLUSIONS

In this chapter, we have set out an analysis of why and how central banks can and should be involved in addressing the financial risks associated with environmentally unsustainable activity, consistent with their existing mandates and objectives. Environmental sustainability risks affect central bank primary objectives through monetary conditions, banknotes, financial stability and the prudential requirements of authorised firms, including market conduct regulations where applicable. We recommend that central banks continue to focus on low and stable inflation as a priority, with economic and financial stability being a prerequisite of overall sustainability over the long-term. Within that, they should support national governments in considering whether and how monetary measures can be used to help credit to be provided to support climate adaptation and mitigation strategies. And they should consider whether to adopt polymer banknotes, making those deliberations public.

Regarding financial stability, central banks should be responsible for promoting a transition to a sustainable and hence lower carbon economy, as part of their existing primary objectives. The full recognition of secondary objectives, to support the government's wider economic policies, can be invoked as necessary. Central banks should also engage constructively with their governments around the use of expanded balance sheets to discuss and explain in what ways they can, or cannot, be used to support wider government social and economic objectives. Central banks should not (for now) purchase large quantities of green assets as part of QE portfolios, as that could crowd out private sector investors from investing in nascent green markets. But they could and should consider buying green assets (perhaps through a sovereign wealth or other investment tranche) as part of the routine assets needed, to the extent that their balance sheets are likely to remain expanded.

In addition, central banks should help coordinate regulatory bodies to ensure that disclosures by authorised financial firms are in line with TCFD recommendations and that such firms are (a) either completely transparent about all their holdings of assets or (b) regularly commission an independent calculation to establish their portfolio's carbon footprint. The central bank's regulatory function should also ensure that authorised firms are identifying and managing the risks from climate change. For instance, they can help banks build stress tests based on forward scenarios that will help the industry judge what its capital and liquidity requirements should be in the face of future threats to stability (e.g. Bank of England, 2019).

Similarly, where they are responsible for such duties, central banks should ensure that all funds offered to retail investors should disclose simple sustainability metrics. Funds that specifically promote themselves as 'green' or 'low carbon' should be required to provide evidence consistent with that label. All financial sector firms, including asset managers and independent financial advisors, should be able to demonstrate awareness of the issues and risks to financial investments arising from climate change and be required to ask clients about their preferences for investing sustainably (EC, 2018a).

Finally, international bodies consisting of representatives from the official and private sectors should continue to promote policy and regulatory reforms. The *Network for Greening the Financial System*, consisting of over fifty members from central banks, regulatory bodies and firms, was founded in 2017 (NGFS, 2017) and has achieved a remarkable record of facilitating discussions (and debate) involving industry and academia in considering how financial policy and regulation should address sustainability risks in financial markets. These efforts should play an important role in spreading best regulatory practice in this area.

REFERENCES

Alexander, K. (2014), 'Stability and Sustainability in Banking Reform: Are Environmental Risks Missing in Basel III?', Cambridge/UNEP, October. www .cisl.cam.ac.uk/resources/sustainable-finance-publications/banking-regulation.

Alexander, K. and Fisher, P. G. (2019), 'Banking Regulation and Sustainability'. In: Beekhoven van der Boezem, F.-J., Jansen, C. and Schuijling, B. (eds.), *Sustainability and Financial Markets*, pp. 7–32. Law of Business and Finance Volume 17. Wolters Kuwer, Netherland B.V.

Aliber, R. Z. and Kindleberger, C. P. (2015), *Manias, Panics and Crashes*, Palgrave Macmillan, UK, 7th ed.

Bank of England (2013), 'LCA of Paper and Polymer Bank Notes' available, along with other relevant papers at: www.bankofengland.co.uk/banknotes/polymer-banknotes.

Bank of England (2017), 'Carbon Footprint Assessment: Paper vs. Polymer £5 & £10 Bank Notes'. www.bankofengland.co.uk/-/media/boe/files/banknotes/poly mer/carbon-footprint-assessment.pdf?la=en&hash= A2077D4BEF302DF8F8488503DEA041876627ECBD.

Bank of England (2019), 'The 2021 Biennial Exploratory Scenario on the Financial Risks from Climate Change'. www.bankofengland.co.uk/paper/2019/biennial-exploratory-scenario-climate-change-discussion-paper.

Carney, M. (2015), 'Breaking the Tragedy of the Horizon – Climate Change and Financial Stability', speech to Lloyd's of London, September. www .bankofengland.co.uk/speech/2015/breaking-the-tragedy-of-the-horizon-climate-change-and-financial-stability.

Cœuré, B. (2018), 'Monetary Policy and Climate Change', speech at the Bundesbank-NGFS-CEP Conference on 'Scaling up Green Finance: The Role of Central Banks', Berlin, 8–9 November 2018. www.ecb.europa.eu/press/key/ date/2018/html/ecb.sp181108.en.html.

Debelle, G. (2019), 'Climate Change and the Economy', speech, 12 March. www.rba .gov.au/speeches/2019/pdf/sp-dg-2019-03-12.pdf.

Draghi, M. (2020), 'Draghi: we face a war against coronavirus and must mobilise accordingly',Financial Times, March. https://www.ft.com/content/c6d2de3a-6ec5-11ea-89df-41bea055720b?shareType=nongift.

ECB (2018), Transcript of hearing: Committee on Economic and Monetary Affairs monetary dialogue with Mario Draghi, President of the European Central Bank. https://www.ecb.europa.eu/pub/pdf/annex/ecb.sp180709_transcript.en .pdf?d0bd98150affdcbcd1ea9e80f128b90b.

Eichengreen, B. (1999), *Toward a New International Financial Architecture: A Practical Post-Asia Agenda*, Peterson Institute Press, Washington, DC.

European Banking Federation (2018), 'Green Finance: Considering a Green Supporting Factor', January. www.ebf.eu/wp-content/uploads/2017/09/Geen-finance-complete.pdf.

European Commission (2018a), 'Final Report of the High-Level Experts Group on Sustainable Finance', Brussels, January. https://ec.europa.eu/info/publications/180131-sustainable-finance-report_en.

European Commission (2018b), 'Action Plan: Financing Sustainable Growth', March. https://eur-lex.europa.eu/legal-content/EN/TXT/PDF/?uri=CELEX:52018DC0097&from=EN.

Financial Conduct Authority (2018), 'Climate Change and Green Finance', Discussion Paper, October. www.fca.org.uk/publications/discussion-papers/dp18-8-climate-change-and-green-finance.

Fisher, P. G. (2013), 'Financial Markets, Monetary Policy and Credit Supply', speech given at Richmond University, London, October. www.bankofengland.co .uk/-/media/boe/files/speech/2013/financial-markets-monetary-policy-and-credit-supply.pdf?la=en&hash=1AE9D84BD3CC1A8E0B3FCCDB13EDE6063CBA26C9.

Fisher, P. G. and Hughes Hallett, A. J. (2018), 'Can Central Bank Balance Sheets Be Used as a Macroprudential Tool?' King's Business School, DAFM Working Paper, 2018/6. www.kcl.ac.uk/business/assets/pdf/dafm-working-papers/dafm-wp6.pdf.

H M Treasury (2018), 'Remit for the Monetary Policy Committee Attached to a Letter from the Chancellor of the Exchequer to the Governor of the Bank of England'. https://assets.publishing.service.gov.uk/government/uploads/system/uploads/attachment_data/file/752077/PU2207_MPC_remit_web.pdf.

Hornbeck, R. (2012), 'The Enduring Impact of the American Dust Bowl: Short and Long Run Adjustments to Environmental Catastrophe', *American Economic Review* 102 (4), 1477–1507.

Hutley, N. and Hartford-Davies, S. (2016), 'Climate Change and Directors' Duties', Memorandum of Opinion published by the Centre for Policy Development and the Future Business Council via Minter Ellison, Solicitors, Melbourne, October. https://cpd.org.au/wp-content/uploads/2016/10/Legal-Opinion-on-Climate-Change-and-Directors-Duties.pdf.

International Monetary Fund (2019), 'Annual Report on Exchange Arrangements and Exchange Restrictions 2018'. www.imf.org/en/Publications/Annual-Report-on-Exchange-Arrangements-and-Exchange-Restrictions/Issues/2019/04/24/Annual-Report-on-Exchange-Arrangements-and-Exchange-Restrictions-2018-46162.

International Panel on Climate Change (2018), 'Global Warming of 1.5°C: Summary for Policymakers', Geneva. www.ipcc.ch/site/assets/uploads/sites/2/2018/07/SR15_SPM_version_stand_alone_LR.pdf.

Lagarde, C. (2019), 'Hearing at the Committee on Economic and Monetary Affairs of the European Parliament'. www.ecb.europa.eu/press/key/date/2019/html/ecb.sp191202~f8d16c9361.en.html.

Lambert, C., Noth, F. and Schüwer, U. (2017), 'How Do Banks React to Increased Credit Risk? Evidence from Hurricane Katrina', SAFE Working Paper No. 94, Goethe University, Frankfurt. https://papers.ssrn.com/sol3/papers.cfm?abstract_id=2585521.

Landon-Lane, J., Rockoff, H. and Steckel, R. H. (2011), 'Droughts, Floods and Financial Distress in the United States'. In: Libekap, G. D. and Steckel, R. H. (eds.), The Economics of Climate Change: Adaptations Past and Present, pp. 73–84. The University of Chicago Press.

Lloyd's of London (2014), 'Catastrophe Modelling and Climate Change'. www .lloyds.com/news-and-risk-insight/risk-reports/library/natural-environment/catastrophe-modelling-and-climate-change.

Mersch, Y. (2019), 'Back to Stable', Frankfurt am Main. www.bis.org/review/r190529a.pdf.

Nordhaus, W. D. (2013), The Climate Casino: Risk, Uncertainty, and Economics for a Warming World, Yale University Press, New Haven, CT.

Peng, H., Xiaoqing, L. and Chaobo, Z. (2018), 'Introduction to China's Green Finance System', Journal of Social Science and Management 11, 94–100, 96.

People's Bank of China (2015), Notice on Green Financial Bonds, PBOC Document No. 39. www.climatebonds.net/files/files/China_Annual_Report_2017_English.pdf.

Prudential Regulation Authority (2015), 'The Impact of Climate Change on the UK Insurance Sector, a Climate Change Adaption Report by the Prudential Regulation Authority', September. www.bankofengland.co.uk/prudential-regula tion/publication/2015/the-impact-of-climate-change-on-the-uk-insurance-sector.

Prudential Regulation Authority (2018a), 'Transition in Thinking: The Impact of Climate Change on the UK Banking Sector', September. www .bankofengland.co.uk/prudential-regulation/publication/2018/transition-in-thinking-the-impact-of-climate-change-on-the-uk-banking-sector.

Prudential Regulation Authority (2018b), 'Enhancing Banks' and Insurers' Approaches to Managing the Financial Risks from Climate Change, Consultation Paper 23/18. www.bankofengland.co.uk/-/media/boe/files/prudential-regulation/consultation-paper/2018/cp2318.pdf?la=en&hash=8663D2D47A725C395F71FD5688E5667399 C48E08.

Reuters (2014), 'Euro Banknotes Will Remain Paper Not Plastic'. www.reuters .com/article/us-euro-fakes/euro-banknotes-will-remain-paper-not-plastic-idUSBREA0C0JQ20140113.

Stern, N. (2006), The Economics of Climate Change: The Stern Review, https:// webarchive.nationalarchives.gov.uk/20100407172811/http://www.hm-treasury

.gov.uk/stern_review_report.htm. Print edition (2007), Cambridge University Press.

Task Force on Climate-Related Financial Disclosures (2017), 'Final Report: Recommendations of the Task Force on Climate-related Financial Disclosures', FSB, June. www.fsb-tcfd.org/publications/final-recommenda tions-report.

Task Force on Climate-Related Financial Disclosures (2018), '2018 Status Report', FSB, September. www.fsb-tcfd.org/publications/tcfd-2018-status-report.

Task Force on Climate-Related Financial Disclosures (2019), '2019 Status Report', FSB, June. www.fsb-tcfd.org/wp-content/uploads/2019/06/2019-TCFD-Status-Report-FINAL-053119.pdf.

UNEP FI and PRI (2011), 'Universal Ownership: Why Environmental Externalities Matter to Institutional Investors', United Nations Environment Programme Finance Initiative and Principles for Responsible Investment. www.unepfi.org/fileadmin/documents/universal_ownership_full.pdf.

World Economic Forum (2013), 'The Green Investment Report – The Ways and Means to Unlock Private Finance for Green Growth', Geneva. www3.weforum.org/docs/WEF_GreenInvestment_Report_2013.pdf.

World Economic Forum (2019), 'The Global Risks Report 2019', Geneva, January. www3.weforum.org/docs/WEF_Global_Risks_Report_2019.pdf.

4 Sustainable Finance and Prudential Regulation of Financial Institutions

Esko Kivisaari

4.1 INTRODUCTION

Institutional investors channel savings to investments. In this chapter, we will look at banks, insurers, pension funds and, to a limited extent, other institutional investors and their ability to foster sustainability. Their investment decisions have a crucial role in making some activities possible and others not. At the same time, their choices will have impact first on themselves at a micro-prudential level and later on societies on a macro-prudential or systemic level.

While it is self-evident that investment decisions have an impact, we also need to ask two crucial questions:

i. does prudential supervision have a key role in making institutional investors do the right things for sustainability, and

ii. is it reasonable to use institutional investors to turn the world in a sustainable direction, instead of using regulation on the primary industries – to make those industries themselves sustainable, including not only using prohibitions but also setting tax policies and subsidies correctly?

More concretely, if we observe that minced meat is cheaper in the supermarket compared to veggies, do we think that just tinkering with prudential regulation will change the situation? When a pound of meat, before being minced, has eaten maybe ten pounds of veggies, do we believe that changing the parameters of prudential regulation of institutional investors will tilt the balance in the favour of veggies? While prudential rules can and do play a role, we need to recognise their limits.

Institutional investors have different time horizons for their investments. Banks usually borrow with a short duration and invest with a longer duration. With insurers and especially with pension funds, the liabilities are long term and the maturity of their investments is typically shorter. Other institutional investors have different planning horizons based on their liability characteristics that can vary substantially.

Generally, the motivation for an institutional investor is to get as good a return as possible for its investments for the level of risk, often also including the liquidity risk, that it can tolerate with regard to its liabilities. Institutional investors make their investment decisions utilising their own risk management, based on their own preferences.[1] They usually set their economic capital to the level that is enough to sustain possible losses on a certain confidence level and a certain time horizon. Setting the level of the economic capital naturally takes into account the prudential norms.

Institutional investors are subject to certain prudential rules. Prudential rules differ from sector to sector and from jurisdiction to jurisdiction. A general trend has been to align regulatory prudential rules with the rational risk management of a financial institution. This trend has to some extent recently been overridden by rules-based norms (especially in Basel III). Prudential rules can be understood widely to cover a multitude of aspects, or they can narrowly mean only capital adequacy. In this chapter we take the middle ground: we will not only look at the strict limits but also to the crucial so-called second pillar aspects. Prudential rules contain additionally the so-called market discipline aspects that require good disclosure from the investors (the third pillar).

Prudential rules have a role to play when we think of sustainable finance. At least three approaches are possible:

---

[1] A good study on sustainable considerations when it comes just to banking can be found in Alexander and Fisher (2019). The aim of this chapter is to take a more universal look at the possibilities of an institutional investor and not just at banks.

  i. a neutral approach where the norms will as closely as possible reflect risks,
 ii. an approach to incentivise sustainable investments with lower
     requirements (e.g. with a green supporting factor, GSF), or
iii. an approach based on penalising 'brown' investments (a brown penalising
     factor, BPF) which should lead to less investments in activities understood
     to be unsustainable.

It is apparent that the second and third approaches can be used simultaneously.

In this chapter we will analyse the possibility of using these approaches in quantitative prudential supervision. We will look at the following aspects of supervision, with main emphasis on current EU legislation (CRD/CRR,[2] Solvency II, IORP) Directive[3]):

a. measurement – how the valuation of assets and liabilities is defined and
   what is the time horizon of measurement, and what could sustainability
   aspects mean here,
b. how sustainability could be introduced into actual capital
   requirements,
c. what could sustainability mean to stress tests and
d. sustainability aspects of the required own analyses (ICAAP,[4] ORSA[5] and
   Own Risk Assessment (ORA)[6]).

The last aspect mentioned relies heavily on the entities' own risk management and how their risk management is related to prudential norms. This leads to the general question of whether it is easier to achieve sustainability through prudential regulation, or whether it is better to rely on entities' own risk management.

Our conclusion will be that the risk-based approach is the sustainable financial approach. After all, rather than just a climate catastrophe we will prefer not to have a climate catastrophe connected to a financial catastrophe.

---

[2] Capital Requirements Directive and Regulation respectively.
[3] Institutions for Occupational Retirement Provision Directive.
[4] Internal Capital Adequacy Assessment Process.
[5] Own Risk and Solvency Assessment.   [6] Ongoing Regulatory Activity.

4.2   INSTITUTIONAL INVESTORS AND PRUDENTIAL REGULATION

An institutional investor is an entity that pools money to purchase securities, real property and other investment assets or originates loans. Institutional investors include banks, insurance companies, pension funds, hedge funds, real estate investment trusts, investment advisors, endowments and mutual funds. While all of these have their different characteristics, for the purpose of this chapter we concentrate on banks, insurers and pension funds, and categorise the rest simply as funds. The logic for this is that the former types of institutions each have more or less clearly defined prudential regulation, while the latter ones have less content in this area, due to the fact that usually the actual asset owners bear the whole of the investment and other risks. Sometimes banks are not thought to be institutional investors, but we include them in this category.

Prudential regulation is financial regulation that requires financial firms to control risks and hold adequate capital as defined by capital requirements. Consumer protection rules also belong to financial regulation, but they are, however, not usually understood to be part of prudential regulation.

Prudential regulation can be split into micro-prudential regulation that focuses on the individual firms and makes sure they can withstand shocks and macro-prudential regulation that looks at the whole financial system and the systemic risk. Micro-prudential regulation focuses thus on protecting the clients, creditors and owners of a single undertaking. Macro-prudential regulation works on the societal or even higher level, attempting to limit risks to the whole financial system, that is the systemic risk. A general aim of prudential regulation is to limit moral hazard, that is the extent to which the owners of an undertaking can benefit from its profits in good times while leaving taxpayers to cover the costs when this undertaking fails.

Prudential regulation is at different levels of harmonisation across the world and across sectors. In banking we have the rules agreed by the Basel Committee on Banking Supervision (BCBS) that go under the name Basel III (BIS, 2017) which is under implementation currently. Basel rules are therefore the natural basis for the discussion of sustainability and banking prudential regulation. Adoption of Basel rules is to some degree different in different jurisdictions, for example:

i. The European Union uses them as the basis of banking regulation (Capital Requirements Directive (CRD) and Capital Requirements Regulation (CRR)[7]) applicable to basically all banks, whereas
ii. in the United States, Basel rules apply only to largest internationally active banks.

In insurance, the EU seems to be currently leading the development of prudential regulation. The EU implemented the Solvency II directive[8] at the start of 2016 and is currently reviewing it based on the experience to date. At the same time the International Association of Insurance Supervisors (IAIS) is developing its global International Capital Standard (ICS) (IAIS, 2020. The ICS shares many elements with Solvency II, although there are also differences (and it also, at least during the five-year testing period, contains the US's so-called aggregation method). As the main concepts are shared, it seems natural to talk of sustainability with reference to Solvency II, as it can be understood also in the ICS framework.

Pension funds are different from banking and insurance in the sense that there is much less harmonisation even on the European level, let alone the global level. In Europe there is the Institutions of Occupational Retirement Provision (IORP) directive,[9] but its provisions in the area of prudential regulation are weaker than in banking and insurance. The International Organisation of Pension Supervisors (IOPS) and the Organisation of Economic Co-operation and Development (OECD) are advancing the global agenda but there exists nothing comparable to the Basel Accord or the ICS. With respect to sustainability, one can however note recent activity by

---

[7] European Union (2013).   [8] European Union (2009).   [9] European Union (2016a).

the IOPS (IOPS, 2019). Other institutional investors are often actively fostering sustainable development (BlackRock, 2020). This is a result of investor activity as, compared to pension funds, there is even less prudential regulation for them.

4.3   DRIVERS OF INSTITUTIONAL INVESTMENTS DECISIONS: YIELD, RISK, LIQUIDITY

Institutional investors are huge players in the global financial market. A basic characteristic of those investors is that they are investing on behalf of somebody else, the actual asset owner, to achieve the primary goal of that asset owner. The primary goal of the actual asset owner could be the amount of his/her pension, the certainty of the compensation in case of an insured loss or the safety of the deposit.

The institutional investor is doing its investment decisions within the boundaries set by the aspirations of the actual asset owners. These boundaries manifest themselves mainly in the following three ways:

i. the asset owners want to have the best possible yields for their money,
ii. the asset owners want to have certainty that their money is not lost in too risky investments and
iii. the asset owners also want their money back when they need it, that is they want liquidity. A client of a bank wants to be able to draw his/her money when he/she wants it – but also in insurance a policyholder wants to have his/her compensation as soon as possible after his/her house has burnt down.

It is clear that:

• to some extent the requirements of the actual asset owners are contradictory and impossible to fulfil simultaneously, and also
• it is next to impossible for the asset owner to be fully certain that his/her rights are duly observed.

The second factor mentioned means that, from the point of view of the asset owner, markets are imperfect (van Hulle, 2019). The logic of prudential regulation is to do whatever is possible to correct this deficiency, that is to bring the situation as close as possible to the so-called perfect market solution.

Both asset owners and societies are more and more emphasising that institutional investors should, in addition to what is said above, increasingly stress sustainability in their activity. Societies see that the transition to a more sustainable world is not possible without large investments from the private sector. Investors feel the need to advance the transition and also see inaction on their side to be risky, with increasing sustainability risks.

4.4 PRUDENTIAL REGULATION OF INSTITUTIONAL INVESTORS: HOW TO PROTECT ASSET OWNERS AND AVOID SYSTEMIC RISKS?

The Basel framework (BIS, 2017) consists of three pillars:

i. Pillar I sets out the calculations of regulatory capital requirements for credit, market and operational risk,
ii. Pillar II sets out the process by which a bank should review its overall capital adequacy and the process under which the supervisors evaluate how well financial institutions are assessing their risks and take appropriate actions in response to the assessments and
iii. Pillar III sets out the disclosure requirements for banks to publish certain details of their risks, capital and risk management, with the aim of strengthening market discipline.

Modern prudential regulation of different institutional investors is generally built on this three-pillar concept (but certainly risks taken into account in the first pillar are different based on the characteristics of the institution). It could also be noted that the first pillar often gives room for so-called internal models. An institution with a robust risk management system can, to a smaller or larger degree, use its own data and own modelling in calculating its first pillar requirements.

Prudential regulation has a strong emphasis on the second of these three elements. The hard limits of the first pillar are actually thought to be sufficient only when this concept based on the three lines of defence is implemented efficiently:

  i. The first line of defence (functions that own and manage risks) is formed by managers and staff who are responsible for identifying and managing risks as part of their accountability for achieving objectives.
 ii. The second line of defence (functions that oversee or who specialise in compliance or the management of risk) provides the policies, frameworks, tools, techniques and support to enable risk and compliance to be managed in the first line, conducts monitoring to judge how effectively they are doing it and helps to ensure consistency of definitions and measurement of risk.
iii. The third line of defence (functions that provide independent assurance) is provided by internal audit. Sitting outside the risk management processes of the first two lines of defence, its main roles are to ensure that the first two lines are operating effectively and advise how they could be improved.

The main issues to be addressed in the first pillar are:

  a. how prudential factors are taken into account in the measurement of assets and liabilities,
  b. what is the relevant time horizon and
  c. what is the amount of required capital (or, with what confidence level the entity is required to be able to honour its obligations during this time horizon)?

In today's thinking, the safe way to measure assets and liabilities is to use the so-called fair value approach. A fair value is, by definition, the value of an asset or a liability in a transaction between two willing parties in an arms-length transaction. While the definition as such is clear, its application is not straightforward in practice. When there is a deep and liquid market for an asset (or a liability), it is easy to measure the value from the current market price. But often, at least and especially for liabilities of the insurance or pension type, there is no deep and liquid market. One or the other method of marking to the model is needed in these cases. The crucial rule to apply in creating mark-to-model approaches is to avoid arbitrage possibilities.

In addition to the task of taking care of the interests of the actual asset owner, the supervisor has the requirement of seeing that the so-called systemic risks can be managed. Systemic risks arise most often in situations where the investments of an institutional investor have a longer maturity than the liabilities of this investor and this investor is heavily connected to other actors of the market. This is typically a more important question to be addressed in businesses with the characteristics of banking, and less in traditional insurance and even less in pensions.

With respect to time horizons, the characteristics of different institutional investors give grounds for very different approaches. In banking, the time horizon is typically ten days, whereas in insurance normally a one-year time horizon is used. Pension funds differ from one another depending on the guarantee on the pension. When the beneficiary has a guaranteed payout (often called 'firm commitment'), it is natural to use the same horizon for the fund's risk management and capital requirements as in insurance. When a fund instead operates on a 'best effort' basis, the beneficiary bears the risk and hence there is less need for capital to be held by the fund.

The capital requirements are based on the idea of sustaining a certain risk with a given confidence level over the time chosen horizon for each type of an institutional investor. In banking,[10] the required capital corresponds (at least in internal models) to the expected shortfall (conditional expectation of loss for losses beyond the Value at Risk or the VaR level, also called TailVaR) with a confidence level of 97.5 per cent. In insurance[11] the basis is the one-year VaR with the confidence level of 99.5 per cent (but also TailVar can be used in internal modelling). In both banking and insurance, it needs to be noted that this is just the basic principle behind the actual method in Basel IV and Solvency II, respectively. In practice there are details that go beyond the purpose of this chapter. In pensions the situation is the same as in the time horizon described previously: depending on

---

[10] BCBS (2019).   [11] van Hulle (2019).

the commitment either the insurance principles are used, or the requirements can be milder.

In addition to these aspects, prudential norms need to address supervisory actions when the capital of an entity is at different levels compared to the requirements. Requirements will also have to deal with different aspects of assets and liabilities, for example how the risk of equity investments is different from that of lending.

4.5   REGULATORS' VIEWS AND ACTIONS ON PRUDENTIAL NORMS AND SUSTAINABILITY

4.5.1   *Sustainability in the BCBS World*

There seems to be little in the actual BCBS discussions when it comes to sustainability. However, at the Paris One Planet Summit in December 2017, eight central banks and supervisors established the Network of Central Banks and Supervisors for Greening the Financial System (NGFS, 2017). Since then, the membership of the Network has grown dramatically, across the five continents.

The Network's purpose is to help strengthening the global response required to meet the goals of the Paris agreement and to enhance the role of the financial system to manage risks and to mobilise capital for green and low-carbon investments in the broader context of environmentally sustainable development. To this end, the NGFS defines and promotes best practices to be implemented within and outside of the membership of the NGFS and conducts or commissions analytical work on green finance.

The key message of the network is that central banks all over the world acknowledge that climate change is a source of financial risks. For market dynamics to fully unfold, investors need a stable investment framework, including reliable market standards, market indices and transparency. As central banks have a strong advisory role in politics, they have a key role as anchor investors and can serve as catalysts for further market growth. To address central banks' crucial role, the NGFS sees itself as a platform for best practices and for the exchange of views and experience between central bankers and supervisors (Mauderer, 2019).

The four recommendations of the NGFS addressed to central banks and supervisors are:

i. Integrating climate-related risks into financial stability monitoring and micro-supervision. This includes assessing climate-related risks in the financial system and integrating them into prudential supervision.
ii. Integrating sustainability factors into own portfolio management. The NGFS encourages central banks to lead by example in their own operations.
iii. Bridging data gaps. Public authorities are asked to share data relevant to climate risk assessment and make these data publicly available.
iv. Building awareness and intellectual capacity and encouraging technical assistance and knowledge-sharing. The NGFS encourages all financial institutions to build in-house capacity and to collaborate to improve their understanding of how climate-related factors translate into financial risks and opportunities.

Two NGFS recommendations are addressed to policymakers:

i. Achieving robust and internationally consistent climate and environment-related disclosure. Investors need to know about the climate risks in their investments.
ii. Supporting the development of a taxonomy of economic activities. A taxonomy makes investing green easier and prevents 'green washing'. It creates more market transparency on which activities are really green and which are not.

4.5.2 Sustainability in Insurance Supervision

Integrating sustainability into insurance supervision started with the realisation that an increasing number of governments, central banks, regulators and financial sector stakeholders were working, through different measures and actions, to drive climate risks and other sustainability factors into the core of the financial system function. Action on climate change was also a core aspect of many national-level policy processes relating to sustainable finance. These and other developments prompted insurance supervisors to begin examining the relevance of climate change for insurance supervision, both individually and collaboratively through the Sustainable Insurance Forum (SIF, 2016).

The SIF is a network of leading insurance supervisors and regulators seeking to strengthen their understanding of and responses to sustainability issues for the business of insurance.

The SIF was launched in December 2016, as a global platform for international collaboration by insurance regulators and supervisors on sustainability issues, with a special focus on climate change. During 2017, the SIF undertook several joint activities relating to climate risks, including the delivery of a coordinated submission to the TCFD consultation (TCFD, 2017), followed by the release of a joint statement in July 2017 (SIF, 2017) supporting the recommendations and highlighting how supervisors can support uptake.

The SIF has also helped supervisors to share knowledge and compare experience from their efforts to address climate risks. It has started high-level policy engagement with the IAIS on climate risk issues.

At the second meeting of the SIF in July 2017, members requested the SIF Secretariat to develop a guidance document on climate change and insurance supervision. This was done in cooperation with the IAIS and the initial result of this cooperation was an Issues Paper of July 2018 (SIF and IAIS, 2018).

The objectives of the Issues Paper are to raise awareness for insurers and supervisors of the challenges presented by climate change, including current and contemplated supervisory approaches for addressing these risks.

The Issues Paper provides an overview of how climate change is currently affecting and may affect the insurance sector, provides examples of current material risks and impacts across underwriting and investment activities, and describes how these risks and impacts may be of relevance for the supervision and regulation of the sector. It explores potential and contemplated supervisory responses and reviews observed practices in different jurisdictions. The Paper is intended to be primarily descriptive and is not meant to create supervisory expectations.

After this in December 2019 the IAIS and the SIF have published their draft Issues Paper on the Implementation of the Recommendations of the Task Force on Climate-related Financial Disclosures (SIF and IAIS, 2019). They state, among other things, that there are interactions between micro- and macro-prudential objectives. According to the Issues Paper, integrated frameworks could help strengthen understanding of the impacts of climate risks on individual firms, as well as the impacts on the sector as a whole on climate risk resilience within the financial system and broader economy.

As a next step, the SIF and IAIS will develop an Application Paper on Climate Risk in the Insurance Sector. This paper is expected to include a section on disclosures.

4.5.3 Sustainability in Pension Supervision

The International Organisation of Pension Supervisors (IOPS) has issued its Supervisory Guidelines on the Integration of ESG Factors in the Investment and Risk Management of Pension Funds in the autumn of 2019 (IOPS, 2019). The IOPS recognises that ESG factors are key and timely issues for the investment and risk management of pension funds, whose consideration is relatively new in the landscape of regulatory frameworks of pension funds worldwide. They are also dynamically evolving and have different impacts and risks depending on the country. The guidelines address the integration of ESG factors in the investment and risk management process, disclosure of ESG factors in the investment and risk management process and scenario testing of investment strategies.

It was natural for the IOPS, whose mandate is to act as the standard-setting body on pension supervisory issues and on regulatory issues related to pension supervision, to bring the views and experience of their members together on how ESG factors should be considered and integrated in the supervision of investment and risk management of pension funds. The guidelines are the outcome of numerous discussions held at several IOPS meetings over the last two years. They are voluntary in nature and are intended to guide supervisors and other entities involved in supervision of pension fund risk management and investment.

4.5.4   Sustainability in the European Implementation of Basel III

In the Public Consultation Document on the implementation of the final Basel III reforms in the EU (European Commission, 2019), the European Commission consults among other things on the introduction of sustainable finance issues into the implementation. It is noted in the consultation that previously the co-legislators (European Commission, Council of the European Union and EU Parliament) have reflected on the Paris Agreement on climate change and its impact on prudential regulation and agreed on three actions dedicated to sustainable finance:

i. A mandate for the European Banking Authority (EBA) to assess the inclusion of ESG risks in the supervisory review and evaluation process (SREP) and submit a report on its findings to the Commission, the European Parliament and to the Council.
ii. A requirement for large, listed institutions to disclose ESG risks, including physical risks and transition risks.
iii. A mandate for the EBA to assess on the basis of available data and the findings of the Commission High-Level Expert Group on Sustainable Finance (European Commission, 2018), whether a dedicated prudential treatment of exposures related to assets or activities associated substantially with environmental and/or social objectives would be justified.

Further to this work, the Commission has launched a study on the development of tools and mechanisms for the integration of ESG risks into institutions' risk management, business strategies and investment policies as well as into prudential supervision. Final results of this study are expected by beginning of 2021.

As part of its Action Plan on Sustainable Finance, the Commission proposed a regulation for a framework for the establishment of an EU classification of environmentally sustainable economic activities (so-called EU taxonomy). In parallel, the Commission set up a technical expert group on sustainable finance (EU TEG, 2019) that was tasked to already advice on a taxonomy for climate change mitigation and adaptation.

In December 2019, EBA published the report on undue short-term pressure from the financial sector on corporations (EBA, 2019). This report takes into consideration three dimensions and perspectives that relate to short-termism: the banks' perspective, the corporates' perspective and the sustainable finance perspective.

The report provides policy recommendations advocating that policy action should aim to provide relevant information and incentives to the banks to extend the time horizon in their strategies and governance. The EBA especially recommends that the European Commission and the EU legislators:

i. maintain a robust regulatory prudential framework,
ii. foster the adoption of longer-term perspectives by institutions through more explicit legal provisions on sustainability,
iii. continue to enhance disclosures of long-term risks and opportunities by both corporations and banks and
iv. improve information flows and data access and support the role of the banking sector in raising awareness on sustainability challenges and ESG risks.

4.5.5 Sustainability in European Insurance and Pension Supervision

In June 2018, the European Insurance and Occupational Pensions Authority (EIOPA) agreed on an Action Plan on Financing Sustainable Growth (EIOPA, 2018) in order to coordinate different projects with the aim of ensuring that insurers and pension funds operate in a sustainable manner by:

i. Managing and mitigating ESG risks appropriately: this reflects the role of insurers in underwriting risk for the whole economy.

ii. Reflecting preferences of policyholders and pension scheme members for sustainable investments.

iii. Adopting a sustainable approach to their investments and other activities: this reflects the importance of insurers and pension funds as owners of a substantial portion of investments in the European economy.

EIOPA carries out its action plan via several projects in all areas of EIOPA's work and consults with stakeholders, including on the following:

i. Participation in the European Commission's Technical Expert Group to assist the Commission in developing the so-called taxonomy.

ii. Supervisory opinion on the integration of sustainability considerations in fiduciary duty, risk management and public disclosure in IORPs (Institutions of Occupational Retirement Provision).

iii. Technical advice to the European Commission on potential amendments to the Solvency II Directive and the Insurance Distribution Directive with regard to the integration of sustainability risks and sustainability factors (European Union, 2009, 2016b).

iv. Integration of ESG considerations in scenario analysis and as an element of analysis in EIOPA's stress testing, starting with the Pension Funds Stress Test of 2019 (EIOPA, 2019a).

EIOPA also contributes to the cross-sectoral work regarding the impact of short-term pressure on financial corporates as well as the impact of IFRS standards on long-term and sustainable investments.

EIOPA published its Opinion on Sustainability within Solvency II in September 2019 (EIOPA, 2019b). EIOPA is of the opinion that within a risk-based framework like Solvency II, any change to capital requirements must be based on a proven risk differential compared to the status quo. Assessment of the underlying risk is therefore also the starting point and guiding principle for the analysis and opinion on capital requirements related to sustainability.

EIOPA is of the opinion that undertakings should assess their exposure to sustainability risks which will increasingly impact the insurance sector over the coming years and decades. For example, the transition risk of revaluation of assets could arise suddenly, with important consequences, affecting potentially long-term illiquid investments. The increasing costs of natural catastrophe risks are already impacting the (re)insurance industry today.

EIOPA does not consider that the one-year time horizon of Solvency II should be changed, but rather complementary tools such as scenario analysis and stress testing would be more appropriate to capture impacts of climate change. EIOPA is of the opinion that further work is needed to define a consistent set of quantitative parameters that could be used in climate change-related scenarios that undertakings can then adopt as appropriate in their ORSA, risk management and governance practices.

4.6 INDUSTRY VIEWS ON SUSTAINABILITY AND PRUDENTIAL NORMS

4.6.1 Industry View in Banking

The European Banking Federation (EBF) strongly supports the Commission agenda for a sustainable future. It has published in September 2017 its recommendations in Towards a Green Finance Framework (EBF, 2017). According to the EBF, a common taxonomy, set of minimum standards and disclosure framework on green finance are essential for efficient allocation of financial resources to green projects and assets, market and risk analysis, benchmarks and development of new products that could be offered on a comparable basis. Comparable disclosures on environmental and climate change performance and related risks are a prerequisite to addressing climate change risks and reaching the objectives set out in the Paris Agreement. While the compliance with the proposed disclosure framework will require significant internal capacity building, the European banking sector calls for the European Commission to take steps, in cooperation with the private sector, towards the adoption of a common disclosure framework consistent with the recommendations of the TCFD (TCFD, 2017).

While banks are clearly increasing their engagement in financing sustainable activities, the EBF thinks that more needs to be done to attract private capital to support the transition to a sustainable economy. Fostering long-term finance is currently constrained by regulatory requirements, challenges to perform risk assessment on the long-term horizon or demand for higher risk and liquidity premiums, making projects less viable from an economic and finance perspective. Some of these constraints can be addressed by targeted regulatory or policy decisions to incentivise long-term sustainability finance. The clarity and stability of the regulatory environment and public policies are essential for banks to engage in long-term business models and decision-making.

In the key recommendations the EBF mentions considerations of changes to prudential regulations based on the risk sensitivity and evidence of the macro-prudential benefits of green assets in reducing the probability of the climate-related risks and mentions also in this area that introducing a green supporting factor should be discussed.

4.6.2   Industry View in Insurance

In its comments[12] in July 2019 on the EIOPA opinion on sustainability within Solvency II, the European insurance industry supported the transition to a more sustainable economy and is committed to integrating sustainability further into its business model. Current examples of sustainable practices by insurers include prevention and adaptation, loss protection/compensation and long-term sustainable financing of the economy by increasingly investing in sustainable assets.

The insurers think that the current Solvency II framework is not a barrier to the integration of sustainability. In particular, sustainability risks are incorporated into the current Solvency framework, through an undertaking's risk management, governance and the own risk and solvency assessment (ORSA).

[12] Insurance Europe (2019a).

With respect to the EIOPA's draft opinion, the insurance industry appreciates that:

i. The general valuation principles of Solvency II already allow insurers to integrate financially material sustainability risks. The valuation focus in Solvency II should remain on market values.
ii. Continued improvement in the quality and scope of public disclosure on sustainability risks is appreciated. Provided there is available quantitative evidence, this will allow better incorporation of climate change risks on the asset and liability sides of an undertaking.
iii. With respect to capital requirements, the sector believes that any differential treatment between green assets or brown assets should be based on a proven difference in the underlying risks.

However, *Insurance Europe* notes that:

i. The direct incorporation of a uniform quantitative approach into the ORSA, based on a standardised set of climate change scenarios, would contrast with the very nature of the ORSA, which is company-specific and with a unique time horizon.
ii. With respect to the use of a forward-looking approach insurers should be given maximum flexibility to use the most suitable tools to deal with sustainability risks in line with their undertakings' specificities.
iii. Good practices should be based on high-level non-binding principles.
iv. Proportionality should be duly considered in any proposed requirements.

Insurers do not see Solvency II as such limiting activity in the sustainability area. In the industry joint letter[13] to the President-in-office of the ECOFIN the industry is however concerned over the general prudency of the regime. The sector thinks that its risk-based approach remains strongly supported and it has been instrumental to ensure very high standards of risk management and customer protection across Europe. However, insurers think that Solvency II requires targeted important improvements and the current review process is necessary and welcome. Without these changes the regime creates

---

[13] Insurance Europe (2019b).

constraints on the industry, unnecessarily limiting its ability to write long-term business, invest long-term and its capacity to cover risks for customers.

4.6.3   Industry View in Pensions

PensionsEurope in its position paper on the Commission's Legislative Package on Sustainable Finance[14] welcomed the EU's agenda on sustainable finance. Pension funds are long-term investors that aim to deliver adequate pensions for their members and beneficiaries. This means they naturally take the long view and are required to consider the long-term risks that may affect their portfolios. Targeted policy initiatives on sustainable finance can catalyse ongoing initiatives within the financial sector. In this respect, according to *PensionsEurope*, better data on companies and other investments, clearer definitions on what is considered sustainable and more transparent financial services will help to address some of the barriers pension funds face when wanting to invest more sustainably.

PensionsEurope sees the taxonomy as an enabler for integrating ESG factors in investment decisions. If designed properly, it can help pension funds to better understand and measure the sustainability risks in their portfolios. It can also serve as a basis for discussions with investment managers about ESG integration when agreeing mandates or selecting investment funds. Finally, it can be a valuable tool to provide information to members and beneficiaries.

According to *PensionsEurope*, the current understanding of fiduciary duty already today fosters sustainable investments. Moreover, under the most recent codification of the fiduciary duty for pension funds, that is the 'prudent person' rule in IORP,[15] specifically allows for the consideration of ESG factors and requires pension funds to take into account the long-term interest of their members and beneficiaries. Over the last years, there has been a clear trend in the pensions sector towards sustainable investment. There are many

[14] PensionsEurope (2018).   [15] European Union (2016a).

best practices and approaches of how pension funds consider sustainability factors. *PensionsEurope* believes that the EU should not harmonise how pension funds manage their sustainable investments.

PensionsEurope thinks that the ESG framework for IORPs is the most advanced amongst financial market actors. IORPs are required to incorporate ESG factors in their governance and risk management systems. The EU should first assess how the IOPR Directive's ESG provisions are put into practice, before making amendments. According to *PensionsEurope*, delegated acts are an inappropriate legislative tool to regulate occupational pensions. The IORP Directive only provides for minimum harmonisation, recognising the diversity of the IORP landscape in Europe and the role of national social and labour law for occupational pensions. An EU-wide requirement would also struggle to take account of the specific national governance structures of pension funds, as well as the responsibilities entrusted to trustees or board members, including member representatives.

4.7 DO PRUDENTIAL NORMS DRIVE INSTITUTIONAL INVESTORS TO SHORT-TERMISM?

In many instances it is argued, including by institutional investors themselves, that because of prudential regulation, institutional investors are driven to short-termism as they are not able to make long-term investments that would be good for sustainability. In this context reference is made to the fairly short time horizons that are the basis of banking and insurance prudential norms. It is additionally argued that the whole concept of fair value valuation drives investors to short-termism. Support to this can be found from statistics that show the holding periods of different assets are over time becoming shorter.

A fairly easy issue to be tackled is the shortening of the average holding period. This is probably true because of the development of new technology: it is fairly easy to create automated systems that benefit from even the smallest market imperfections. A very different question is whether this results into generally shorter holding periods and less financing for longer-term sustainable projects. As such shortening average holding periods do not provide sufficient evidence to conclude that the investment horizon of institutional investors is getting shorter. In the availability of longer-term finance there seems to be a lot of variation already among European countries which makes it difficult to say that prudential regulation as such would shorten the horizons.

One should also think what it would mean if the prudential regulation in banking or in insurance would be based on longer time horizons than what is the case today. Let us think about insurance with its one-year time horizon. What would happen if the time horizon would be, say, two or five years? As long as the confidence level would be maintained at the level of 99.5 per cent, this would lead to substantially higher capital charges for all longer-term investments. This would most certainly lead to a substantial pressure to adjust investment portfolios so that the emphasis is on the shorter term.

It needs to be noted that the time horizons used in prudential regulation do not refer to the actual planning horizons in corresponding sectors. Instead, the time horizons used are the basis for the risk measures used in setting the capital requirements. Additionally, while already in the valuations longer time horizons are used, the different prudential regimes for banking, insurance and pensions contain the so-called second pillar regulation requiring a longer-term analysis from undertakings.

The time horizons used in setting the prudential requirements do not result from the idea that only the short term is important. Instead, they result from the idea that entities need to be prepared with capital buffers to bear the risks during these time periods. For longer time periods, undertakings have other means of taking care of their risks and these should be analysed with the second pillar tools.

In the financial market there are sometimes arguments that a longer time horizon makes the risk smaller (this is often called 'diversification over time'). This can fairly easily be proven wrong with rigorous mathematics. One can also think what it means to say that the risk gets smaller with time. Apparently, the risk should then be getting higher when time is shortened which leads to paradoxes.

There are thus important factors indicating that the true reason for any short-termism in not a result of the time periods utilised in setting the parameters of prudential rules. More probable drivers for short-termism could result from:

i. markets generally rewarding short-term gains more than possible long-term rewards,
ii. valuations principles making longer-term effects more visible also on the shorter term, and
iii. risk management practices getting more scientific.

One can also say that valuation with the fair value principle does not mean the use of a point value. Instead, it usually means the discounting of future probability-weighted cash flows with the best available interest rate curve to the present. Creating these future cash flows means not only looking at the present, but looking very far into the future. In this area, in former years with clearly positive real interest rates, it was argued that discounting makes all longer-term implications vanish. In today's interest environment one can hardly say that discounting works like this.

In addition to holding capital, a range of other risk mitigation tools are available. These tools include, for example, at the least the following:

i. advanced risk management,
ii. (in insurance) reinsurance, and other risk mitigation and risk transfer/financing tools,
iii. raising capital and
iv. changing of the investment portfolio.

Today's prudential rules take these different risk mitigation techniques into account. This is done in the second pillar of prudential regulation. The main tools in this area are

i. the Internal Capital Adequacy Assessment Process (ICAAP) in banking,
ii. the Own Risk and Solvency Assessment (ORSA) in insurance and
iii. the ORA in pensions.

All these tools rely heavily on the requirement that institutional investors should have their own risk management operating in an appropriate manner. One part of this risk management is that the assets and liabilities must be matched in a manner that reduces the risks.

4.8   ALIGNING PRUDENTIAL SUPERVISION WITH STATE-OF-THE-ART RISK MANAGEMENT OF INSTITUTIONAL INVESTORS

Mark Carney, then Governor of the Bank of England and FSB Chair used the concept of 'The Tragedy of the Horizon'.[16] The idea of the concept is that costs of taking action are borne in the short run, but the benefits accrue to future generations. This mismatch of time horizons has challenging implications for prudential regulation.

From a prudential regulation point of view there are two basic approaches to advance the agenda of sustainable investment. These approaches can crudely be described as follows:

i. create incentives (say, in the form of a green supporting factor, GSF) or disincentives (say, in the form of a brown penalising factor, BPF) to support sustainable investments with smaller capital requirements compared to 'brown' investments, or
ii. rely on the usual role of investors as mediators of finance from savers to investments with their risk management practices, but strengthen the role of sustainability in this area by, say, requiring better disclosure, including sustainability factors in stress testing and so forth.

The idea of modern prudential regulation is to align the regulation with the risk management that any sensible undertaking would do even without regulation. From the previous discussion it seems that

---

[16] Carney (2015).

supervisors would prefer continuing on the risk-based approach, amplified with stress tests and scenario analyses. It can however be noted
that in the European implementation of the Basel III regime EBA is
asked to look also at the possibility of a GSF/BPF. From the industry
point of view there are some sector-specific differences:

i. banks generally support the risk-based approach but would like to see an
   evidence-based GSF.
ii. insurers strongly support the risk-based approach and they are very
    sceptical of either a GSF or a BPF. Insurers do not see a reason to treat the
    sustainability issue in isolation but think that current regulation is
    generally overly conservative when it comes to the longer-term.
iii. pension funds have generally tried to avoid harmonised quantitative rules
     due to differences from country to country and do not see a reason to have
     harmonised rules in the area of sustainability.

It is interesting to analyse how a GSF/BPF would fit into this area:

i. If the GSF/BPF would be introduced without good evidence that risks
   are smaller/larger, undertakings would mainly continue decisions
   based on their own risk management – therefore the result could not be
   guaranteed.
ii. Again, without good evidence the GSF could result in a systemic
    bubble.
iii. If the GSF/BPF would be implemented in one sector and not in the others
     the impact in that sector could be neutralised by other sectors (i.e. if banks
     would have the GSF, other sectors would know that banks do not base
     their decisions on actual risks and they could therefore take their money
     out of the green area – the overall result could be even negative).

It is therefore difficult to find sound support for the GSF or the BPF. It
must however be noted that at least in theory there is some good logic
with the BPF. The BPF could be the tool to internalise unsustainable
externalities into investment decisions. This would however again
need good evidence on the areas it should be used. One can also ask
that if something is against the good of societies should it not be
prohibited as such and not just be penalised.

4.9   CONCLUSIONS

In the EU context the regulators have fairly strong tools in financial regulation while they are substantially weaker in some other areas, like taxation and different product rules and subsidies. There is the possibility that the regulators are using financial regulation in attempts that could be more successful with other tools – if you have a hammer, everything looks like a nail.

It seems generally that both supervisors and industries recognise the merits of risk-based supervision. Supervisors think that when risks are taken into account as well as possible this is already enough to make the investors to fulfil their role in sustainable development. Industries have some reservations in this area: banks would still consider a GSF and insurers think that supervisors generally take a too conservative view on longer-term risks (i.e. insurers agree on the risk-based idea but have difficulties in agreeing with supervisors on how the risks are valued).

Institutional investment is important in our efforts to try to reach a more sustainable world. But the limits of finance need to be recognised. Finance is important for different areas of economic activity. But tuning finance alone cannot make a particular economic activity sustainable. It is important to first see that the basic incentives in an economic activity are pointing to the right direction.

REFERENCES

Alexander, K. and Fisher, P. (2019), 'What Happens When Nobody Is Watching: Regulation, Bank Risk Culture and Achieving Environmental Sustainability'. In: Taafe, O. (ed.), *Banking on Change, the Development and Future of Financial Services.* John Wiley, London, pp. 27–42.

Bank of International Settlements (BIS) (2017), 'Basel III: Finalising Post-Crisis Reforms'. www.bis.org/bcbs/publ/d424.pdf.

Basel Committee on Banking Supervision (BCBS) (2019), 'Minimum Capital Requirements for Market Risk'. www.bis.org/bcbs/publ/d457.htm.

BlackRock (2020), 'Making Sustainability Our Standard'. www.BlackRock.com/us/individual?locale=en_US&switch=y.

Carney, M. (2015) 'Breaking the Tragedy of the Horizon – Climate Change and Financial Stability', speech to Lloyd's of London, September 2015. www .bankofengland.co.uk/speech/2015/breaking-the-tragedy-of-the-horizon-climate-change-and-financial-stability.

European Banking Authority (EBA) (2019), 'EBA Report on Undue Short-Term Pressure from the Financial Sector on Corporations'. https://eba.europa.eu/eba-calls-banks-consider-long-term-horizons-their-strategies-and-business-activities.

European Banking Federation (EBF) (2017), 'EBF Report: Towards a Green Finance framework'. www.ebf.eu/ebf-media-centre/towards-a-green-finance-framework.

European Commission (2018), 'Final Report by the High-Level Expert Group on Sustainable Finance'. https://ec.europa.eu/info/sites/info/files/180131-sustain able-finance-final-report_en.pdf.

European Commission (EC) (2019), 'Public Consultation Document Implementing the Final Basel III Reforms in the EU'. https://ec.europa.eu/info/sites/info/files/ business_economy_euro/banking_and_finance/documents/2019-basel-3-con sultation-document_en.pdf.

European Insurance and Occupational Pensions Authority (EIOPA) (2018), 'Sustainable Finance'. https://eiopa.europa.eu/Pages/About-EIOPA/ Organisation/Sustainable-Finance-.aspx.

European Insurance and Occupational Pensions Authority (EIOPA) (2019a), 'Occupational Pensions Stress Test 2019-1'. https://eiopa.europa.eu/Pages/ Financial-stability-and-crisis-prevention/Occupational-Pensions-StressTest-2019 .aspx.

European Insurance and Occupational Pensions Authority (EIOPA) (2019b), 'Occupational Pensions Stress Test 2019-2, Opinion on Sustainability within Solvency II'. https://eiopa.europa.eu/Publications/Opinions/2019-09-30% 20OpinionSustainabilityWithinSolvencyII.pdf.

European Union (2009), *Official Journal of the European Union*, L 335, 17 December 2009. https://eur-lex.europa.eu/legal-content/EN/TXT/?uri=OJ: L:2009:335:TOC.

European Union (2013), *Official Journal of the European Union*, L 176, 27 June 2013. https://eur-lex.europa.eu/legal-content/EN/TXT/?uri=OJ:L:2013:176:TOC.

European Union (2016a), *Official Journal of the European Union*, L 354, 23 December 2016. https://eur-lex.europa.eu/legal-content/EN/TXT/?uri=OJ: L:2016:354:TOC.

European Union (2016b), *Official Journal of the European Union*, L 26, 2 February 2016. https://eur-lex.europa.eu/legal-content/EN/TXT/?uri=OJ: L:2016:026:TOC.

EU Technical Expert Group on Sustainable Finance (EU TEG) (2019), 'Taxonomy Technical Report'. https://ec.europa.eu/info/sites/info/files/business_economy_euro/banking_and_finance/documents/190618-sustainable-finance-teg-report-taxonomy_en.pdf.

van Hulle, K. (2019), *Solvency II – Solvency Requirements for EU Insurers – Solvency II Is Good for You*. Intersentia, Cambridge.

Insurance Europe (2019a), 'Insurance Europe Comments to the EIOPA Opinion on Sustainability within Solvency II'. www.insuranceeurope.eu/sites/default/files/attachments/Comments on EIOPA opinion on sustainability within Solvency II.pdf.

Insurance Europe (2019b), Joint IE, PEIF, CFoF, CRoF, Amice Letter to EU Council Presidency. www.verzekeraars.nl/media/6838/joint-ie-peif-cfof-crof-amice-letter-to-eu-council-presidency-20191209.pdf.

International Association of Insurance Supervisors (IAIS) (2020), Insurance Capital Standard (ICS). www.iaisweb.org/page/supervisory-material/insurance-capital-standard.

International Organisation of Pension Supervisors (IOPS) (2019), 'IOPS Supervisory Guidelines on the Integration of ESG Factors in the Investment and Risk Management of Pension Funds'. www.iopsweb.org/iops-supervisory-guidelines-esg-factors.htm.

Mauderer, S. (2019), 'Scaling Up Green Finance – The Role of Central Banks', Speech. www.bis.org/review/r190617i.htm.

Network of Central Banks and Supervisors for Greening the Financial System (NGFS) (2017), 'Origin and Purpose'. www.ngfs.net/en/about-us/governance/origin-and-purpose.

PensionsEurope (2018), 'PensionsEurope Paper on Sustainable Finance'. www.pensionseurope.eu/pensionseurope-paper-sustainable-finance.

Sustainable Insurance Forum (SIF) (2016), 'Promoting Supervisory and Regulatory Leadership on Sustainability Challenges and Opportunities for the Insurance Sector'. www.sustainableinsuranceforum.org.

Sustainable Insurance Forum (SIF) (2017), 'Leading Insurance Supervisors Support Adoption of Climate Disclosure Recommendations'. http://unepinquiry.org/wp-content/uploads/2017/07/SIF_TCFD_Statement_July_2017.pdf.

Sustainable Insurance Forum (SIF) and the International Association of Insurance Supervisors (IAIS) (2018), 'Issues Paper on Climate Change Risks to the Insurance Sector', International Association of Insurance Supervisors (IAIS), Basel.

Sustainable Insurance Forum (SIF) and the International Association of Insurance Supervisors (IAIS) (2019), 'Draft SIF/IAIS Paper on TCFD Recommendations'.

www.iaisweb.org/page/consultations/current-consultations/draft-issues-paper-on-the-implementation-of-the-tcfd-recommendations.

Taskforce for Climate-related Financial Disclosures (TCFD) (2017), 'Final Report: Recommendations of the Task Force on Climate-related Financial Disclosures'. www.fsb-tcfd.org/publications.

5 Transparency and Accountability Standards for Sustainable and Responsible Investments

Flavia Micilotta

5.1 INTRODUCTION

The 2008 financial crisis was an eye-opener. It highlighted just how little investors understood financial products, which they often dismissed as too complex. There was a significant lack of financial literacy among consumers, which had hitherto gone unnoticed. Consumers simply did not have the necessary skillset to make sound financial decisions and achieve stable financial well-being. The financial industry in general has always been characterised by low levels of literacy, and that holds true not only on a European scale but also at an international level. Low individual financial literacy has been repeatedly identified as one of the main causes behind the most recent financial crises. 'Financial institutions, experts and sometimes regulators' have been held mostly responsible for this state of affairs.

The rise of the Sustainable and Responsible Investment (SRI) industry has gone hand in hand with a growth in information asymmetry which has involved all its key actors and investment areas. This is set to have severe repercussions, which will also be felt at the level of investment products. It has now been more than two decades since investment managers and institutional investors were confronted with the concept of sustainability for investments. Unfortunately, sustainability criteria for financial products and their underlying, relevant sustainable information and analysis have only become less clear in the intervening years. In the early days, there was no coordination or standardisation in the industry. Now, there is a proliferation of actors, each with their own particular methodology. The dire state of things first became apparent for the institutional sector, followed over time by the retail segment.

The policy discourse has also evolved in recent years to come out very much in favour of sustainable finance. This has meant a substantial increase in product offering and in the number of players active in this space. But this fortunate momentum now needs to be backed by serious standards and codification mechanisms in order to prevent it from becoming a bubble. At present, the industry needs to shift its approach to sustainable finance and SRI from a niche interest or an optional extra to part of its mainstream offer. The time for enhancing credibility has come. The industry has become sophisticated enough to self-regulate itself and embrace upcoming new developments which are geared in this direction.

At a time when, more than ever, there is a global sense of urgency around the climate, and a general acknowledgement that considerable private investments are required for the transition towards a Paris-compliant economy, sustainable finance and SRI are key. As evidence of that, the assets under management allocated to these funds ramped up to over $30trn at the end of 2018 (GSIA, 2018), at global level. Nevertheless, since portfolio managers are free to determine what is 'green', 'social' or 'sustainable', the result is that oil, airlines and other activities deemed controversial are still included in SRI portfolios.

The efforts of the European Commission with the Action Plan on Financing Sustainable Growth are geared towards eliminating 'greenwashing' and bringing clarity into the market on products that can be considered as clean financial products, with the aim of funding a sustainable economy. The financial system is about to enter a new era in which investments are deemed to be more closely linked to the real economy and able to solve the issues that society is faced with today. This will translate into a higher level of education for investors and a deeper level of transparency, traceability and accountability for the financial products of this next generation.

5.2   FINANCIAL LITERACY

Simply put, financial literacy is financial education. This covers subjects such as basic economics, statistics and numeracy skills, combined with the ability to employ these skills in making financial decisions. Research has given evidence of people making better saving and borrowing results as a direct result of becoming more knowledgeable about finance. They are more likely to plan for retirement and hold more diverse assets in their portfolio.

A strong push in favour of deregulation and easier access to credit has inevitably led to the increased significance, over the years, of financial literacy. The increasing number and complexity of financial products, the continuing shift in responsibility for providing social security from governments and financial institutions to individuals and the growing importance of individual retirement planning make it imperative that financial education be provided to all. In the context of competition, financial institutions still offer favourable conditions, credit and other various financial products and services. Being confronted with easier access to personal loans and different payment options has led to an increase in spending and consumption and a rapid rise in personal and household debt levels.

More and more households are being asked to make their own decisions about their financial investment choices. When it comes to savings, and pensions in particular, financial illiteracy can become a serious threat to their life-time welfare.

Furthermore, increased life expectancy means longer working lives are becoming necessary to enable men and women globally to acquire adequate pensions. Regulators have carried out extensive research[1] that shows the extent to which, being increasingly confronted with a rapidly ageing population, the pressure on the pension system could be somewhat eased by reorienting the system towards more occupational and personal insurance schemes. This shifts more

---

[1] See Batsaikhan and Demertzis (2018).

and more responsibilities to the individual who can greatly enhance their decision-making with higher levels of financial literacy. For these reasons, complementing statutory pensions with broad and well-designed supplementary schemes[2] can help support adequate pension outcomes. Member states in Europe already offer varying degrees of such instruments; being able to consider supplementary pension schemes will play a pivotal role in guaranteeing a good quality of retirement for Europe's citizens. The ability to think ahead and assess different options are directly linked to levels of financial literacy.

Investing in financial literacy can help citizens access the benefits of economic development and contribute to the inclusive growth agenda in the EU. More importantly, it can also help citizens understand the sustainable finance investment space and be able to differentiate the offerings available, while finding the product that best matches their needs. The final report drafted by the European Commission's High-Level Expert Group on Sustainable Finance (HLEG) has highlighted some interesting research that stresses the timeliness of these findings: 'there is strong evidence that Europe's citizens overwhelmingly believe that social and environmental objectives are important for their savings and investments'.[3] Nevertheless, in order to empower European citizens with sustainable finance issues, there needs to be a sustainable financial system in place, which is transparent and accountable. 'Improving access to information on sustainability performance and promoting financial literacy are essential elements of that effort'.[4] Citizens need to be given the possibility to opt for sustainable investment products and for that to happen those products need to be readily available, highly recognisable and comparable.

[2] European Commission (2018b), p. 18.
[3] HLEG Final Report, European Commission (2018a), p. 10.
[4] HLEG Final Report, European Commission (2018a), p. 13.

5.3   LACK OF SUSTAINABILITY DEFINITIONS

The SRI component, typically linked to a notion of 'sustainability' in general terms and 'transparency', renders the problem of information even more complex, mainly due to two main factors. On the one hand, we have another layer of complexity that comes into play. In fact, the discourse around sustainability, closely linked to sustainable development, since its inception, has mostly been characterised by a high degree of confusion resulting from a multitude of definitions. It was the Brundtland Report for the World Commission on Environment and Development (1987), which for the very first time, introduced the notion of sustainable development. The SRI industry has evolved rather substantially over the years since the report came out and is slowly evolving from a rather 'social' approach, closely linked to ethics and moral considerations, to one that is looking at a larger set of criteria that embraces the wider spectrum of sustainability which today is better known under the ESG considerations. On the other hand, the evolution of ESG has been similarly hindered by a general lack of set definitions, which has served the industry's creativity, while also slowing down, to a certain extent, its ability to enter the mainstream.

Investors should be able to rely upon the assumption that the money they place in a product that has been labelled as 'sustainable' or 'SRI-compliant' should respect some minimum parameters of quality and screening criteria, differentiating this investment choice from another product which does not carry this denomination.

Today, most of the fund managers offering SRI funds use a certain terminology linked to this investment tool, common to most players, and which largely draws from a codification[5] around investment strategies originally devised by the European Forum for Responsible Investment – Eurosif. The seven investment strategies

[5] As defined by Eurosif: www.eurosif.org/responsible-investment-strategies.

that have been identified include ESG integration, which is the most generic one, most often used as a proxy for all SRI investing.

ESG integration specifically refers to the

> explicit inclusion by asset managers of ESG risks and opportunities into traditional financial analysis and investment decisions, based on a systematic process and appropriate research sources. This type covers explicit consideration of ESG factors alongside financial factors in the mainstream analysis of investments. The integration process focuses on the potential impact of ESG issues on company financials (both positive and negative), which in turn may affect the investment decision.[6]

As cited in the biennial Eurosif Study 2018, 'the biggest growth (registered across all other investment strategies for the same period – 2016–2018) for ESG integration with a Compound Annual Growth Rate of 27%, sustains the view that integrating sustainability criteria within investments is increasingly the norm'. This exponential growth[7] is reflecting several different investment approaches on the part of fund managers whose practices range from a box-ticking exercise to a well-defined integration strategy as part of their investment process. A method needs to be adopted to assess and determine exactly what it means to integrate ESG considerations for all investors. Several KPIs have already been tested to successfully determine the different practices: the number of SRI analysts that are part of the investment team, the formalisation of ESG integration in the investment policy and so forth. Nevertheless, such elements do not constitute real evidence of clear practice. Furthermore, the underlying answer to these issues is ultimately a good level of standardisation of practices across the industry, with a particular focus on the process. The recent rise in interest for SRI, particularly with regard to the retail

---

[6] Eurosif (2018), p. 82.
[7] Eurosif (2018) presents a sample of forty investment firms which have formalized a policy on ESG integration as part of their investment process.

segment[8] which has grown by 800 per cent in the last four years alone, gives rise to new possibilities for the industry as a whole, but at the same time poses new challenges.

The Action Plan on Financing Sustainable Growth defined by the European Commission pursues a twofold ambition: to increase the capital flow towards the transition economy while avoiding green-washing. In this respect, the retail segment is one of the most promising leads. Until very recently, regulation[9] has never looked at providing specific guidance on how to embed sustainability as part of the investment preferences discussed with the client; this state of things has deprived retail investors in particular of opting for this choice. On top of that, research has shown how little incentive investment advisers have to pitch sustainable investment options, mainly because they are somewhat less knowledgeable about the topic and they fail to grasp the main arguments to raise the topic with their clients. A consequence of this is that financial advisers perceive sustainability-oriented products as some kind of trade-off with returns[10] and are either unable or unwilling to explain these products to their clients.

If more investors need to opt for SRI investments in the future,[11] the financial industry needs to work to ensure making this choice is easier for clients. Understanding the implication of investment products represents a key issue in this respect and investment products should disclose information regarding their sustainability potential.

Today, products that carry sustainability denominations are self-assessed. In this chapter, we have looked, albeit briefly, at the lack of clarity as per ESG integration techniques on the part of asset

---

[8] Eurosif (2018), p. 76.

[9] As part of its Consultation Paper on integrating sustainability risks and factors in MiFID II, 19 December 2018, the Commission clarified that its objective is 'to explicitly require the integration of sustainability risks (i.e. environmental, social and governance risks) in the investment decision or advisory processes'.

[10] There is ample evidence today of the opposite in fact, see for example Balanced Rock Investment Advisors (2014).

[11] HLEG Final Report, European Commission (2018a), p. 29.

managers in the structuring of their portfolios. This reality extends to the application of methodologies and processes of the different products available in the market. This leaves us with a range of different products, mostly SRI-denominated, with significant differences in quality. This situation clearly distorts competition among market players. One tool which has been developed as a proxy for a quality indicator are the SRI labels, which have begun to rapidly populate the market. The aim of these tools, developed either at government level by some member states, or by private players in the market, has been to inform and guide investors as to the qualities of the different financial products (in this case mostly funds) and what they can actually deliver. Labels have taken general denominations such as SRI or ESG, whereas in some instances labels have focussed on a more specific issue, towards achieving a particular goal or making an impact. Different labels are hard to compare. Some are rather more focussed on exclusions, some favour impact or ESG integration, whereas yet others are also focussed on the investment approach and process.

Nevertheless, the proliferation of labels has created a high level of fragmentation in the SRI market, instead of increasing transparency and providing useful guidance for investors.

5.4   EUROSIF'S WORK

The question around the transparency and accountability that should be inherent to sustainable investment products further points to another factor, and that is the notion that the 'added' value attached to SRI funds is conveyed by the sustainability element and its quality. This latter component is also strictly linked to a mix of plausibility and objectivity, hence demonstrable transparency. In fact, the 2008 financial crisis witnessed an important rise and major changes in the SRI industry, which pushed investors to raise questions around the relevance of sustainable finance and what role SRI can play in helping to strengthen it. France, which was already an important hub for SRI investments in Europe, registered at the time a continued growth in assets under management which had reached around €30bn at the end of 2008 (i.e. up 37 per cent versus 2007-end), while, at the same time, the markets experienced a sharp fall and 'traditional' management saw significant outflow (Novethic, 2009). SRI soon became a byword for transparency and quality not just in the investments but also in the process as a whole. To answer all these new and pressing questions, the European Sustainable and Responsible Investment Forum, Eurosif, started devising a solution which could bring some 'transparency' to the industry and the players involved. This led to the development of some specific investment guidelines back in 2004.

The purpose of these guidelines, launched with the backing of the European Commission, was to provide greater transparency and to clarify SRI processes for mutual funds. The ultimate aim was to ensure that investors would be better informed as to their choices while giving fund managers an opportunity to report and compare best practice among themselves in anticipation of future legislation on SRI funds. In April 2008, around 50 signatories representing over 140 SRI funds had signed up to these guidelines. Building on the growing interest from market players, the work to improve the process used by managers answering the questionnaire continued and four years later, in 2008, Eurosif launched the European SRI Transparency Code, dedicated to enhancing clarity and transparency with regard to the principles and processes governing SRI funds. Its prime objectives were to help investors make more informed choices, instil confidence in this special asset class, encourage best practice among fund managers and pre-empt legislation on SRI mutual funds that would not otherwise integrate the perspective of practitioners.

The set-up of the Transparency Code, as the framework of reference for funds that carry an SRI denomination, has quickly been picked up by different players, at both a European and international level, who have launched SRI product labels with precise, geographic connotations and have seen an uptake by most SRI asset managers active in this space. These developments have helped provide a certain level of guidance to the market for investors that intend to become active in this space. However, the diversity and sheer multitude of labels that came to the fore in the last years has also translated into a certain degree of fragmentation of the market. In other words, the multiplication of these guidance mechanisms has itself contributed to information asymmetry.

The SRI industry today has grown to the tune of several trillions of assets under management and yet, in spite of the several labels and transparency tools available in the market today, it seems difficult to determine exactly what is a SRI fund and what is behind this exponential and continued growth. The European Commission has started working on developing standards to support the growth of sustainable financial tools. The SRI industry has today reached significant proportions and it can be considered the backbone of sustainable finance. To this end, it is important for the industry to be able to rely on a key set of common criteria, which at a European level can serve as the standards for SRI investors.

5.5   WHAT THE INDUSTRY NEEDS

Sustainability is big business. Today more than ever, financial players are highly interested in marketing their products as 'sustainable', choosing one of the available denominations to differentiate their approach from the next financial adviser. Confusion is still high over what an SRI fund can deliver and, perhaps more worryingly, what an SRI fund is exactly. Some asset managers use the SRI denomination as a marketing tool. They have developed their own offer, which does not match at all the expectations of certain SRI purists or more simply, is not able to account for all the different aspects of SRI. At a time when not having a sustainable offer would indicate simply 'being out of the game', we need to use this momentum to develop further and take the industry to a level of maturity that will inscribe sustainable finance as part of the mainstream financial offer permanently. Nevertheless, we still have a long way to go, and reputation is key. Ratings, labels and green financial products are set to deliver a more sustainable economy, but are we ready for more and better and what does that mean? The answer is disclosure of course! We don't need more, we need better; a functional set of disclosures that will allow market players to communicate easily and find their answers.

Investors deserve and expect transparency and clarity about what they are buying. The question remains whether or not they can get it and if they can fully understand it, given the lack of uniform knowledge around the sustainable investing denominations floating around today. If savers will need to decide for themselves as to what constitutes sustainable investment and specifically what matches their preferences, it means that we are going to need much higher standards for disclosure rather than a one-size-fits-all approach.

As we have seen, there are several competing sets of norms, coupled with an endless alphabet soup coming from different parts of the industry and different geographies. Unfortunately, the industry is more or less built on these foundations.

In the past, the application of one or more SRI strategies were thought to be enough for an investment fund to fall within the cat-egorisation of 'sustainable'. The SRI approaches were considered a proxy for the quality and a guarantee of deliverable to a certain extent. Although a practical approach on the commercial side, this develop-ment did not add much in terms of clarity on the products, nor did it help in shaping the demand of investors, who were simply on the receiving end. Things have rapidly evolved for the better. The level of sophistication of investors is increasing at the same pace as the con-ceptualisation of the investments themselves.[12] We see this phenom-enon clearly with SRI funds. Historically relying largely on exclusion concepts, today's investors are increasingly leaving this concept far behind, along with the selection of standards as international bywords for sustainability.[13] The preference has shifted in favour of

---

[12] Exclusions as defined by Eurosif (www.eurosif.org/responsible-investment-strategies).

[13] Norms-based investments as defined by Eurosif (www.eurosif.org/responsible-investment-strategies).

better-defined investment criteria, where the investor is no longer satisfied with merely avoiding certain kinds of investments and opting for companies that comply with international standards of best practice. To prove it, the investment trend for these strategies has started going down in the last years, shifting increasingly in support of more active strategies.[14] Progressively, investors are positioning themselves closer to the centre of the investment decision and want to be able to make investment decisions that not only match their preferences but that can also have a defined impact. In that respect, impact investing is rapidly outgrowing its niche and will only continue to grow faster to match that kind of appetite.

Certainly, the investment strategy that best embodies the key elements of responsible investment, impact investing, is a combination of a positive impact linked with the commitment to return. This strategy has grown with a positive compound annual growth rate of 52 per cent over the course of the past six years but it is mainly since 2013 that we noticed a substantial shift (Eurosif, 2018, p. 36). Thanks to the notions of intentionality, additionality and measurement, impact investing could become the preferred tool for investors who are keen on making a difference with their investment choice. Nevertheless, many hurdles still need to be overcome, and an ideal set of recognised parameters for the measurement and comparison of impact investing are yet to be defined. The policy work undertaken by the European Commission[15] has already done much to ensure the foundations are there. The fundamental work undertaken for the development of a climate taxonomy was the first important step in that direction.

Going forward, there will be a need for continuing to develop a complete sustainability taxonomy, in order to include all the aspects linked to sustainable finance. Building on that, the European policy

---

[14] Exclusions have registered a decrease in the last two years, by 7 per cent (Eurosif, 2018).

[15] Various materials on the EC website: https://ec.europa.eu/info/business-economy-euro/banking-and-finance/green-finance_en.

work has also included standards for products. We have so far seen the recent development around the set-up of a Green Bond Standard (GBS)[16] as part of the Action Plan on Financing Sustainable Growth, in parallel with a European Ecolabel for investment funds. In line with the recommendations of the HLEG and in order to develop important signals for the market, the European Commission decided to set a standard, sending a strong signal in favour of green bonds as an important instrument to mobilise capital towards the transition economy. 'The EU green bond market has yet to reach its full potential, currently representing a relatively modest percentage of overall outstanding bonds from EU issuers. But it has attracted significant public interest, and it has had a disproportionate demonstration effect in support of green finance.'[17] Beyond acting as a guarantee of a more unified market in the EU, the hope for the standard was for it to bring unity and ultimately be regarded as the market reference.

In parallel to the EU GBS, the Commission has also started its work on an EU Ecolabel[18] for green financial products. The aim of the Ecolabel would be to cover a variety of green financial products as well as to provide information to retail investors on whether a financial product respects a green standard. It is clear from this work that regulators understand that the industry still needs guidance and empowerment in order to reach its full potential. 'The EU Ecolabel criteria for retailed financial products aims at facilitating the identification and comparison among retail investments towards green investments and supporting a sustainable financial market' ... and again 'the EU Ecolabel would be particularly helpful for retail investors that are typically interested in investing in products covered by the Regulation on Packaged Retail Investment and Insurance-based Products (PRIIPs) or simpler savings products'.[19] The financial industry needs to rely on a set of clear standards based

---

[16] Technical Experts Report on the Proposal for a Green Bond Standard, European Commission (2019b).
[17] HLEG Final Report, European Commission (2018a), p. 30.
[18] European Commission (2010).   [19] European Commission (2019a).

on recognisable references that all the market operators can use when they create and distribute their products. Guaranteeing a common language and transparent standards of quality is crucial to ensure trust and stimulate investor demand. Concerning the responsible investment industry, an important tool to facilitate investment decisions would entail highlighting the correct framework that these kind of investments should use. What are the processes that need to be followed? Which criteria are the most relevant? Looking at the existing wealth of labels, standards and benchmarks existing today, one might think that the market is heading in the right direction. But as we have explored, this state of things has mostly led to a high level of fragmentation which has possibly hampered industry players, notably investors, from choosing sustainability in their investments choice.

A set of minimum standards for SRI products is the answer to the information asymmetry that dominates the market today and which poses a significant risk to its reputation and sustainability.

The standard would define the quality and determine the process that a product should fulfil to deserve the 'SRI' denomination. In order to leave space for the manager to shape their products freely, the standard should not indicate one specific way to achieve the expected result. A set of processes and requirements would need to be fulfilled together with specific metrics that would help consumers, in the end, to easily be able to determine the quality of the process in place and the achievement of stipulated targets. A mix of different components and strategies would characterise the standard itself, which would be adapted to reflect the evolving expectations of investors and the needs of society, and the legislative translation of these needs and expectations. The end result would be a standard targeting not just retail but also private and institutional clients in Europe; a framework able to translate the needs and expectations of the market in a way that is easy to grasp even for investors with little or no knowledge of sustainable finance. Particular attention should be given to the way in which the integration process takes place. As previously mentioned, much of the uncertainty around sustainable investment products has to do with asset managers' ESG integration. The process could be characterised by a due diligence system carried out throughout the whole value chain. Due to the crucial element this represents for the veracity of the standard itself, compliance with the defined criteria should be externally verified on a regular basis in order to ensure that a valid process is in place and that all the elements are up to date.

5.6 POLICY DEVELOPMENTS AND THE WAY FORWARD

The last five years have seen a series of rapid strides in the context of sustainable finance. The Paris Accord has been a detonator which resonated deeply in the financial community. In order to guarantee limiting global temperatures to 1.5°C, the Accord aimed to empower countries to deal with the impact and consequences of climate change. There was official recognition that in order to achieve this task, we need to be able to count on financial flows which can significantly contribute as successful enablers. This inspired European regulators to take a series of actions which culminated in the development of an Action Plan on Financing Sustainable Growth and a regulatory framework for the development of new financial tools.

The HLEG, set-up by the European Commission in 2016, was given the task of starting this work and determining the key elements that needed to be in place in order to make this change happen.

The pervasive lack of transparency across the investment chain was one of the main focus areas of the Group's work, together with the need to clarify the role of each player involved in order to determine their potential to change the status quo. Each actor needs to play a role to change the course of finance and contribute to the shift towards more sustainable ways to finance the economy. Information asymmetry greatly hampers sustainable finance and the real lack of understanding about the key elements and components among the actors that are part of the investment cycle need to be addressed.

Regulation can do a lot in this sense and the European Commission took an important stand in January 2019, when it published draft rules on how investment firms and insurance distributors should *'take sustainability issues into account when providing advice to their clients'*. These included amended delegated acts under the Markets in Financial Instruments Directive (MiFID II) and the Insurance Distribution Directive (ESMA, 2019). Even if the integration of sustainability risks within the MiFID II requirements will likely be through a high-level principle-based approach, similar to the management of the other kinds of risks, it will constitute an important change in the relation between service providers and clients and is likely to facilitate the discussion around sustainability going forward. This represents a major change in the consideration of financial products as we have known them so far.

These changes represent a true innovation in the financial system which will have a ripple effect that involves business players at large. Regulation is a powerful enabler of this shift in favour of enhanced transparency, which together with fiduciary duties represents an essential feature of principle-based regulation. Regulation of retail funds can contribute to increasing investors' protection, and transparency about both financial and non-financial risks is what is most necessary for investors.

Another major shift in the last years which has coincided with this enhanced focus on sustainability has certainly been the rethinking of fiduciary duty, which became one of the major keys to unlocking such potential. In the past, the extent to which fiduciary duties are compatible with taking ESG criteria into account has been much debated from a legal standpoint. The constructive elaborations on this matter that followed in the last four years have been cementing a good degree of compatibility with these duties when certain conditions, particularly the material financial impact on the investment performance and the beneficiaries' support, are met.

These changes call for a systematic integration of climate risks and ESG considerations in fiduciary duties.

In this chapter, we have argued that in spite of claims from asset managers that they account for these considerations, the reality is rather different. As with every new development and change, we will need some time before this becomes the 'new normal'. For this reason, investors' comprehension and their requesting sustainability to be an integral part of their investments is necessary. Clear standards set by European regulators, accessible products and easy to decipher processes can do much to bring about the needed changes.

REFERENCES

Balanced Rock Investment Advisors (2014), 'ESG Isn't a Trade-Off It's a Trade-Up'. https://balancedrockinvestmentadvisors.com/2014/12/22/esg-isnt-a-trade-off-its-a-trade-up.

Batsaikhan, U. and Demertzis, M. (2018), 'Financial Literacy and Inclusive Growth in the European Union'. Bruegel, Brussels. www.bruegel.org/2018/05/financial-literacy-and-inclusive-growth-in-the-european-union.

European Commission (2010), 'EU Ecolabel Regulation (Regulation (EC) No 66/2010) of 25 November 2009'. Brussels. https://eur-lex.europa.eu/legal-content/EN/TXT/PDF/?uri=CELEX:32010R0066&from=en.

European Commission (2018a), 'Final Report of the High-Level Expert Group on Sustainable Finance'. Brussels. https://ec.europa.eu/info/sites/info/files/180131-sustainable-finance-final-report_en.pdf.

European Commission (2018b), 'EU Pension Adequacy Report: Key Conclusions'. Directorate-General for Employment, Social Affairs and Inclusion. Brussels. https://ec.europa.eu/social/main.jsp?catId=738&langId=en&pubId=8084&furtherPubs=yes.

European Commission (2019a), 'Ecolabel Criteria for Financial Products'. JRC Technical Reports, p. 10. Brussels. https://susproc.jrc.ec.europa.eu/Financial_products/docs/1AHWG%20meeting_Financial%20Products%2004042019.pdf.

European Commission (2019a), 'Report on the Green Bond Standard'. Brussels. https://ec.europa.eu/info/sites/info/files/business_economy_euro/banking_and_finance/documents/190618-sustainable-finance-teg-report-green-bond-standard_en.pdf.

European Security and Markets Authority (2019), 'ESMA's Technical Advice to the European Commission on Integrating Sustainability Risks and Factors into MiFID II'. Final Report, p. 4. ESMA, Paris. www.esma.europa.eu/sites/default/files/library/esma35-43-1737_final_report_on_integrating_sustainability_risks_and_factors_in_the_mifid_ii.pdf.

Eurosif (2018), 'Eurosif SRI Study 2018'. Brussels. www.eurosif.org/wp-content/uploads/2018/11/European-SRI-2018-Study.pdf.

Global Sustainable Investment Alliance (GSIA) (2018), 'Global Sustainable Investment Review'. GSIA. www.gsi-alliance.org/wp-content/uploads/2019/03/GSIR_Review2018.3.28.pdf.

Novethic (2009), 'The Challenges Facing SRI Money Market Funds'. Paris. www.novethic.com/fileadmin/user_upload/tx_ausynovethicetudes/pdf_complets/SRI_Money_Market.pdf.

6 Environmental Risk Analysis by Financial Institutions

Nina Seega and Andrew Voysey*

6.1 INTRODUCTION

The G20 'Green Finance Study Group' (GFSG) created under the Finance Track of the G20 was established in 2016 with two co-chairs, the People's Bank of China and the Bank of England, on behalf of the Chinese and UK governments respectively. The GFSG's objective was to identify institutional and market barriers to green finance and, based on country experiences and best practices, analyse options on how to enhance the ability of the financial system to mobilise private green investment, thereby driving the green transformation of the global economy.

This required a global stock-take of the tools and techniques that financial institutions are developing to analyse environmental risks, a summary of which forms the basis of this chapter. At its heart is the question of how environmental sources of financial risk can be more effectively integrated into mainstream decision-making by financial institutions. To answer this question, based on the research commissioned and published by the GFSG, this chapter lays the practical and theoretical foundations of mainstreaming environmental risk analysis, analyses the trends emerging from the stock-take, presents challenges preventing uptake of innovative practice by mainstream actors and offers ways forward.

* This work was generously supported by a grant of the United Nations Office for Project Services.

6.2 PRACTICAL AND THEORETICAL FOUNDATIONS OF MAINSTREAMING ENVIRONMENTAL RISK ANALYSIS

6.2.1 The Rationale for This Research

If risks arising from environmental sources are being inadequately incorporated into financial decision-making, that is of strategic significance to G20 financial systems for at least two reasons. First, managing risk is central to the effective functioning and stability of financial institutions. Inadequate understanding of growing environmental sources of risk could allow threats to financial institutions to accumulate. Second, all capital is deployed on the basis of expected 'risk-adjusted' returns. If environmental risk is being underestimated, capital can be over-allocated to higher risk activities and limit progress towards sustainable global growth associated with a green transition. Improving environmental risk analysis can therefore support more efficient allocation of capital for long-term stability.

History has shown that 'environmental' events can affect the efficiency and effectiveness of markets, the safety and soundness of financial institutions and even the performance of wider financial and economic systems. Further, efforts to address environmental threats can also create financial risks. As a result, financial institutions have been addressing environmental sources of risk for many years. For instance, spurred by a series of major natural catastrophes in the late 1980s and early 1990s, the global (re)insurance industry encoded resilience to extreme natural catastrophes into its capital regime.

There is a growing recognition, however, that traditional approaches to incorporating environmental factors into risk management systems are insufficient in the face of environmental sources of risk, which now exist at new levels of scale, likelihood and interconnectedness. Today's risk environment is increasingly seeing risks that were previously considered by financial institutions to be inconsequential becoming, or threatening to become, more material. At the same time, increased interdependencies within the global financial system both open up new opportunities and increase vulnerability to second-order effects through contagion.

6.2.2   An Approach Grounded in Mainstream Risk Management

This research uses a long-established typology of financial risks to categorise the ways in which financial institutions can be exposed to environmental sources of risk. Market risk refers to the 'risk of losses in on- and off-balance sheet positions arising from movements in market prices' (Basel Committee on Banking Supervision, 1996). Credit risk is comprised of issuer and counterparty risk. Issuer risk is the possibility that an issuer/borrower is not able to fulfil its obligations due to its default. Counterparty risk comprises the risk that a counterparty defaults and is not able to fulfil its obligations (Christoffersen, 2003). Underwriting risk is the risk of insured losses being higher than expected. In property and casualty insurance products, significant components of such risk are the reserve and premium risks. In life and health insurance products, biometric and customer behaviour risks are important (Bennett, 2004). Business risk refers to the possibility that changes in circumstances undermine the viability of business plans and business models. Operational risk is the risk of losses due to 'physical catastrophe, technical failure, and human error in the operation of a firm, including fraud, failure of management, and process errors' (Christoffersen, 2003). Legal risk is the risk of significant legal consequences that flow from actions attributable to business (Moorhead and Vaughan, 2016). These are the risks that may arise when parties suffer losses related to environmental change, or their failure to manage appropriately their contribution to it. Some risk taxonomies add liquidity, country and reputational risks to these categories.

For simplicity in this research, 'business risk' and 'operational risk' are combined into one category, labelled 'business risk'. In addition, rapidly changing societal views of corporate behaviour relating to many environmental sources of risk mean that financial institutions often highlight reputational risk as a material factor in their decision-making. This research therefore also includes reputational risk in the 'business risk' category. Similarly, 'underwriting risks' that are faced by insurers and 'counterparty risks' are collated into the category of 'credit risks'. Thus, the category of credit risks would contain issuer and counterparty risks faced by banks and institutional investors and credit and underwriting risks faced by (re)insurance companies.

The research then uses two broad categories for how environmental threats, and efforts to address them, can create financial risks. There is a range of ways to conceptualise environmental sources of risk (e.g. Mercer's 'TRIP' framework). The roots of the typology used in this research lie in the Bank of England's Prudential Regulation Authority (PRA) 2015 report 'The impact of climate change on the UK insurance sector'. That report identified 'physical risks', which we elaborate arise from the impact of climatic (i.e. extremes of weather), geologic (i.e. seismic) events or widespread changes in ecosystem equilibria (e.g. soil quality or marine ecology). These sub-categories are informed by the Cambridge Centre for Risk Studies 'Taxonomy of Macro-threats' (Coburn et al., 2014). As the Financial Stability Board notes, physical risks can be event-driven ('acute') or longer-term in nature ('chronic'). The PRA also identified 'transition risks', which arise from efforts to address environmental change, including but not limited to abrupt or disorderly introduction of public policies, technological changes in investor sentiment and disruptive business model innovation.

An analytical framework derived from these mainstream approaches to risk identification was developed to underpin this research (Figure 6.1). Pockets of expertise exist around the world in many of the cells of this matrix. The focus of this research is to gather experiences and learning from across this spectrum, without preference to any one in particular, in order to identify cross-cutting lessons. Importantly, interlinkages can emerge *between* different environmental sources of risk (e.g. extreme events triggering policy change) as

	Financial risks			
	Business	**Credit**	**Market**	**Legal**
Physical: **-Climatic** **-Geologic** **-Ecosystems**				
Transition: **-Policy** **-Technology** **-Sentiment**				

*(left axis label: **Environmental sources**)*

FIGURE 6.1 An analytical framework for understanding environmental sources of financial risks

well as between the risks that result for different financial sectors (e.g. the impact of uninsured losses on the collateral values of bank loans).

6.2.3 Are Environmental Risks New?

This research is based on the premise that 'environmental risks' are not fundamentally new categories of risk for financial institutions. Rather, seeing these as sources of existing types of risk, rather than fundamentally new types of risk is a critical distinction, which highlights the importance of understanding existing mainstream risk management analytical frameworks and practices.

Many of the environmental threats, and efforts to address them, that trigger the risks faced by financial institutions today exhibit new characteristics. The experiences submitted by financial institutions as part of this research point to at least three distinctions – larger scale, increased likelihood and deeper interconnectedness. Evolutions in risk management tools and practices need to contend with all of these. Each one of these three characteristics is testing in its own right but in combination they can result in environmental sources of risk being material to financial institutions within traditional time horizons. The increasing scale, likelihood and interconnectedness of today's environmental sources of risk mean that they can no longer be considered peripheral to the risk management agenda and that traditional views that these are only long-term threats beyond the time horizon of interest to financial institutions are increasingly open to challenge. This manifests in moving baseline averages and increased likelihood of low probability, high-impact extremes. For example, Holland and Bruyère (2014) observe an upward trend in the global proportion of category 4–5 hurricanes, offset by a similar decrease in the proportion of category 1–2 hurricanes.

The possibility of abrupt transitions adds a further layer of complication to environmental risk management. Developments in technology and science (e.g. low-cost battery storage at scale) can prompt an abrupt shift in investor sentiment about future climate trajectories, which in turn could lead to economic shocks, causing substantial losses in financial portfolio values within traditional investment horizons (CISL, 2015; DNB, 2018). An abrupt transition might also be spurred by sudden and potentially irreversible changes in Earth systems, such as the disappearance of summer Arctic sea ice or disruptions to monsoon circulations (King et al., 2015). In these circumstances late adjustment would result in a 'hard landing' (Gros et al., 2016), which, exacerbated by a lack of technological progress, would amplify the physical costs of climate change.

6.2.4 The Backbone of Risk Management Processes

Traditional risk management processes proceed along several widely recognised stages. First, potential risk factors that could affect the portfolio or firm in question are identified, including the channels through which those risks could create financial impacts. Second, the overall significance of the risk factors on the portfolio or firm is calculated in order to come up with an exposure at risk. More detailed assessment of the impact of different scenarios is performed for higher priority risks, which relies on sufficient availability or disclosure of risk exposure information. Third and finally, exposure at risk is compared to the firm's risk appetite and a risk mitigation action plan is composed and executed.

One risk assessment tool that was mentioned by numerous financial institutions during the course of this research is 'stress testing', which is 'a risk management tool used to evaluate the potential impact on a firm of a specific event and/or movement in a set of financial variables' (BIS, 2005: 3). Stress testing has its roots in scenario analysis, which helps decision-makers assess the impacts of plausible, extreme futures. A scenario describes possible futures in sufficient detail, while remaining concrete, internally consistent and causally connected (Schoemaker, 1991). Stress testing is broader in application than regulatory assessments of threats to financial stability; in this research, financial institutions are found to be using stress testing to model impacts mainly at the client/investee or portfolio level.

6.2.5   Research Methodology

In light of the preliminary nature of work in this area, the approach taken is one of stock taking of existing tools and applications being developed by financial institutions in particular. Such an approach is timely because financial institutions around the world, as well as a variety of experts working with them, are currently developing relevant tools and approaches, often triggered by broader policy and regulatory interventions. Some of the learning from this work is made publicly available, but much of it is not. There is certainly no comprehensive global review of current practice, from which to derive lessons about the barriers to the effective incorporation of environmental sources of risk into financial decision-making and review options, concepts and potential methodologies for further development.

The research was conducted in four stages. In the first stage a review of available expert literature was undertaken. Thereafter an open invitation was issued to countries, financial institutions and private sector stakeholders through official G20 channels to submit examples of leading practice. In the third stage a deeper look at a subset of illustrative examples, and the analytical techniques therein, from around the world was undertaken. Finally, the fourth stage synthesised common lessons, challenges and options. The results of the synthesis were tested and refined with private sector representatives through webinars and workshops.

The selection of case studies was designed to demonstrate a variety of evolving risk management tools and approaches worldwide from different financial sectors and relating to different environmental sources of risk. The case studies are neither an exhaustive list of current practice, nor necessarily an indication of best practice. Rather, they are a selection from the submissions provided to the research team designed to reflect the diversity of experiences evident across markets of interest to the G20. They suffer from selection bias in that they illustrate the submissions received to showcase what is currently happening, rather than what is not. Given that this is intended as an initial stock taking exercise, this work should be taken in the spirit of laying the groundwork for future, more specific research.

The stock-take was informed by a variety of submissions from across the world, from institutions in countries such as Australia, Brazil, Canada, China, Colombia, France, Germany, India, Mexico, Netherlands, UAE, the UK, the US, Spain, Switzerland and South Africa, as well as a variety of industry bodies and international organisations.

6.3 ANALYSIS

A range of illustrative case studies was developed through this research process to demonstrate innovative market practice across a range of geographies, financial sectors and risks. They are detailed in Table 6.1, listed in alphabetical order by country.

In combination, these illustrative case studies, together with the supporting material submitted, the literature review and the private sector consultation events, allow us to draw a range of lessons. They are presented subsequently in three sections: those that are

Table 6.1 *Illustrative case studies of climate risk assessment*

	Country	Sector	Focus
1.	**Brazil**	Banking	Measuring the exposure of the Brazilian banking system to environmental risks.
2.	**China**	Banking	Stress testing the impact of environmental factors on a Chinese commercial bank's credit risk.
3.	**Germany**	Investment	Using scenario analysis to assess the impact of different carbon and energy regulation in equity analysis.
4.	**India**	Banking	Measuring and managing an Indian bank's exposure to natural capital risks.
5.	**International**	Ratings agency	Integrating the impacts of climate change into sovereign debt ratings.
6.	**International**	Banking and investment	Integrating water stress into corporate bond analysis.
7.	**Italy**	Banking	Using stress testing and ratings models to align risk analysis with a 2° climate scenario.
8.	**Netherlands**	Financial sector	The Dutch Central Bank's review of sectoral exposure to energy transition risks.
9.	**South Africa**	Insurance	Understanding the impact of climate change on a locality in South Africa.
10.	**Switzerland**	Banking	Stress testing balance sheet and client vulnerability to climate change risks.
11.	**United Arab Emirates**	Banking	Integrating environmental risk, including technology change, into credit approval processes in the Gulf.
12.	**United Kingdom**	Banking	A scorecard approach to integrating environmental performance into pricing decisions for real estate.

Table 6.1 (cont.)

	Country	Sector	Focus
13.	United Kingdom	Insurance	A realistic disaster scenario of the micro- and macro-economic effects of a global food system shock.
14.	United States	Banking	Stress testing a US bank's energy clients against regulation and incentives driving the energy transition.

cross-cutting, those that relate to specific financial sectors and those that relate to possible gaps in current practice.

6.3.1 Cross-Cutting Lessons

While national legal, market and environmental contexts give rise to local variations, a broad range of financial firms across markets and sectors are demonstrating meaningful engagement and early progress on this topic. Figure 6.2 shows how this range of examples can be understood in the context of the analytical framework developed by this study. The primary focus was at the firm level, however there are also examples of firms deferring at this stage to innovation being driven at the industry level, often in response to new regulations on environmental and social risk management (for instance in Bangladesh, Brazil, Colombia and Peru).

Innovation focussed on physical sources of risk is clustered around climatic events. Illustrative examples include a global reinsurer collaborating with a ratings agency to analyse the impact of climate change on sovereign credit ratings (Case Study 5; S&P Global Ratings (2015)), an insurance market study on the micro- and macro-economic impacts of global food price shocks triggered by an intense El Niño phase (Case Study 13) and systems analysis led by a non-life insurer to understand the drivers of growing risk exposure in the context of climate change in a particular region (Case Study 9).

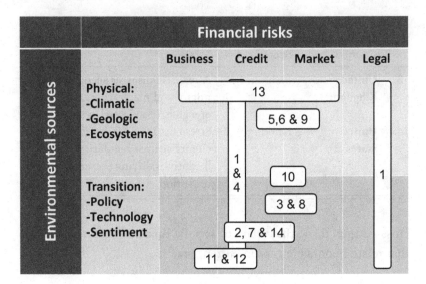

FIGURE 6.2 The focus of the illustrative case studies featured in this study

One major international collaboration is focussed on how to incorporate water stress into corporate bond analysis (Case Study 6; GIZ et al.,
(2015)), an example of an overlap between climatic and ecosystem
sources of risk. None of the cases represented here deal with geologic
sources of physical risk. However, these sources of risk have long been
analysed by insurance companies as part of their catastrophe modelling as well as by other financial institutions when considering their
operational risks and business continuity plans.

Innovation focussed on transition sources of risk is clustered
around policy or regulatory change. Examples of innovation in China
(Case Study 2), Germany (Case Study 3), Italy (Case Study 7), the
Netherlands (Case Study 8) and the United States (Case Study 14) all
focus on understanding the impact of policy change, to achieve decarbonisation, cleaner air or both. One example from the UAE considered the
role of technology change (Case Study 11), although the impact of this
specific analysis on financial decision-making so far has been modest.

Qualitative approaches are the starting point, but quantitative
analysis is a shared goal. Virtually all of the private and public submissions received indicated that financial institutions are already

engaged in some sort of qualitative assessment and management of the impact of environmental sources of risk. Approaches include, but are not limited to, strategic reviews, upgrades to risk governance structures and the tightening of internal risk management policies, including adopting international principles-based frameworks. Some early progress is being made with respect to innovative approaches to quantifying these impacts, which is clearly the direction of travel for risks to be properly managed.

A variety of tools and techniques are emerging, across every stage of traditional risk management. There are four common stages of a risk management process, starting with risk identification, moving through risk exposure and risk assessment and concluding with risk mitigation. Within each stage, this study has found examples of innovation emerging.

6.3.2   Risk Identification and Exposure

Strategic reviews are a common first step. One example not featured as an illustrative case study here was the UK PRA's study into the impacts of climate change on the insurance industry (PRA, 2015). To estimate total exposure, either at the firm or industry level, proxies are being used. In Case Study 4, for example, a bank analysed its total exposure to 'natural capital' risks, that is negative externalities created by the companies it finances that could in the future be internalised by a range of interventions, by using an 'environmentally extended input output (EEIO) model'. In Case Study 1, a banking association carried out the same exercise at the sector level and estimated that 33 per cent of Brazil's top ten banks' corporate lending is to sectors exposed to high levels of environment-related legal risk. Finally, in Case Study 8, a central bank also wanted to assess its financial sector's exposure, this time to transition sources of risk, finding that up to 12.4 per cent of the country's pension fund assets are in fossil fuel or carbon-intensive industries. All of these approaches are designed to obtain high-level overviews of exposure within the current data constraints based on a number of, sometimes quite significant, assumptions. Nevertheless, they can play an important role in informing decision-makers about the magnitude of risk that they need to consider.

6.3.3 Risk Assessment

For risk assessment, different scenario-based tools are being evolved according to the context, including stress testing, realistic disaster scenarios and probabilistic modelling. Where financial institutions are trying to assess the potential impact of risks on individual clients or investees and subsequently aggregate the results to a portfolio level, stress testing techniques are being adapted. In Case Study 14, for example, a bank has developed a carbon stress testing methodology to model the impact of increased carbon regulation and market responses to low carbon transition incentives on specific industry sector client portfolios, ultimately to inform decisions about credit risk. Case Study 2 sees another bank develop a very similar methodology, albeit the motivator here is air quality regulation. Case Study 3, developed by a group of investors, takes a similar approach while also explicitly factoring in the ability of investee companies to react to tighter regulation and thus reduce the impact on their performance, including the reduction by more than 10 per cent of the margins of poorly prepared energy-intensive companies in a strong carbon price scenario.

To analyse impacts that may propagate through entire economies, realistic disaster scenarios have been deployed. In Case Study 13, an analysis of the impact of global food price shocks on both micro- and macro-economic performance concluded that such a shock could supress European stock markets by 10 per cent, and US stocks by 5 per cent, over a sustained period. The probability of occurrence of such a scenario was estimated as significantly higher than the benchmark return period of 1:200 years applied for assessing insurers' ability to pay claims against extreme events.

Where data allows, probabilistic modelling can help to navigate uncertainty. In Case Study 5, a global reinsurer worked with a ratings agency to integrate the impacts of climate change into sovereign debt ratings. The research estimated that the damage-to-value ratio for a sovereign of a major climatic catastrophe could increase by an average of 25 per cent as a result of climate change. The negative ratings impact of the catastrophes due to climate change increases accordingly, on average by about 20 per cent compared to a scenario not including climate change.

6.3.4 Risk Mitigation

For risk mitigation, an important innovation is the use of systems modelling to identify 'no-regrets' actions that institutions can prioritise in the context of complexity. When it comes to risk mitigation, most financial institutions are focussed on what is within their control, such as decisions to engage with their clients/investees so that they reduce their own risk exposure. All of these options are perfectly valid, but many are limited in their ability to respond in situations of marked complexity. Case Study 9 sees an insurance company use a systems modelling approach to determine that human-induced changes to ecosystems are likely to be as important a driver of increased risk exposures as hazards that are made more intense or frequent by climate change. What has emerged as a response is collaboration with local authorities to address the human-induced ecosystem change.

Credit and market risks are receiving the most attention and analysis is revealing some material impacts. Early stage evidence exists of financial institutions acting on the findings of such risk analysis in their financial decision-making. In Case Study 2, for instance, a major Chinese bank reports that the findings of its analysis of the impact of tighter air quality standards on the financial performance of thermal power and cement companies have informed a recalibration of the bank's risk appetite in those sectors. In Case Study 12, a UK bank is offering corporate real estate clients pricing incentives on loans when they can evidence their action to reduce their exposure to transition risk.

6.3.5   Sector Trends

The insurance industry has the deepest experience of innovation in analysing physical sources of risk, having developed coherent metrics, methodologies and models to manage the financial impacts of natural catastrophes such as hurricanes, storms and floods. One key question for the sector relates to the fact that it is less clear whether these tools and techniques are being applied to transition sources of risk.

Investor innovation appears most focussed on transition sources of risks, specifically as they impact heavy polluting and energy-intensive sectors. Innovation is focussed at the investee and portfolio level, driven by concerns around market, credit (counterparty) and business (reputation) risk. Policy and regulatory change, rather than technological advances or sentiment shifts, appear to be of greatest concern, though it is notable that specialist investment funds have been launched specifically to benefit from disruptive technologies and business models.

In the banking industry, transition sources of risks affecting energy-intensive sectors are also a focus, with some broader innovation too. Driven by their potential exposures to all forms of financial risk, banks are certainly focussed on transition sources of risk related to the decarbonisation of the economy. Discussions in political fora about the possibility of regulatory 'carbon stress tests' and the introduction in 2019 of such tests for the UK insurance sector will no doubt be spurring this. In addition, though, it is notable that banks in various countries are focussing innovation on a broader set of risks, including those derived from physical sources like water stress and transition sources where regulatory or other efforts seek to internalise the negative externalities created by companies they finance.

6.3.6   Possible Gaps in Current Practice

While attention is widely being applied to transition risks, the possibility of abrupt shocks is rarely considered in practice. Expert bodies such as the Advisory Scientific Committee of the European Systemic

Risk Board (Gros et al., 2016) consider the possibility of a delayed and abrupt transition away from a high emission energy system to be a plausible scenario. Meanwhile, research has shown that the impact of short-term, abrupt shifts in market sentiment induced by awareness of future climate risks could lead to material economic shocks (CISL, 2015; DNB, 2018). When looking at transition sources of risk, most innovation is focussed on policy or regulatory change. While scenario analysis does allow for 'strong' policy interventions to be modelled, these are rarely assumed to be introduced in a sudden manner. A tension between the literature and current practice therefore appears to exist. This is despite experience such as the Tohoku earthquake of 2011 that led, albeit indirectly, to abrupt changes in the German government's policy towards nuclear energy. A notable exception here is the work conducted by De Nederlandsche Bank on the impact of abrupt transitions on the Dutch financial system (DNB, 2018).

Limited work to assess interlinkages between sectors and subsequent aggregation appears to be happening. Across the spectrum of financial risks that can be driven by environmental sources, the majority of work is concentrated on assessing direct impacts to financial institutions via the companies they insure, finance or own. Meanwhile, some regulatory authorities and academic experts are already considering the indirect channels through which network effects could see impacts propagate through the financial system and affect financial institutions indirectly. Researchers at the Bank of England, for example, are considering the impact of uninsured losses from natural catastrophes on collateral values securing loans in the property and small business market (Batten et al., 2016), while a group of international academics has developed a methodological framework to assess the exposure of the financial system to climate policy risks including through indirect channels such as energy-intensive sectors, housing and finance (Battiston et al., 2017).

Of all the financial risks, the biggest knowledge gap may be around legal risk. Despite featuring prominently in legal contexts or strategic reviews of markets such as Brazil, China and the UK, legal risk does not appear as the primary focus of any of the quantitative analysis submitted to this study, nor of any discrete scenario-building work. This may be because of the uncertainties involved or because legal risks tend to be derived from failures to manage physical or transition risks, or both. Nevertheless, experts and industry bodies alike argue that this is a significant risk (Barker, 2013; Geneva Association, 2011).

6.4 THREE CHALLENGES TO MAINSTREAM INTEGRATION

The illustrative case studies highlighted in this stock-take show that innovation in risk analysis is emerging but is far from integrated into mainstream decision-making. The stock-take has drawn attention to pockets of innovation in risk analysis tools and techniques across financial sectors. Most examples are in the development stage, where new methodologies are being trialled on subsets of relevant exposures financial institutions may have. Where the results of this innovation are being implemented in risk management practice, these are the exceptions rather than the rule. On the one hand, such innovation by major incumbent players shows how significantly the need for new analytical tools and techniques is being felt at the heart of the financial system. On the other hand, given the importance of this agenda, the fragmented and early stage nature of such innovation should be cause for motivation to address challenges preventing quicker mainstream uptake. This research has identified three challenges to mainstreaming. These challenges are raised consistently across the illustrative case studies, appear regularly in the expert literature and have been validated as priorities in engagements with private sector institutions convened for this study.

6.4.1 Lack of Capacity

Developing credible analyses on how environmental sources can create financial risks is complex and requires expertise that is often not found in one institution. Assembling the insight required to convert threats, transmission mechanisms and impacts into useable scenarios may require financial institutions to form new partnerships with experts from a range of sectors. In the vast majority of illustrative case studies profiled in this research, the financial institution in question had to work with at least one other type of stakeholder to fill knowledge and skill gaps or clients/investees to acquire relevant data. Justifying investment in collaborative approaches, required to connect disparate pockets of expertise, with no guaranteed return and associated opportunity costs, is challenging to envisage at scale.

One option to build capacity is the convening of multi-sector, multi-disciplinary fora to develop environmental risk scenarios that represent priorities within a national context. Examples of such fora are present in the United Kingdom, the Netherlands and Japan. Countries have different exposures to environmental sources of financial risks according to their geographies, the structure of their economies and financial markets, their liability regimes and their public policy contexts, to name just a few factors. Ensuring adequate prioritisation of capacity building at the country level is therefore important. Further, to build capacity more industry and academic research is required to deepen collective understanding, ideally in a quantitative manner, of how the impacts of different risks can aggregate, how interlinkages between sectors may allow risks to propagate and how abrupt shocks may impact different pools of capital. These are all questions that individual financial institutions find it difficult to prioritise and so their relative potential impact remains unknown.

6.4.2 Inadequate Data

Data is a critical input to risk analysis. The lack of comprehensive and consistent data dissuades financial institutions from investing in tool development. In order to incorporate environmental sources of risk into mainstream analysis, a variety of types of data are required, but significant challenges are associated with the comprehensiveness and consistency of data that is available. The data on the exposure of financial institutions' clients or investees to the risks in question is most often cited as lacking. Further, industry classifications vary across different assets and institutions, making it problematic to measure exposure to carbon and related energy regulation in a consistent and comparable manner. It is at this level of data disclosure that some countries have introduced legislation (e.g. France through its Energy Transition Law, 2015). At least two other types of data are needed by individual financial institutions. The first is data on environmental sources of risk, for example the kind of datasets compiled by the insurance industry relating to changing weather-related extreme events. The second is data that gives financial institutions insights into how the impacts of different hazards or transition-related events propagate. For example, the consortium behind Case Study 6, which developed a methodology to integrate water stress into corporate bond analysis, notes that it could not access data relating to how water infrastructure and ownership rights (e.g. arrangements to pump water into a given region from a different basin during a period of stress) influence how drought impacts different regions.

In parallel, but related to the need for better data, many traditional risk assessment methodologies need to be adapted to analyse risk arising from environmental sources. This is not just a question of having the right data, but of having the tools and expertise that is required to interpret complex datasets and make them compatible with mainstream financial risk management tools. In private submissions to this study, different types of institution shared that they are trying to adapt scenario-based tools to analyse risks with environmental sources but are struggling, for instance, with which transmission mechanisms to prioritise or with how to present the output of such tools in a decision-ready manner given the uncertainties involved.

One option to improve data is to ensure work to improve data disclosure focusses on all types of data required for effective risk analysis. This would include firm- and asset-level disclosure as well as data related to how impacts may propagate through different systems. The FSB's Task Force on Climate-related Financial Disclosures (TCFD) is one preeminent body focussed in this area.

6.4.3 Lack of a Level Playing Field

If risk is being mis-priced, or if short-termism means risks are not being taken into account sufficiently by financial institutions, a competitive market may force a 'race to the bottom'. Where enhanced risk analysis reveals risk has been mis-priced, a competitive market context can act as a disincentive for individual firms to act unilaterally. Just as one anecdotal example, in the United States, the City of Norfolk (Virginia) invested in analysis to enhance its understanding of its own exposure to sea level rise. When it published its findings, this triggered ratings agencies to downgrade its credit rating. While it is true that consequential work to manage this risk exposure may result in the 'reward' of its credit rating being uplifted again, in the near term this has been seen as a clear disincentive to action.

Similarly, short-termism in financial decision-making is a challenge cutting across many issues but particularly relevant to risk analysis (Chenet, Thoma and Janci, 2015; Mercer, 2015; WEF, 2014). However, the stock-take has shone light on helpful experiences that already exist. For instance, the non-life insurance industry is typically oriented around one-year insurance contracts and yet regulatory requirements to ensure that insurance companies hold sufficient capital to be resilient to a natural catastrophe event with a 1 in 200 annual probability has brought the management of high-impact, low-likelihood risks into short-term decision-making that affects both the safety and soundness of firms and financial stability.

Scenario-based environmental risk analysis, when deployed appropriately to manage tail risks in particular, can help to address some aspects of uncertainty and time horizon issues. Experience is emerging around the world, in different sectors, focussed on different environmental sources of risk. A concerted effort to share knowledge and experience across such boundaries could accelerate action.

6.5 SUMMARY AND LOOKING AHEAD

This research makes several contributions to the research on sustainability transitions (Markard et al., 2012). First, it proposes a simple framework for understanding environmental sources of financial risks. Such a framework helps financial actors understand and engage with environmental sources of risk. Second, it underlines the role of financial firms in sustainability transitions. The agency of particular actors during transitions is a fertile area, where more research is needed (Markard et al., 2012; Raven et al., 2011). Given the capital requirements of such transitions, financial institutions are particularly important in ensuring that environmental risks are priced correctly, which means that sufficient capital is allocated to such transitions. Therefore, continued research and collaboration in this space is of utmost importance. In the time since this research was conducted, a number of developments have emerged to move the field forward. One example of particular importance is the work of the Network for Greening the Financial System, a network of over fifty (at the start of 2020) central banks and regulators across the world, which continues to drive forward the GFSG's work on adequate incorporation of environmental risk analysis into mainstream financial risk management.

REFERENCES

Barker, S. (2013), 'Directors' Duties in the Anthropocene – Liability for Corporate Harm due to Inaction on Climate Change', Corporate Law, Economics and Science Association, December. http://responsible-investmentbanking.com/wp-content/uploads/2014/11/Directors-Duties-in-the-Anthropocene-December-2013.pdf.

Basel Committee on Banking Supervision (1996), 'Amendment to the Capital accord to Incorporate Market Risks', pp. 1–54. Basel Committee on Banking Supervision, January. www.bis.org/publ/bcbs24.htm.

Batten, S., Sowerbutts, R. and Tanaka, M. (2016), 'Let's Talk about the Weather: The Impact of Climate Change on Central Banks', Working Paper 603, Bank of England. www.bankofengland.co.uk/working-paper/2016/lets-talk-about-the-weather-the-impact-of-climate-change-on-central-banks.

Battiston, S., Mandel, A., Monasterolo, I., Schuetze, F. and Visentin, G. (2017), 'A Climate Stress Test of the Financial System', *Nature Climate Change* 7, 283–288. www.nature.com/articles/nclimate3255.

Bennett, C. (2004), *Dictionary of Insurance*. Pearson Education, Harlow.

BIS (2005), 'Stress Testing at Major Financial Institutions: Survey Results and Practice', Committee on the Global Financial System, pp. 1–36.Bank for International Settlements, Basel. www.bis.org/publ/cgfs24.htm.

Chenet, H., Thoma, J. and Janci, D. (2015), 'Financial Risk and the Transition to a Low Carbon Economy: A Carbon Stress Testing Framework', 2i Investing Initiative, July. www.dnb.nl/binaries/OS_Transition risk stress test versie_web_tcm46–379397.pdf.

Christoffersen, P. F. (2003). *Elements of Financial Risk Management*. Academic Press, London.

CISL (2015), 'Unhedgeable Risk: How Climate Change Sentiment Impacts Investment'. University of Cambridge Institute for Sustainability Leadership, Cambridge. www.cisl.cam.ac.uk/resources/publication-pdfs/unhedgeable-risk.pdf.

Coburn, A. W., Bowman, G., Ruffle, S. J. et al. (2014), 'A Taxonomy of Threats for Complex Risk Management', Cambridge Risk Framework. Cambridge Centre for Risk Studies, University of Cambridge. www.jbs.cam.ac.uk/fileadmin/user_upload/research/centres/risk/downloads/crs-cambridge-taxonomy-threats-complex-risk-management.pdf.

DNB (2018), 'An Energy Transition Risk Stress Test for the Financial System of the Netherlands'. De Nederlandsche Bank, Amsterdam. www.dnb.nl/en/binaries/OS_Transition risk stress test versie_web_tcm47–379397.pdf.

Geneva Association (2011), 'Liability Issues Related to Climate Risk'. www.genevaassociation.org/sites/default/files/publications-document-type/pdf_public/sys_ga2011-rmsc5_0.pdf.

GIZ, NCD, VfU (2015), 'Integrating Water Stress into Corporate Bond Credit Analysis'. www.globalcanopy.org/sites/default/files/documents/resources/INTEGRATING WATER STRESS REPORTFINAL.pdf.

Gros, D., Schoenmaker, D., Langfield, S. and Matikainen, S. (2016), 'Too Late, too Sudden: Transition to a Low-Carbon Economy and Systemic Risk', Reports of the Advisory Scientific Committee, Vol. 6: European Systemic Risk Board. www.esrb.europa.eu/pub/pdf/asc/Reports_ASC_6_1602.pdf.

Holland, G. and Bruyère, C. L. (2014). 'Recent Intense Hurricane Response to Global Climate Change', *Climate Dynamics* 42, 617–627.

King, D., Schrag, D., Dadi, Z., Ye, Q. and Ghosh, A. (2015), 'Climate Change: A Risk Assessment'. www.csap.cam.ac.uk/media/uploads/files/1/climate-change-a-risk-assessment-v11.pdf.

Markard, J., Raven, R. and Truffer, B. (2012), Sustainability Transitions: an Emerging Field of Research and Its Prospects', *Research Policy* 41(6), 955–967. www.sciencedirect.com/science/article/abs/pii/S004873331200056X.

Mercer (2015), 'Investing in a Time of Climate Change'. www.mercer.com/.../ mercer-climate-change-report-2015.pdf.

Moorhead, R. and Vaughan, S. (2016), 'Legal Risk: Definition, Management and Ethics', UCL Centre for Ethics and Law. https://papers.ssrn.com/sol3/papers .cfm?abstract_id=2594228.

Prudential Regulation Authority (PRA) (2015), 'The Impact of Climate Change on the UK Insurance Sector: A Climate Change Adaptation Report by the Prudential Regulation Authority', September. www.bankofengland.co.uk/-/ media/boe/files/prudential-regulation/publication/impact-of-climate-change-on-the-uk-insurance-sector.pdf.

Raven, P., Chase, J. and Pires, J. (2011), 'Introduction to Special Issue on Biodiversity', *American Journal of Botany* 98, 333–335. www.researchgate .net/publication/51165770_Introduction_to_special_issue_on_biodiversity1

Schoemaker, P. (1991), 'When and How to Use Scenario Planning: A Heuristic Approach with Illustration', *Journal of Forecasting* 10, 549–564.

S&P Global Ratings (2015), 'The Heat Is On: How Climate Change Can Impact Sovereign Ratings', November 25. S&P Global Ratings Services, McGraw Hill Financial. www.agefi.com/uploads/media/S_P_The_Heat_Is_On_How_Climate_ Change_Can_Impact_Sovereign_Ratings_25-11-2015.pdf.

WEF (2014), 'Integrating Natural Disaster Risk into the Financial System Private Workshop Summary', 16 June. Geneva, Switzerland: World Economic Forum. www3.weforum.org/docs/WEF_ENV_NaturalDisasterRiskFinancialSystem_ WorkshopSummary_2014.pdf.

7 Sustainable Governance and Leadership

Claudia Kruse and Michael Schmidt

7.1 INTRODUCTION

For the financial sector to play its necessary, supportive role in a more sustainable economy, with less resource-intensive and more resilient growth, enduring change is needed in the sector's system of values, beliefs and behaviours. This required change in culture represents an opportunity for all players in the financial industry to reinstall a positive purpose in their role in society at large.

The rules of engagement of any system are based on implicit or explicit governance principles and driven by leadership actions. Our chapter therefore explores three aspects of governance principles.

First, the requirements of education, training and qualifications in respect of sustainability issues for leaders and finance professionals, to enable them to take a wider and longer-term perspective in their decision-making processes. That includes the relevant and material ESG risks and opportunities affecting their business.

Second, the changes needed in the governance framework of financial institutions, with a particular focus on the concept of stewardship, in a new, more encompassing understanding, as a key mechanism:

a. to manifest the service role towards beneficiaries and end investors by taking their preferences into account more stringently and

b. to guide their role as active stewards of capital towards investee companies.

Third, the necessary modifications to director duties in general, so that the intended stewardship action can be effective with a view to rendering the real economy more sustainable over time. These changes include a clear commitment to transparency and address the governance rules related to company management, supervision and incentive structures.

7.2   CHANGES TO EDUCATION, TRAINING AND QUALIFICATION REQUIREMENTS

Ultimately, the business culture in the financial sector needs to shift to align decisions and actions more closely with long-term perspectives in terms of risks and client preferences, and establish the norms and values needed to deliver on the promise of a sustainable financial system that is useful to society.

Knowledge and skills related to long-term risks, sustainability and governance are essential preconditions for changing the way organisations are run and allocate capital. A new generation of leadership and investment professionals will have to be trained and assessed differently.

In order to attract talent in the future, companies need to be much clearer about their purpose and also show how they allow their employees at every level of seniority to have a socially and environmentally positive impact and how sustainability permeates all aspects of a company from procurement to performance assessment. For younger generations these aspects of company performance weigh heavily in their choice of employer, research shows.

7.2.1   *Degrees and Teaching*

Many people who work in the corporate and financial sector have been to business school. Hence, they play a crucial role in shaping the next generation of professionals. They could make a real difference were they to have a greater focus on teaching long-term systemic perspectives, sustainability, ethics and social purpose. A number of global business schools have already been actively engaged.[1] Some schools have started to offer modules and even dedicated degrees, for example the University of Maastricht offers an MSc Finance and

---

[1] www.ft.com/content/b6bcfa02-ef37-11e9-ad1e-4367d8281195.

Sustainability; Cambridge,[2] Oxford,[3] Harvard and several others offer executive education.

Business school rankings are crucial to their future success. If these rankings were to be modified to include how well ESG-related topics were incorporated into teaching, this could change the way future staff are being taught to think (Pitt-Watson and Quigley, 2019). Initiatives such as the UN Principles for Responsible Management Education (2007) and the UN Higher Education Sustainability Initiative (2012) have helped advance the teaching of sustainable development and for business schools to take a leading role. Still, sustainability is not yet integral to core curricula or integrated into finance and business degrees. While further education institutions can play a key role, they still have way to go. One way forward is to develop partnerships with the financial and business sector to create dedicated programmes catering for future needs.

The drive for change can also come from the financial sector itself. In the Netherlands, the financial sector, under the aegis of the Sustainable Finance Platform of the Dutch Central bank, helped develop a course offered by University of Nyenrode, which is targeted at board members on advancing their comprehension of sustainability and long-term issues.[4] Erasmus University has since followed suite with a dedicated sustainable finance course,[5] and at the University of Groningen it is part of the accounting faculty. Many financial institutions, like ABN Amro or APG, have incorporated sustainability into their own internal leadership training programmes.

Finance professionals often require certifications, such as Chartered Financial Analyst (CFA), Certified International Investment Analyst (CIIA) or Certified Alternative Investment Analyst (CAIA).

---

[2] www.cisl.cam.ac.uk/centres/centre-for-sustainable-finance.
[3] www.smithschool.ox.ac.uk/research/sustainable-finance/global-advisory-council .html.
[4] www.nyenrode.nl/opleidingen/p/finance-in-transitie.
[5] www.rsm.nl/executive-education/open-programmes/programmes/sustainable- finance/overview.

The CFA programme has a strong focus on ESG integration and, together with the Principles for Responsible Investment (PRI), has developed an ESG integration framework.[6] The CFA Institute is looking to incorporate more ESG-related components into its curriculum, and in its 2019 review of the state of ESG integration it emphasises the talent gap.[7] The CFA-accredited PRI academy offers three courses (RI Fundamentals, RI Essentials and Enhanced Financial Analysis) which qualify for Permanent Education points. Likewise, the European Federation of Financial Analyst Societies (EFFAS) offers a dedicated qualification for financial analysts and portfolio managers, the Certified EFFAS Environmental Social and Governance Analyst (CEESGA) and since 2019 the Certified Sustainable Investing and Finance Professional (CSIF).[8] The International Corporate Governance Network (ICGN) has been offering an in-person programme on how to integrate ESG factors in investment decision-making, as part of investor stewardship, since 2012, which is focused on learning from practitioners.[9]

As previously shown, while not yet mainstream there is a growing number of courses and programmes which have a sustainability and governance component or are even dedicated to the topic. Importantly, they have to cater for both technical skills and leadership competencies in this area.

7.2.2   Governing Bodies and Competencies

Company boards (and other governing bodies) play a leadership role in setting the tone at the top and communicating ethical values. The Financial Stability Board (FSB, 2017a, p. 3) noted that 'Where norms

[6] www.unpri.org/the-esg-integration-framework/3722.article.
[7] As well as a problem of lack of knowledge, there is a talent gap. ESG teams often lack professionals with investment experience and application, and investment desks largely consist of professionals with limited ESG knowledge and research skills.
[8] www.dvfa.de/finanzakademie/programme/csif-certified-sustainable-investing-and-finance-professional.html.
[9] www.icgn.org/education.

and values are not clearly defined and enforced, the culture of an institution can defeat its formal governance.'

Supervisors' work on culture is evolving and does not merely focus on financial outcomes of culture but takes a broader perspective. The FSB also noted that: 'Interplay can be seen between culture and governance frameworks. [...] While firms are responsible for shaping their culture, supervisors and regulators could play a role in promoting culture as a mitigant to misconduct risk' (FSB, 2017b, p. 7).

To influence culture one therefore needs to address the composition of the very governance bodies that set the tone at the top, not only with regard to norms and values, but also with regard to an institution's relationships with its stakeholders and the incorporation of long-term and sustainability risks into how the business is run. Arguably supervisory authorities ought to assess this ability as part of assessments of director appointments at the institutions under their direct supervision.

Current guidance on assessment regimes for board members of financial institutions, the so-called fit and proper regimes define in very broad terms what the board as a collective should comprise. Likewise, sectorial regulations for the finance sector define risk in broad terms. Fit and proper assessments cover topics such as understanding of market risks and risks to one's institution. This arguably would include climate and other sustainability risks.

Supervisors, including the European Central Bank (ECB), develop Supervisory Manuals which include checklists for assessing the ability to manage the risks identified. Since board assessment processes seek to determine a board's capacity to deal with key risks to an institution, and an individual's contribution to this, the interplay between the definition of risks, the management thereof and fit and proper assessments is evident.

At the time of writing the EC was consulting on the role of the European Supervisory Agencies (ESAs) and as their mandates with regard to sustainability get extended, this ought to effect how board members' suitability to run institutions is assessed.

De Nederlandsche Bank (DNB) is also working to take into account climate-related risk in its supervisory framework. DNB recognises climate risks as a significant long-term risk and institutions under its supervision are subject to a stress test on climate.[10] They see scope for insurers to take all material risks into account in the Own Risk and Solvency Assessments (ORSAs). DNB has developed and published a good practice document that gives insurers more guidance on how to deal with these risks as part of their risk management and through scenario analyses. While sustainable investing is part of the DNB's interview guidance for appointments to investment committees, it is not included in the Policy Rules or Dutch Law.[11]

In the United Kingdom, the Prudential Regulatory Authority's (PRA) supervisory statement SS 3/19 (PRA, 2019) creates director liability for climate change. The PRA requires banks and insurance companies 'to have clear roles and responsibilities for the board and its relevant sub-committees in managing the risk from climate change'. Under the Senior Managers Regime, firms need to submit Responsibility Statements for a number of controlled functions. Individual senior managers must now accept personal responsibility also for climate change.

As SS 3/19 states: '... the board and the highest level of executive management should identify and allocate responsibility for identifying and managing financial risks from climate change to the relevant existing Senior Management Function(s) (SMF(s)) most appropriate within the firm's organisational structure, enhancing banks' and insurers' approaches to managing the financial risks from climate change.'

In its 2015 analysis of the specific impact of climate change on the UK insurance sector, the PRA highlights the potential liability risk (PRA, 2015):

---

[10] www.dnb.nl/binaries/Working%20paper%20No.%20625_tcm46-382291.pdf.
[11] www.toezicht.dnb.nl/binaries/50-235985.pdf.

Potential causes of action against directors and officers may include, for example, shareholder derivative actions for breach of statutory or fiduciary duties or seeking compensation for a loss of corporate value attributable to a failure to mitigate or adapt. Claims may also be based on a failure to disclose (or misleading disclosure) in relation to the risks associated with climate change, particularly as the requirements for related disclosure and reporting become more stringent.

... it would seem increasingly difficult to argue that impacts on corporate value arising from a failure to manage risks associated with climate change are not reasonably foreseeable – on the basis of prevailing scientific and economic evidence . . ..

... failure to adapt' claims could be distinguishable from those arising from the corporate collapses relating to the global financial crisis, which were often viewed as 'sudden' and broadly 'unforeseen'. Rather, such claims may be more closely analogous to other cases of alleged failure to manage structural or systemic transition risks.

Likewise, the PRA warned (PRA, 2015, p. 7) that:

Liability risks may take a long time to crystallise compared to catastrophe claims as it can take years to establish whether the insured party was at fault and to determine the true amount of loss that has arisen as a result. The true cost of liability claims can often be uncertain and complex to determine. This is compounded by the fact that claims are commonly settled out of court – often for the sum insured.

Directors are the stewards of companies. Recognising the link between disruptive climate change and business, the World Economic Forum has published a set of Climate Governance Principles designed to help non-executive directors address and steer on climate risks and opportunities. The eight principles cover: climate accountability on boards, command of the subject, board structure, material risk and opportunity assessment, strategic integration, incentivisation, reporting and disclosure, and exchange.[12] Since the launch of the principles in Davos in 2019, a number of networks of non-executive directors have been established, for example in Italy, hosted by the National Institute of Directors; in Malaysia, hosted by the Institute of Corporate Directors and supported by the Securities Commission Malaysia; and in the United Kingdom, the Directors' Climate Forum 'Chapter Zero', hosted by Cambridge University. These fora allow for an exchange of good practices and advancing knowledge. As directors emerge as drivers of change, we are likely to see a growing demand for high-quality education by a variety of providers and the exchange with experts from different fields, outside of the boardroom, will increase.

7.3   STEWARDSHIP AND GOVERNANCE

A sustainable financial system works for the benefit of the real economy and its citizens. Those who are entrusted to invest money on behalf of others need to ensure that they invest in line with the preferences of those end beneficiaries.

In the Netherlands, for example, it is required by law that the boards of pension funds be representative of their constituency. Moreover, pension funds have to establish a dedicated 'Verantwoordingsorgaan', a body to whom the board of the pension fund is accountable and where beneficiaries and other stakeholders are represented. This means that within the governance structure of pension funds the interests of beneficiaries are structurally represented, and their representatives are part of the decision-making and oversight.

Beyond the formal mandated governance, a number of Dutch pension funds actively pursue the dialogue with beneficiaries. One example is ABP, the pension fund for the Dutch civil servants.

---

[12] www3.weforum.org/docs/WEF_Creating_effective_climate_governance_on_corporate_boards.pdf.

The fund regularly organises roundtables with societal stakeholders and uses them as a sounding board for the review of its Responsible Investment Policy. In 2018, for example, it decided to add tobacco to the list of excluded products. Board members meet with participants and during live webinars stand ready to answer participant questions. This commitment to being accountable goes hand in hand with transparency about how the fund invests, engages and votes, and which dilemma it faces. It requires openness and resources to handle this. The fund has been publishing an annual Responsible Report since 2008 and asking its key stakeholders ('our participants and employers in the pension fund, ABP board members and organisations that are directly or indirectly involved in our sustainable and responsible investment policy')[13] what they would like to read about in the report since 2013.[14] Many more funds seek more direct connections with their beneficiaries, a good example is the Australian pension fund CBUS.

As part of the EU Commission's Action Plan on Financing Sustainable Growth (European Commission, 2018), delegated regulations were proposed that require investment firms under MiFID II and distributors of insurance products under IDD to ask their clients about sustainability preferences more explicitly within the suitability assessment. These preferences then ought to be reflected, alongside the financial objectives, in the recommendations on the choice of financial products. Moreover, advisers need to be transparent and explain to clients how ESG preferences have been taken into account. The new requirements are expected to come into force at the

---

[13] The latter group comprises, for example trade unions, NGOs, knowledge institutions, legislators, politicians, media and other pension funds and pension providers.

[14] 'ABP aims for a good pension for its participants. And it aims for a sustainable world in which to enjoy that pension. We pay attention to returns, risks, costs and to how the companies we invest in deal with people, the environment and good governance (ESG – Environmental, Social and Governance). A good and affordable pension is and remains the point of departure for our investment choices. Attention for people, the environment and good governance is also important. Financial returns and sustainable and responsible investing can go hand in hand.'

beginning of 2021 and should help better address the sustainability preferences of retail investors. This could be a game changer in terms of a systematic approach that may stimulate demand for sustainable and responsible products, which in turn need to provide credible information to the consumer.

Many asset owners have parts or all of their assets managed by external investment firms. It is therefore essential that stewardship and governance form a core part of the investment management agreement. The International Corporate Governance Network (ICGN) in 2012 published a Model Mandate which includes contract terms to achieve an alignment between the asset owner's and the asset manager's stewardship objectives, integration of long-term factors including ESG issues, systemic responsibility, stewardship and engagement, voting and other key commitments. This has since been incorporated into the ICGN Global Stewardship Principles.[15] Arguably such provisions should form a mandatory part of any agreement, in particular with the EU Shareholder Rights Directive II (SRD II) imposing obligations on stewardship, engagement and voting upon investors with the goal in mind that the provisions 'contribute to a proper alignment of interests between the final beneficiaries of institutional investors, the asset managers and the investee companies and potentially to the development of longer-term investment strategies and longer-term relationships with investee companies involving shareholder engagement'.[16]

7.3.1   Evolution of Governance Structures and Director Duties

It is crucially important, in order for the EU's, and by extension, the UN's sustainability objectives and climate goals to be achieved, that all corporates systematically consider the related risks and opportunities in their business strategies and governance arrangements.

---

[15] www.icgn.org/sites/default/files/ICGNGlobalStewardshipPrinciples.pdf.
[16] Directive (EU) 2017/828, L 132/4.

Investors have leverage over their investee companies through active engagement in their role as providers of equity and debt financing. However, their actions as responsible stewards could be greatly supported by integrating a clear commitment to sustainability in the duties of companies' directors and in the governance rules related to companies' management, supervision and incentive structures. As the OECD underlines (OECD, 2015):

> The board is not only accountable to the company and its shareholders but also has a duty to act in their best interests. In addition, boards are expected to take due regard of, and deal fairly with, other stakeholder interests including those of employees, creditors, customers, suppliers and local communities. Observance of environmental and social standards is relevant in this context.

While references to sustainability aspects in governance can increasingly be found in both the OECD and the ICGN principles, as well as in many national corporate governance codes, they have yet had limited impact. It is therefore welcome that 'fostering sustainable corporate governance' constitutes a dedicated action point in the EU Commission's Action Plan on Financing Sustainable Growth. However, no concrete proposals that would go beyond the current provisions already in place through SRD II have so far emerged.

7.3.2 Key Principles to Address the Wider Principal–Agent Problem

Across a broad range of countries globally it is now widely understood that for the effective functioning of economic systems and for building trust in their decision makers the existence of and adherence to good governance standards – in law, rules and principles – play an essential role. While good governance should not be confined to joint-stock corporations, the principal–agent problem is of particular relevance there. The management board, especially of big corporations, typically has a substantial information advantage over the often-widespread shareholder base. While the shareowners (the 'principal') bear the full economic risk of the business activity indefinitely, company management (the 'agent') is only employed for a comparatively short period – with limited economic risk. This asymmetry constitutes the danger that without adequate control mechanisms, management may not act in the best interest of their shareholders. Management might for example take short-term rewarding decisions that have, however, detrimental effects on the long-term success of the company. At the time when those long-term negative impacts are felt by shareholders (and often also by other stakeholders like employees, clients, suppliers and communities around the corporate) the responsible management may no longer be in place.

The good news is that, according to the OECD, which monitors the global development of corporate governance against their principles, corporate governance frameworks have further evolved (OECD, 2019). However, given the increasing complexity and accelerating change in many areas relevant to shareholders, not least in technology and society, the need for responsible corporate governance has not abated, thus requiring continuous improvements in the way companies are led and managed, including the interplay between management and investors – today more so than ever, as the economic and financial world is faced with an enormous transformational task that is posed by the need for ecological and social sustainability in the face of climate change, resource depletion, burdening demographics and the uncertainties of digitalisation.

Institutional shareholders, as professional stewards of capital, have an elevated responsibility in accompanying the corporate sector in this transition with an active engagement policy that takes an encompassing, long-term perspective. In doing so they can and should assume a leadership role for all shareholders, thereby nurturing their own purpose in society.

Against this background, and for investors' stewardship role to be effective, a solid set of key principles, such as put forward in the OECD or ICGN principles, are necessary but not sufficient for addressing the principal–agent problem in our times. Most of them are already implemented in a reasonable number of jurisdictions but to differing degrees. In the context of the sustainability debate, it is worthwhile highlighting areas of greatest importance and need for improvement.

7.3.2.1 Protection of (Minority) Shareholder Rights

As institutional investors typically are minority investors in companies, the protection of minority shareholder rights is important in order to avoid potential abuse of asymmetric information and influence. As ICGN puts it (ICGN, 2019):

> Concerns can be particularly acute in companies with controlling shareholders – a common theme of ownership around the world. While controlling shareholders in many cases can be strong long-term partners with minority shareholders, there is also the risk that the interests of the controlling shareholder might conflict with those of minority shareholders. These challenges can be particularly difficult in developing or emerging markets, where enforcement of minority shareholder rights can be challenging.

Appropriate measures to protect (minority) shareholder rights are (amongst others):

- To uphold the principle of 'one share – one vote', that is a clear rejection of differential ownership rights through loyalty shares or dual class shares. After years of retrenchment of dual class shares, this has again become an area of increasing concern, most notably in markets like Canada, Brazil and Hong Kong as well as in the US technology sector. It appears as though stock exchanges with their listing criteria play a decisive role as to the acceptance of dual class shares in financial markets. In fact, one could argue that any quality stock market segment or index should not include companies that apply differential ownership or voting rights to their share capital.
- To ensure that shareholders have the right to vote on major decisions which may change the nature of the company in which they have invested. This

pertains in particular to mergers and acquisitions in developing as well as some developed markets.
- To avoid dilution of existing shareholders when increasing the share capital.
- To limit and manage transparently conflicts of interest, in particular with regard to related party transactions.

7.3.2.2   Effective Board Composition and Interaction

The board, be it in a single board or dual board structure, is the most important management and control body for a (listed) company. The board is the most important addressee and lever for shareholders into the company they own. Its composition, its modus operandi and its proceedings should therefore be of utmost interest to institutional shareholders in fulfilling their stewardship role. Given the need for transformational change in many industries as described above the right board composition remains a major challenge.

Appropriate measures to render boards effective are (amongst others):

- To ensure a sufficiently competent and diverse board with regard to the knowledge and experience relevant for and reflective of the company's business model. Diversity should be understood as a concept that extends beyond gender mix, equally considering education, ethnicity, age and social background. Competence should also not be defined too narrowly but specifically include the understanding of both the sustainability risks affecting the company and the external effects of the company's economic activity on the environment and society.
- To ensure a sufficient share of independent non-executive directors commensurate with the shareholder structure. For a widely held joint stock company this typically requires a majority of independent non-executives.
- To apply limits to the age and tenure of directors in order to allow for appropriate board renewal as the company evolves and needs to adapt to changes in its ecosystem of doing business.

The particular importance of director duties is discussed in more detail in Section 7.3.3.

7.3.2.3 Adequate Management Incentives and Remuneration

While most executives can be assumed to be driven by intrinsic motivation, incentives and financial rewards are important instruments ideally to align the interests of a company's management with its shareholders and stakeholders for long-term sustainable value creation. Logically, this is an important area of attention by investors in their pursuit of stewardship. And there still is big room for improvement as ICGN states (ICGN, 2019):

> Executive remuneration remains a corporate governance problem in many jurisdictions and an ongoing challenge for boards to oversee equitably. As ESG factors are increasingly identified as material risks or opportunities, investors should encourage executive incentive schemes to include relevant ESG related key performance indicators (KPIs). The issue of quantum of executive pay can be an uncomfortable subject for investors, but it is becoming particularly sensitive given growing global attention to the social problem of income inequality. Investors should be prepared to challenge high levels of pay in engagement with corporate boards and to use vote against remuneration plans which are not responsibly structured.

The debate around appropriate measures to establish the desired alignment of executive compensation with long-term interests of shareholders and stakeholders has been particularly intense over the last few years, thanks to the general media attention to the subject worldwide, high-profile shareholder revolts and the introduction of SRD II in Europe. Various guidelines[17] have been published and it

---

[17] See for example the Guidelines for Sustainable Management Board Remuneration Systems published in Germany by an industry Working Group in 2018 at: www .guidelines-executivecompensation.de/wp-content/uploads/2018/08/Leitlinien_ EN_Web.pdf and the provisions in the updated German Corporate Governance Code (2019) at www.dcgk.de/en/home.html.

appears as though there is increasing agreement at least around a few key principles, which can be summarised as:

- To keep the remuneration system simple (ideally three components: fixed remuneration, short-term variable and long-term variable), all-encompassing (i.e. no separate fringe benefits, pensions schemes etc.) and long-term oriented (over three years for long-term components).
- To emphasise long-term variable components over short-term and fixed elements.
- To set ambitious, mostly quantifiable targets that also take sustainability goals into account.
- To set terms and hurdles for payout that allow to take detrimental long-term effects of management action into account (bonus-/malus and claw-back provisions).
- To put an overall remuneration cap in place (absolute and relative).
- To encourage long-term share ownership by management through complementary share ownership guidelines.

7.3.2.4 Transparent Reporting and Open Investor Dialogue

Given the information asymmetry between shareholders (as well as other stakeholders) and company management, institutional investors rely for their value and risk assessment of investee companies on correct information that is relevant and material to the business model and its future prospects. Transparent reporting and an open dialogue therefore form decisive elements in the stewardship process. In this context, ICGN cautions against the virtue of too much information: 'For investors to monitor, vote and to engage with companies effectively, accurate unbiased and relevant information must guide investor decisions. Detailed disclosure does not always ensure transparency, nor does it ensure the integrity of the accounting and auditing process' (ICGN, 2019).

In relation to the best way, how to report there seems to be a growing sense among investors (and corporates) that the audited financial statements are by no means sufficient and adequate for the needs of investors, particularly with regard to gauging investee companies' prospects in the sustainability transition highlighted earlier. As ICGN puts it: 'It is important to link financial statements and accounting matters to broader factors that affect sustainable corporate value creation.' Various initiatives have emerged to address the apparent gap, among them the International Integrated Reporting Council (IIRC), Sustainability Accounting Standards Board (SASB) and, more recently, the International Accounting Standards Board (IASB) have been more vocal in this field, too. The latter is an important development. To address the challenges of climate change in reporting, the TCFD has gained broad recognition as a global framework, proposing forward-looking scenario analysis as an innovative yet unconventional approach.

The evolution of reporting and filling the data gaps, particularly for information on relevant and material sustainability factors, should be an important area of engagement by stewards of capital with their investee companies. The demands should be threefold:

i. Sustainability data and information have to be relevant and material with regard to the business model and should be presented in the context of the business strategy and the financial effects.
ii. Sustainability data, particularly related to climate, should have a forward-looking perspective and be suitable for scenario analysis (e.g. under TCFD).
iii. Sustainability data should be embedded in the business strategy, planning process and in the remuneration system of senior management.

7.3.3   A New Statement of Director Duties

While governance structures provide an important formal framework for good corporate governance and help foster the implementation of sustainability considerations in a company, it is the role and conduct of a company's directors which is arguably most decisive. Therefore, director duties should be an area of special focus for attenuating a sustainable corporate governance as for example intended by the EU Commission's Action Plan and as recognised in ICGN's current policy priorities.

ICGN highlights (ICGN, 2019):

> In addition to facing traditional challenges relating to boards in their oversight of companies, directors increasingly recognise that the 'boundaries' of corporate governance are often fluid and bring new risks and opportunities that require board attention and oversight. Many of these newer challenges relate to business interface with society, including its interactions with customers, employees and other key stakeholders. Related to this, the so-called 'soft' issues of ethics and culture have been shown to have hard impacts on companies – particularly as they emerge as risks and opportunities. Examples include the emissions scandal at Volkswagen, the loss of confidence in the banking sector in the global financial crisis and the pernicious effects of bribery and corruption in both developed and emerging markets. Trust in business is low, and social concerns including income disparity are attracting significant public attention.

Thus, in order to reflect the wider responsibility of directors required by a sustainable business orientation a new statement of director duties could be mandated, which is informed by a cross-sectional international analysis of existing laws, codes and principles:

7.3.3.1   Duties for All Directors

i. To act in a way the director considers in good faith is most likely to promote the success of the company for the benefit of its owners and other stakeholders. In performing this duty, a director must have regard to all relevant matters, but the following are specifically important for the sustainable development of a company:
   a. the likely consequences of any decision in the long term (beyond five years);
   b. the interests of the company's employees;
   c. the need to foster the company's business relationships with suppliers, customers and others;
   d. the impact of the company's operations on the community and the environment (externalities);

SUSTAINABLE GOVERNANCE AND LEADERSHIP   163

    e. the integrity of the business partners in the company's supply chain (e.g. no corruption, no child labour, observing human rights);

    f. the desirability of the company maintaining a reputation for high-standard business conduct.

ii. To exercise reasonable care, skill and diligence. This requires a director to be diligent, careful and well informed about the company's affairs, including the impact of the company's business model, production and sales processes on directly and indirectly affected stakeholders as well as the environment. In order to fulfil this duty, the director is required to participate in adequate education and training measures. Directors should be educated on material sustainability issues by:

    a. Involving (new) directors with sustainability competence in important board deliberations, especially on business strategy and risk. For sustainability to be integrated into board decision-making, directors that have expertise and experience in sustainability matters must participate in board functions, structures and processes.

    b. Requiring ongoing education on material sustainability issues for the whole board. Boards and company leadership should mandate that all directors have at least a minimum up-to-date knowledge about material sustainability issues. Education, training programmes and site visits should build knowledge over time and make connections to operational or management realities.

    c. Providing boards with information on the materiality of sustainability to their business. Boards need information to help them understand the materiality of specific sustainability issues to their business, so they can make the connection between sustainability and corporate strategy and risk. Materiality analyses could prove useful in helping directors understand how certain environmental and social issues relate to business strategy and how they may materially affect operations.

    d. Driving board discussion on how sustainability impacts corporate risk, strategy and business models. Identifying risks and opportunities created by environmental and social issues helps companies adapt their models. By becoming more resilient, integrated and circular, businesses can tap into more sustainability-related business opportunities.

iii. To exercise independent judgement. This means not to subordinate the director's power to the will of others. This does not prevent directors from relying on advice, so long as they exercise their own judgement on whether or not to follow it.

iv. To avoid conflicts or possible conflicts between the interests of the director and those of the company. The prohibition will not apply if the company consents (and consent meets the necessary formal requirements).

v. Not to accept benefits from third parties by reason of being a director or doing anything as director. The company may authorise acceptance (subject to its constitution), for instance to enable a director to benefit from reasonable corporate hospitality.

vi. To declare any interest in a proposed transaction or arrangement. The declaration must be made before the transaction is entered into and the prohibition applies to indirect interests as well as direct interests.

7.3.3.2   Specific Demands on Non-executive Directors and Supervisory Boards

vii. To demand and control an explicit strategy by the company's management as to how the company contributes to achieving the Sustainable Development Goals and climate goals taking into account its specific business model.

viii. To ensure that remuneration policies as well as individual executive compensation contracts include long-term sustainability performance targets consistent with the company's sustainability goals, particularly climate goals. These targets should be company-specific and not be linked to for example the position in a sustainability index.

ix. To ensure that in the board nomination process, competency in relevant sustainability matters is systematically considered and the board composition regularly reviewed in this regard. Sustainability could be integrated by:

a. Creating regular opportunities to bring new directors with relevant expertise onto corporate boards. To remain relevant, especially with a view to including sustainability priorities, boards must be periodically 'refreshed'. The board nominating or governance committee could affirm the importance of board refreshment in their charters by developing mechanisms that ensure consideration of refreshment, for example, through a regular board evaluation process.

b. Incorporating material sustainability issues into qualifications for potential board candidates. By thinking about recruiting for sustainability in a systematic way, boards can look beyond their short-term needs. Nominating committees can make sustainability issues important qualifications they consider when recruiting new directors and track the qualifications via a board skills matrix.

c. Finding directors that can make the connections between environmental and social issues and the business context. Nominating committees should recruit effective sustainability competent directors that can assess the potential impact of sustainability issues on a business and 'translate' it to provide context for a board's decision-making. Directors who cannot make the connections between the appropriate social and environmental issues and the relevant business context risk will be marginalised.

d. Identifying directors who represent key stakeholder groups relevant to a company's sustainability impacts. Nominating committees should recruit directors who have experience with interacting or representing stakeholder groups that offer insights into a company's material sustainability impacts. This provides the advantage of bringing both relevant expertise and background diversity to the boardroom.

e. Recruiting candidates representing a diversity of backgrounds and skills to improve decision-making. Nominating committees should seek out candidates who bring a range of attributes, expertise and desired skills to the table and represent a mix of gender, ethnicity, nationalities and backgrounds. This will help the board avoid 'group think' and foster robust, thoughtful deliberations when making a decision. Research also shows that diverse boards are better boards.

x. To demand regular reporting to the Board and relevant stakeholders about the sustainability strategy, its evolution and the development of the business against specific, measurable sustainability targets. Engagement with stakeholders and experts on relevant sustainability issues could be deepened by:

a. Finding regular opportunities for boards to engage stakeholders on environmental and social issues. Regular participation in stakeholder engagements with internal and external stakeholders – including investors and advocacy groups – can help boards gain a holistic understanding of the key issues that affect a company. This can help the company to not only mitigate adverse impacts on external shareholders, but also pinpoint opportunities for creating long-term value.

b. Incorporating external advice. Some companies have chosen to set up sustainability advisory councils or other stakeholder fora. Boards can leverage these bodies as a critical resource. To deepen communication between them and a company's board, board members could be involved in the deliberations more systematically. Such fora could also provide recruitment opportunities for new board members.

  c. Incorporating material sustainability issues into board–investor dialogues. Investors increasingly expect boards to engage directly and systematically with them on critical issues. Given the growing focus of the investor community on sustainability in general and the role of boards for sustainability in particular, material environmental and social factors should be made a part of any board–investor dialogue.

xi. To engage to remove technical obstacles in exercising voting rights.

7.4 CONCLUDING REMARKS

For the financial sector to play its role towards a more sustainable economy, it needs to focus on its purpose and be inclusive towards its stakeholders. We argue that current and future leaders and professionals need to be fully equipped to understand and address sustainability and other long-term risks and opportunities. Building those competencies has to be integral to all stages of formal – and informal – education and hence it is imperative for universities, and other further education institutions to embrace this as part of their teaching and research. Likewise, a different understanding of governance which is stakeholder centric is emerging. Fundamentally, good governance is a core element of sustainable finance which supports society in its transition towards a low carbon, less resource intense and more inclusive economy.

REFERENCES

European Commission (2018), 'Action Plan: Financing Sustainable Growth', March. https://ec.europa.eu/info/publications/180308-action-plan-sustainable-growth_en.
Financial Stability Board (2017a), 'Reducing Misconduct Risks in the Financial Sector Progress Report to G20 Leaders', June. www.fsb.org/2017/07/reducing-misconduct-risks-in-the-financial-sector-progress-report-to-g20-leaders.

Financial Stability Board (2017b), 'Stocktake of Efforts to Strengthen Governance Frameworks to Mitigate Misconduct Risks', May. www.fsb.org/wp-content/uploads/WGGF-Phase-1-report-and-recommendations-for-Phase-2.pdf.

International Corporate Governance Network (2019), 'ICGN Policy Priorities 2019/20'. www.icgn.org/sites/default/files/ICGN Policy Priorities 2019-20.pdf.

OECD (2015), 'G20/OECD Principles of Corporate Governance'. www.oecd.org/daf/ca/Corporate-Governance-Principles-ENG.pdf.

OECD (2019), 'Corporate Governance Factbook'. www.oecd.org/corporate/corporate-governance-factbook.htm.

Pitt-Watson, D. and Quigley, E. (2019), 'Business School Rankings for the 21st Century'. United Nations Global Compact. January. https://www.unprme.org/resource-docs/60555MBAREPORT0119pr03.pdf.

Prudential Regulation Authority (2015), 'The Impact of Change on the UK Insurance Sector', September. www.bankofengland.co.uk/prudential-regulation/publication/2015/the-impact-of-climate-change-on-the-uk-insurance-sector.

Prudential Regulation Authority (2019), 'Enhancing Banks' and Insurers' Approaches to Managing the Financial Risks from Climate Change', Supervisory Statement SS/19. www.bankofengland.co.uk/prudential-regulation/publication/2019/enhancing-banks-and-insurers-approaches-to-managing-the-financial-risks-from-climate-change-ss.

8 ESG Risks and Opportunities

A Fiduciary Duty Perspective

Will Martindale, Elodie Feller and Rory Sullivan[*]

8.1 INTRODUCTION

Fiduciary duties (or equivalent duties and obligations) underpin the operation of the investment system. These duties are intended to ensure that those who manage other people's money act in the interests of beneficiaries, rather than serving their own interests. Fiduciary duties have played, and continue to play, a critical role in ensuring that fiduciaries are loyal to their beneficiaries and carry out their duties in a prudent manner.

The manner in which fiduciary duty is defined and interpreted affects the entire investment chain, from asset owners to companies (PRI, 2016). It informs the way in which asset owners select, appoint and monitor investment managers. It influences investment decision-making processes and ownership practices. It affects the way in which companies are managed. It influences the relationship between investors and society. Ultimately, it affects financial stability and sustainability, and strongly influences our global response to climate change and sustainable development.

In recent years, interpretations of fiduciary duty have undergone rapid evolution. It is now widely accepted that investors need to take account of environmental, social and governance (ESG) or

---

[*] This chapter builds on the work and analysis of the Fiduciary Duty in the 21st Century project, led by the PRI, UNEP FI and The Generation Foundation. The project aimed to end the debate on whether fiduciary duty is a legitimate barrier to the integration of ESG issues in investment practice and decision-making. It did so through developing the evidence base that analysis of these issues can enhance investment performance and through supporting the development and implementation of policy and regulatory measures to embed ESG factors into the fiduciary duties of investors across the major global capital markets. For further information, see www.fiduciaryduty21.org.

sustainability issues in their investment practices. This chapter discusses and analyses the changes in the interpretation of fiduciary duty and the implications for investment practice. It starts with a discussion of the traditional definition of fiduciary duty (in particular, the duties of loyalty and care). It then identifies four factors – the work of the United Nations Environment Programme Finance Initiative (UNEP FI) and the Principles for Responsible Investment (PRI), the changing legal and policy landscape for responsible investment, the understanding of the financial significance of ESG issues to investment performance and the changes in investment practice – that have challenged and led to change in this traditional definition of fiduciary duty. The chapter then proposes a modern definition of fiduciary duty, a definition where ESG issues are at the heart of the duties owed by investors to their beneficiaries. The chapter concludes with some reflections on whether this modern definition of fiduciary duty is a sufficient response to the social and environmental challenges faced by society today.

8.2   FIDUCIARY DUTY: THE TRADITIONAL DEFINITION

In the modern investment system, organisations or individuals (fiduciaries) often manage money or other assets on the behalf of beneficiaries and savers. Beneficiaries and savers rely on these fiduciaries to act in their best interests, where these best interests are usually defined exclusively in financial terms.

In practice, these fiduciaries have varying degrees of discretion as to how they invest the funds they control. The scope of that discretion varies. It may be narrow, for example, in the case of tailored mutual funds where the beneficiary specifies the asset profile and only the day-to-day stock selection and other management tasks are left to the investment decision-maker. It may be wide, as with many occupational pension funds. Further, some public funds are subject to considerable state control and the discretion afforded to these decision-makers may be further narrowed by parameters set by government.

Within the scope of discretion left to the investment decision-maker, fiduciary duties – and equivalent obligations in civil law jurisdictions – exist to ensure that those who manage other people's money act responsibly in the interests of beneficiaries or savers, rather than serving their own interests. These duties are of particular importance in asymmetrical relationships, that is those situations where there are imbalances in expertise and where the beneficiary has limited ability to monitor or oversee the actions of the person or entity acting in their interests.

The way these duties are framed differs between countries and between common law and civil law jurisdictions (see Box 8.1).

While the specific sources and mechanisms of enforcement differ, there is broad agreement between civil and common law jurisdictions that the most important duties owed by fiduciaries to savers and beneficiaries are the duty to act prudently and the duty to act in accordance with the purpose for which investment powers are granted (also known as the duty of loyalty). These traditional fiduciary duties are set out in more detail in Box 8.2.

BOX 8.1   Common and civil law (Adapted from PRI et al., 2019)

In general terms, jurisdictions use two distinct legal systems – common law or civil law. In practice, most are a hybrid of the two, and some also incorporate additional systems of customary and religious law; for example, a combination of common and civil law exists in South Africa, and civil law is influenced by customary law in China.

Common law systems are led by decisions made in the courts based on previous court decisions and statute. These decisions are binding on the parties in the case and on third parties, until overturned by a higher court or statute. In contrast, civil law systems are led by written codes containing general principles supplemented by detailed statutes, and consider previous court decisions as being of secondary importance.

In many common law jurisdictions – examples include Australia, Canada, South Africa, the United Kingdom (in respect of England and Wales) and the United States – fiduciary duties provide the key

BOX 8.1 (cont.)

framework governing the discretion of investment decision-makers, aside from any specific constraints imposed contractually or by statute/regulation. These fiduciary duties were originally developed by the courts with some subsequently being articulated in statute. The courts will interpret the duties in deciding on specific cases, and over time, the duties are open to re-interpretation by the courts when applied to new facts and circumstances. Governments may also pass new statutes in response to new circumstances or a particular decision of the courts. In the United States, for example, the decision-maker's duty is to exercise reasonable care, skill and caution in pursuing an overall investment strategy that incorporates risk and return objectives reasonably suitable to the trust.

In jurisdictions where civil law applies – examples include Brazil, China, the EU, France, Germany and Japan – any obligations equivalent to 'fiduciary duties' will be set out in statutory provisions regulating the conduct of investment decision-makers, and in the governmental and other guidelines that assist in the interpretation of these provisions. The content of these obligations differs slightly between jurisdictions and tends to depend on the type of institutional investor, but common themes include:

- The duty to act conscientiously in the interests of beneficiaries – this duty is expressed in different terms, with jurisdictions using terms such as 'good and conscientious manager' (Japan) or 'professionally' (Germany).
- The duty to seek profitability.
- Recognition of the portfolio approach to modern investment, which may be an explicit requirement or may be implicit in the form of requirements to ensure adequate diversification.
- Other duties relating to liquidity and limits on the types of assets that may be selected for certain types of funds.

In all jurisdictions, the rules that affect investment decision-making take the form of both specific requirements (e.g. the types of assets that are permitted for certain types of investment, the extent to which the assets of a fund may be invested in specific asset classes or categories of issuers) and general duties (such as duties to ensure investments are adequately diversified).

BOX 8.2   **The traditional fiduciary duties**

Fiduciary duties (or equivalent obligations) exist to ensure that those who manage other people's money act in the interests of beneficiaries and do not serve their own interests. The most important of these duties are:

- Loyalty: Fiduciaries should act honestly and in good faith in the interests of their beneficiaries, should impartially balance the conflicting interests of different beneficiaries, should avoid conflicts of interest and should not act for the benefit of themselves or a third party.
- Prudence: Fiduciaries should act with due care, skill and diligence, investing as an 'ordinary prudent person' would do.

These duties require fiduciaries to concern themselves with risks, trends, innovation and the short-term and long-term future (which may be many decades in the case of pension funds). Fiduciary duty itself is not a static concept. It evolves and adjusts in response to changes in knowledge, in market practices and conventions, in regulation and policy, and in social norms.

8.3   FIDUCIARY DUTY AND RESPONSIBLE INVESTMENT: THE EVOLUTION OF A DANGEROUS IDEA

The evolution of thinking on fiduciary duty and responsible investment comprises four separate but overlapping strands: (a) the work of UNEP FI, PRI and their partners, (b) changes in investment policy and regulation, (c) the evidence that ESG issues can be important drivers of investment performance and that investors can use this insight to create value in their investment portfolios and (d) changes in investment practice. We discuss each of these subsequently.

8.3.1   The Work of UNEP FI, PRI and their Partners

In 2005, the United Nations Environment Programme Finance Initiative (UNEP FI) together with the law firm Freshfields Bruckhaus

Deringer published a ground-breaking report titled 'A Legal Framework for the Integration of Environmental, Social and Governance Issues into Institutional Investment' (commonly referred to as the 'Freshfields Report'). The report, in what was seen as a radical conclusion at the time, argued that '. . . integrating ESG [environmental, social and governance] considerations into an investment analysis so as to more reliably predict financial performance is clearly permissible and is arguably required in all jurisdictions' (Freshfields Bruckhaus Deringer, 2005).

This report was followed, in 2009, by another UNEP FI report, 'Fiduciary Responsibility: Legal and Practical Aspects of Integrating Environmental, Social and Governance Issues into Institutional Investment' (UNEP FI, 2009). This report extended the Freshfields report by exploring legal options on how best to integrate ESG issues into investment processes, particularly with respect to investment mandates and investment management contracts. It also analysed how practice in relation to the integration of ESG issues into investment processes had changed, focussing on the extent to which institutional investors had adopted, and could adopt, longer-term and more sustainable investment approaches.

In 2015, the Principles for Responsible Investment (PRI), United Nations Environmental Programme Finance Initiative (UNEP FI), the UNEP Inquiry into the Design of a Sustainable Financial System and the United Nations Global Compact launched a major report on fiduciary duty. The report – 'Fiduciary Duty in the 21st Century' (PRI et al., 2015) – analysed investment practice and fiduciary duty in eight countries: Australia, Brazil, Canada, Germany, Japan, South Africa, the United Kingdom and the United States. The report was informed by interviews with over fifty asset owners, asset managers, lawyers and regulators across the eight countries, a comprehensive review of law and policy in each country and a series of roundtables, conferences and webinars, where the findings were discussed with institutional investors and global experts on fiduciary duty and responsible investment. The report argued that: 'Failing to consider all long-term investment value drivers, including ESG issues, is a failure of fiduciary duty'. It also acknowledged that, despite significant progress, many investors had yet to fully integrate ESG issues into their investment decision-making processes. The report called on investors to integrate ESG issues into their investment practices and decision-making, and to reinforce and re-emphasise the obligations that investment organisations owe to their beneficiaries and clients. It also noted that progress was critically dependent on the formal codification of investors' duties in relation to ESG issues in regulatory and legal frameworks.

Following on from this report, in January 2016, PR, UNEP FI and The Generation Foundation launched a three-year project, Fiduciary Duty in the 21st Century, to encourage legal clarification of investors' obligations and duties in relation to the integration of ESG issues in investment practice and decision-making. Between 2016 and 2019, the project team[1]:

- Engaged with over 400 policymakers and investors to raise awareness of the importance of ESG issues to the fiduciary duties of investors.
- Published the Global Statement on Investor Obligations and Duties which, by December 2019, had been signed by 124 institutional investors from 22 different countries.[2]
- Published and started to implement almost twenty country- or region-specific roadmaps on the policy and regulatory changes required to achieve full integration of ESG issues into investment processes and practices. The jurisdictions covered included Australia, Brazil, Canada, China, the European Union, France, Germany, India, Ireland, Japan, Malaysia, Singapore, South Africa, the United Kingdom and the United States.
- Published reports on the relevance of ESG issues to investment decision-making and on the role of investment consultants.
- Contributed to policy discussions and policy development in a range of jurisdictions, notably through its support of the European Commission's High-Level Expert Group on Sustainable Finance.[3]

---

[1] See, www.fiduciaryduty21.org.
[2] www.fiduciaryduty21.org/investor-statement.html.
[3] https://ec.europa.eu/info/business-economy-euro/banking-and-finance/sustainable-finance_en.

- Hosted over twenty workshops and conferences with investors and regulators in fifteen countries to discuss regulatory clarification and investor practice on ESG integration as part of their fiduciary duty.

The Fiduciary Duty in the 21st Century project has played a key role in encouraging governments to adopt policies and regulations that clarify investors' duties as they relate to ESG matters (see, further, PRI et al., 2019). The changing policy landscape is discussed further subsequently.

8.4   THE CHANGING POLICY LANDSCAPE

Across the world's fifty largest economies, the PRI estimated that, as at September 2019, there were over 730 hard and soft law policy revisions across 500 policy instruments which supported investors to consider long-term value drivers, including ESG factors (PRI, 2019). Of these economies, forty-eight (48) had some form of policy designed to help or encourage investors to consider sustainability or ESG-related risks, opportunities or outcomes.

The introduction of regulation and policy relating to ESG and to responsible investment is very much a 21st Century phenomenon.[4] Of the hard and soft law instruments identified in PRI's Responsible Investment Database,[5] 97 per cent were developed after the year 2000. As illustrated in Figure 8.1, the rate of adoption has accelerated in recent years.

These policy instruments can be divided into three broad categories. The first are pension fund regulations, with the most common types being disclosure requirements (where pension funds are required to disclose their responsible investment commitments and/or how these commitments have been implemented), requirements encouraging pension funds to adopt responsible investment

---

[4] In 2000, the United Kingdom introduced the world's first regulation requiring disclosure by occupational pension funds of their policies on ESG issues. For a useful historic perspective, see Sparkes (2002).

[5] www.unpri.org/sustainable-markets/regulation-map.

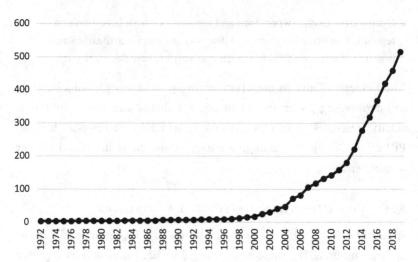

FIGURE 8.1 The growth in responsible investment regulation and policy
y-axis label: Cumulative number of policy interventions per year
Source: PRI responsible investment regulation database, www.unpri.org/
sustainable-markets/regulation-map.

practices and, to a lesser extent, requirements to take account of the
needs and interests of beneficiaries. Some examples are presented in
Table 8.1 and Box 8.3. The second are stewardship codes which aim to
govern or steer the interactions between investors (asset owners and
asset managers) and investee companies, with a view to promoting
long-term value creation strategies. The third are requirements for
companies to discuss ESG issues in their annual reports and accounts
and to provide disclosures on specific ESG issues.

These policies and regulations have played an important role in
encouraging investors to act on ESG issues and to report on the
actions that they have taken. They have also, through improving
corporate disclosures, helped address some of the key barriers to
investors integrating ESG issues in their investment research and
decision-making processes. Policy implementation, however, remains
a challenge in many jurisdictions. Many of these policies are either
voluntary or 'comply or explain', where non-compliance is permitted
so long as investors explain why they do not comply. Furthermore,

Table 8.1 *Examples of policy instruments promoting sustainable investment by pension funds (Adapted from PRI et al., 2019)*

Country	Title	Date	Relevant Text or Requirements
UK	The Pension Protection Fund (Pensionable Service) and Occupational Pension Schemes (Investment and Disclosure) (Amendment and Modification) Regulations 2018	2019	'Appropriate time horizon" means the length of time that the trustees of a trust scheme consider is needed for the funding of future benefits by the investments of the scheme.' 'Financially material considerations" includes (but is not limited to) environmental, social and governance considerations (including but not limited to climate change), which the trustees of the trust scheme consider financially material.'
USA	EBSA: Field Assistance Bulletin No. 2018-01	2018	'To the extent ESG factors, in fact, involve business risks or opportunities that are properly treated as economic considerations themselves in evaluating alternative investments, the weight given to those factors should also be appropriate to the relative level of risk and return involved

Table 8.1 (*cont.*)

Country	Title	Date	Relevant Text or Requirements
			compared to other relevant economic factors.'
Brazil	Resolution 4661	2018	Resolution No. 4661/ 2018 states that, in their risk analysis processes, pension funds shall consider ESG aspects whenever possible, in addition to economic sustainability analysis. This recommendation was reinforced by 'Instrução Previc n. 6/2018', which stated that pension funds' investment policies shall include guidelines for complying with ESG, preferably by economic sector.
EU	Directive (EU) 2016/2341 of the European Parliament and of the Council of 14/12/2016 on the activities and supervision of institutions for occupational retirement provision (IORPs)	2016	'The system of governance shall include consideration of environmental, social and governance factors related to investment assets in investment decisions and shall be subject to regular internal review.'
Ontario, Canada	Pension Benefits Act	2016	Under Section 78(3), a plan's statement of investment policies and

Table 8.1 (*cont.*)

Country	Title	Date	Relevant Text or Requirements
			procedures (SIPP) is required to include information as to whether environmental, social, and governance (ESG) factors are incorporated into the plan's investment policies and procedures and, if so, how those factors are incorporated.
Korea	National Pension Service Act	2015	The National Assembly passed amendments to the National Pension Act of Korea, requiring the National Pension Service to consider ESG issues and to declare the extent to which ESG considerations are taken into account.
Australia	SPG 530	2013	The Australian Prudential Regulation Authority (APRA) expects that a registrable superannuation entity (RSE) licensee would have a reasoned basis for determining that the investment strategy formulated for such an investment option is in the best interests of beneficiaries and that it

Table 8.1 (*cont.*)

Country	Title	Date	Relevant Text or Requirements
			satisfies the requirements of s. 52 of the SIS Act for liquidity and diversification. While ESG considerations may not be readily quantifiable in financial terms, APRA expects an RSE licensee would be able to demonstrate that it has conducted appropriate analysis to support the formulation of an investment strategy that has an ESG focus.
South Africa	Pension Fund Act	2013	The Pension Fund Act codifies fiduciary duty and states that it applies to trustees of pension funds. Sections 7(c) and 7 (d) cover the duties (avoiding conflicts, duty of care, diligence, good faith, independence). In 2011, Regulation 28 was revised to require an investment process for which trustees are responsible for developing with respect to the funds circumstance and monitoring. This

Table 8.1 (cont.)

Country	Title	Date	Relevant Text or Requirements
			revision requires funds to consider all factors (including ESG factors) that may be relevant to the long-term success of the fund.

BOX 8.3   **EU regulation on sustainability-related disclosures in the financial services sector[6]**

The Regulation requires financial institutions and financial advisers to publish on their website:

- Policies on how they integrate sustainability risks in their decision-making or advisory processes.
- A statement on how they consider the principal adverse impacts of investment decisions on sustainability factors. For investors, this would include details of their policies on how they identify and prioritise adverse sustainability impacts, a description of the principal adverse sustainability impacts identified and of the actions taken to manage these impacts, a summary of their engagement policies, a summary of their adherence to standards for due diligence and reporting, and where relevant, the degree of alignment with the Paris Climate Agreement.
- Information on how their remuneration policies are consistent with the integration of sustainability risks in their decision-making.

The European Supervisory Authorities (ESAs) will develop regulatory technical standards setting out sustainability indicators on climate

---

[6] Regulation (EU) 2019/2088 of the European Parliament and of the Council of 27 November 2019 on sustainability-related disclosures in the financial services sector. https://eur-lex.europa.eu/eli/reg/2019/2088/oj.

BOX 8.3   **(cont.)**

change, other environment-related adverse impacts, adverse impacts in
the field of social and employee matters, human rights, anti-corruption
and bribery matters.

For financial products, financial institutions and financial advisers
shall, on a comply or explain basis, disclose for each financial product
how sustainability risks are integrated into investment decisions or
advice, the likely impacts of sustainability risks on the financial
products and whether and how a financial product considers principal
adverse impacts of the investment approach on sustainability factors.

For financial products targeting sustainability objectives, financial
institutions are required to disclose:

- How the sustainability objectives are met, and, if an index has been
  designated as a reference benchmark, whether and how it is consistent with
  the sustainability objectives of the product.
- The extent to which sustainability objectives are attained, the overall
  sustainability-related impact of the financial product and – where an index
  has been designated as a reference benchmark – a comparison through
  sustainability indicators of the respective impacts of the financial product and
  a broad market index.
- A description of the sustainability objectives of the product, information on
  the methodologies used to assess, measure and monitor the sustainability
  objectives.

The ESAs shall develop regulatory technical standards on the details of
the content and the presentation requirements.

many of the formal (or mandatory) obligations are relatively weak; for
example, the 2016 Canada Pension Benefits Act requires pension
plans to publish information as to 'whether ESG factors are incorporated into the plan's investment policies' and, if so, how those factors
are incorporated. These issues are compounded by the fact that many
jurisdictions have not yet allocated the resources and attention
needed to ensure effective implementation. These criticisms should,
however, be qualified by acknowledging that responsible investment-

related legislation is relatively new in most jurisdictions and, as a consequence, has yet to receive significant regulatory attention.

In jurisdictions where regulation or policy on responsible investment is more mature, these issues are starting to be addressed. Regulators are extending the concept of comply or explain to require investors to explain how they propose to address the non-compliance. In other cases, regulators are introducing new policies and regulations designed to remove ambiguity around the relationship between sustainability and finance. For example, the 2019 EU investor disclosures regulation (see Box 8.3) requires investors to disclose how sustainability risks are integrated in investment processes. In parallel, the EU is working to amend the rules underpinning key sectoral legislation (such as MiFID II and Solvency II) to clarify that sustainability should be considered for an investor to be seen to have fulfilled its duties.

These changes in investors' duties and in financial system regulation are not occurring in a vacuum. Policymakers, regulators and governments recognise that issues such as climate change and sustainable development represent systemic risks and opportunities that require explicit and targeted interventions. Many countries have started to implement the Paris Climate Agreement[7] and the Sustainable Development Goals[8] in national policy and regulations. While the details differ, these domestic policies generally involve the setting of national targets, the development of national policy plans and implementation programmes, the adoption of regulation and other policy instruments (e.g. economic instruments, self-regulation), the allocation of responsibilities to different actors and the creation of incentives for action. Some governments have formally incorporated sustainability in the mandates of their financial regulators.

Many of these strategies – see Box 8.4 for examples – now explicitly focus on the finance sector. They recognise that the capital required to deliver policy commitments on climate change and

---

[7] http://unfccc.int/paris_agreement/items/9485.php.
[8] www.un.org/sustainabledevelopment/sustainable-development-goals.

BOX 8.4   **Examples of integrated finance and sustainability policy**

In 2016, the People's Bank of China, in collaboration with six other government agencies, issued guidelines establishing the green financial system. The guidelines included proposals on:

- Developing green lending.
- Enhancing the role of the securities market through improving the rules and regulations for green bonds and guiding international investors to invest in green assets.
- Launching green development funds and public–private partnerships.
- Developing green insurance.
- Improving and extending environmental rights trading markets.

In France, the 2015 Energy Transition for Green Growth Energy Transition Law set long-term goals to reduce greenhouse gas emissions, reduce energy consumption, improve buildings energy efficiency and increase renewable energy generation. The law on energy and the climate prepared in 2019 aims to set long-term goals to achieve carbon neutrality by 2050. The French government has also been developing strategies and shared framework to achieve more sustainable growth, including enhancing biodiversity protection and supporting the circular economy.

---

development cannot be delivered by governments alone and that decisions made in the financial system influence the sustainability of the real economy. This integration of finance into sustainability policy, and the integration of sustainability considerations into finance policy, suggest that we are moving towards a much more integrated and aligned approach to policy across these two areas.

This trend towards alignment and integration is reinforced by other changes. For example, at a multilateral level, the central banks' Network for Greening the Financial System acknowledged in April 2019 that climate change is a source of financial risk. With support from the World Bank, finance ministers from more than twenty countries launched, in April 2019, a coalition to promote climate action through mainstream financial policies at a national level. In early 2019, IOSCO, the international securities regulators' organisation, and IOPS, the international pensions supervisors' organisation, launched consultations on ESG integration and disclosure, for listed companies and for pension fund regulators.

These policy interventions materially alter the economics of the decisions that companies and investors make. They mean that investors need to pay attention to the changes that these measures catalyse (e.g. the economics of specific investments may alter, companies may find that they need to change their business models). They also mean that investors need to consider whether and how these incentives will alter over time. This may lead to them altering their views on the financial characteristics of particular assets or investments and potentially taking action (e.g. changing investment holdings, company engagement) to minimise downside risk or take advantage of opportunities.

8.5   THE INVESTMENT RELEVANCE OF ESG ISSUES

There is growing evidence of the positive relationship between ESG and investment performance. A study by Friede et al. (2015) analysed more than 2,000 empirical studies on the relationship between ESG criteria and investment performance, dating back to the 1970s. The paper concluded that approximately 90 per cent of studies had found a non-negative relationship between ESG performance and corporate financial performance, with a large majority reporting positive findings.

This finding is reinforced by studies into the relationship between ESG and corporate financial performance. For example, the 2014 paper 'The Impact of Corporate Sustainability on Organisational Processes and Performance' (Eccles et al., 2014) investigated the long-term effect of corporate sustainability on organisational processes and performance. The authors concluded that corporations that had voluntarily adopted sustainability policies had generated significantly higher stock returns, suggesting that the integration of such issues into a company's business model and strategy may be a source of competitive advantage for a company in the long run. Similarly, Khan et al. (2016) found that firms with good ESG ratings on material issues tended to outperform those with poor ratings. Better ESG performance can also provide wider financial benefits to companies, such as a lower cost of capital (Cheng et al., 2014; El Ghoul et al., 2011).

The converse also applies as the consequences of failing to effectively manage ESG-related risks can be significant. One analysis of the financial costs of corporate fines and settlements showed that the ten largest fines and settlements in corporate history together amounted to US$45.5bn, that banks had paid out US$100bn in US legal settlements alone since the start of the financial crisis and that global pharmaceutical companies had paid US$30.2bn in fines since 1991 (University of Oxford and Arabesque Partners, 2015). Individual incidents and events can also have major impacts on corporate value. For example, the share prices of Vale S.A. fell by almost a quarter in the immediate aftermath of the Brumadinho mine disaster in 2019, and Volkswagen AG lost almost a quarter of its market value in 2015 after it admitted to cheating on US air pollution tests for years. In 2015, the share price of oil major BP more than halved following the Deepwater Horizon spill.

There are also significant investment opportunities associated with ESG issues. For example, it is estimated that between now and 2030, between US$5trn and US$7trn a year is needed to achieve the Sustainable Development Goals worldwide (UNCTAD, 2014). At least a further US$1.5trn a year is needed in the same period to meet the Paris goal of keeping the average global temperature rise well below 2°C and as close as possible to 1.5°C.[9]

At the portfolio level, a 2018 study by PRI used ESG data provided by MSCI ESG Research to test equities portfolios that were

[9] https://cop23.unfccc.int/news/bridging-climate-ambition-and-finance-gaps.

optimised with assets that had improving ESG scores (effectively a momentum strategy) and high absolute ESG scores (a tilt strategy) (Nguyen-Taylor and Martindale, 2018). The study concluded that ESG information offers investment outperformance advantages relative to respective benchmarks across all regions. This general finding is confirmed by two other studies. In June 2017, BofA Merrill Lynch Global Research released research that concluded that the stocks in its US universe that ranked within the top third by ESG scores (using ESG research from Thomson Reuters) outperformed stocks in the bottom third by 18 percentage points in the 2005 to 2015 period (Subramanian et al., 2017). A 2015 study from Calvert Investments provided similar findings for fixed income (Nguyen-Taylor et al., 2015), concluding that companies ranked in the top half compared to bottom half entities by aggregate ESG scores delivered significant outperformance as measured by the annual rate of change in CDS spreads.

8.6 INVESTMENT PRACTICE: ESG INTEGRATION IS INCREASINGLY STANDARD PRACTICE

Perhaps the clearest indication of how ESG integration is now a standard expectation of investors is provided by the number that have become signatories to the PRI. As of September 2019, the PRI had over 2,500 signatories representing US$86.3trn in AUM, including 465 asset owners and 1,823 asset managers. The PRI's signatories commit to incorporating ESG issues into their investment analysis and decision-making processes, to acting as active owners and incorporating ESG issues into their ownership policies and practices, and to reporting on their activities and progress towards implementing the Principles.

These commitments are being seen across all asset classes. For example, the results of the 2018 PRI signatory reporting and assessment framework indicated that US$38bn of assets in listed equity had some form of ESG integration (e.g. analysis of ESG issues as an integral part of the investment process, screening, thematic investment) (PRI et al., 2019). These data also showed that there is increasing attention to ESG in other asset classes; for example, 76 per cent of asset owners reported that they considered ESG issues when investing in hedge funds, an increase on 53 per cent in 2017.

These high-level commitments are being seen in capital flows. For example, MSCI reported that the equity assets under management invested in ESG ETFs linked to MSCI's ESG indices increased from US\$2.1bn to US\$16.8bn between 2015 and 2019, and, by the end of 2018, there were over 350 open-end and exchange-traded sustainability themed funds, including equity, fixed income and alternative funds, available to US investors, an increase of almost 50 per cent compared to 2017 (reported in PRI et al., 2019).

Investors' views on fiduciary duty both reflect and are driving this growth in responsible investment. In 2019, as part of its annual reporting and assessment framework, the PRI asked signatories to discuss how they interpret their fiduciary (or equivalent) duties. Over 90 per cent of the respondents explicitly acknowledged the consideration of ESG issues in their investment processes as an integral element of their fiduciary duties (PRI et al., 2019). Interestingly, for most, the analysis of ESG issues was seen as enabling better risk management or the avoidance of downside risk; fewer than half highlighted the investment opportunities (or upsides) associated with such analysis. A majority of the respondents also stated that they saw the consideration of ESG factors as a necessary and important part of fulfilling their fiduciary duty towards their clients or beneficiaries. A smaller number noted that this duty 'allowed' or 'permitted' them to take account of ESG issues where relevant. Only a small minority (around 3 per cent) perceived fiduciary duty as a constraint to the consideration of ESG in some circumstances. Stewardship activities such as engagement and voting were identified by close to 40 per cent of respondents as an important way of enhancing value and of delivering on their fiduciary duty.

These general findings are supported by the interviews that underpinned 2015 "Fiduciary Duty in the 21st Century" (PRI et al., 2015) and the 2016 "Investor Duties and Obligations in 6 Asian

Markets" (PRI et al., 2016) reports. In both cases, those asset owners that had taken a proactive approach to responsible investment did not see fiduciary duty as a particular obstacle to action. Many described fiduciary duty as a practical and pragmatic requirement that informs investment and management practice in a similar manner to aspects such as cost, investment returns and so forth. Some went further arguing that fiduciary duty created a positive duty on them to take ESG issues into account in their investment practices, suggesting that a failure to take account of ESG issues could be seen as a breach of their fiduciary duties.

8.7 MODERN FIDUCIARY DUTY

Where does this leave the debate about fiduciary duty? The 2019 PRI, UNEP FI and The Generation Foundation report, 'Fiduciary Duty in the 21st Century', was in no doubt that the changes in the policy and legislative landscape, in investor understanding of the financial relevance of ESG issues and in investment practice and changes discussed earlier have fundamentally changed the expectations of fiduciaries. That report argued that fiduciaries must:

i. Incorporate ESG issues into investment analysis and decision-making processes, consistent with their investment time horizons.
ii. Encourage high standards of ESG performance in the companies or other entities in which they invest.
iii. Support the stability and resilience of the financial system.
iv. Understand and incorporate beneficiaries' and savers' sustainability-related preferences.
v. Report on how they have implemented these commitments.

These expectations both align with and clarify the traditional duties of loyalty and prudence. Understanding and taking account of the sustainability preferences of beneficiaries/clients, whether these preferences are financially material or not, is clearly a central element of the duty of loyalty. Similarly, any conception of prudence (i.e. acting with due skill, care and diligence) clearly includes requirements both to consider all financially material factors and to act effectively and appropriately to manage these factors. The interests of beneficiaries frequently extend many decades into the future, requiring fiduciaries to pay attention to issues such as demographic change, climate change and other environmental pressures.

These expectations are now sufficiently mature and sufficiently underpinned by legislation and policy, that they can and should be considered central elements of the duties owed by fiduciaries and their beneficiaries. In Box 8.5, we present our modern definition of fiduciary duty.

BOX 8.5   **Modern fiduciary duty (PRI et al., 2019)**

Fiduciary duties (or equivalent obligations) exist to ensure that those who manage other people's money act in the interests of beneficiaries, rather than serving their own interests. The most important of these duties are:

- Loyalty: Fiduciaries should:
  - Act honestly and in good faith in the interests of their beneficiaries or their clients.
  - Understand and incorporate into their decision-making the sustainability preferences of beneficiaries/clients, whether these preferences are financially material or not.
  - Impartially balance the conflicting interests of different beneficiaries and clients.
  - Avoid conflicts of interest.
  - Not act for the benefit of themselves or a third party.
- Prudence: Fiduciaries should act with due care, skill and diligence, investing as an 'ordinary prudent person' would do. This includes:
  - Incorporating financially material ESG factors into their investment decision-making, consistent with the timeframe of the obligation.
  - Being an active owner, encouraging high standards of ESG performance in the companies or other entities in which they are invested.
  - Supporting the stability and resilience of the financial system.

BOX 8.5 (cont.)

Fiduciaries should disclose their investment approach to clients and/or beneficiaries, including information on how preferences are incorporated into the scheme's investment strategy and the potential risks and benefits of doing so.

8.8 MOVING FORWARD

The conceptual debate around whether ESG issues are a requirement of investor duties and obligations is now over. However, further work is required in five areas.

First, there needs to be a continued focus on investor implementation. Despite the growth in the number of investors that have made commitments to responsible investment, many investors have yet to integrate ESG issues into their investment processes or to engage with the companies in which they are invested. Even among those that have made commitments, it is probably fair to say that progress has been somewhat piecemeal; many have yet to extend their commitments to all asset classes and, even where implementation has commenced, it is not uncommon to find that there are often weaknesses in their implementation of these commitments (see, for example, PRI, 2016).

Second, the gaps that remain in policy frameworks need to be filled. While many countries have adopted at least one policy measure, the PRI's regulation database confirms that most countries have yet to establish comprehensive policy frameworks that include pension fund disclosure requirements, requirements for pension funds to adopt responsible investment practices, stewardship codes and corporate disclosure requirements.

Third, policy and regulation need to be implemented effectively and translated into concrete actions. This will involve building capacity and awareness across the investment industry and encouraging asset owners and asset managers to implement these measures. It will involve encouraging investors to be transparent about the actions they have taken, the outcomes they have achieved and the lessons they have learned. It also requires policymakers to ensure the effective implementation of the policies and other measures they have adopted, and to identify and take action where there are weaknesses in adoption or implementation.

Fourth, actors other than the investors have an important role to play. For example, investment consultants advise on the investment practices of trillions of dollars worldwide. They are a recognised source of authority and knowledge on investment practice, and their advice shapes the beliefs and practices of trillions of dollars of invested assets worldwide. The views that investment consultants hold about ESG factors therefore have major implications for the sustainability of the financial system. However, there currently seems to be little commercial imperative for investment consultants to extend the coverage of ESG integrated services among their clients. Another example relates to defined benefit pension schemes. In some cases, regulators have been clear that fiduciary or other duties continue to apply (e.g. in South Africa). However, in other markets, the nature of the duty to beneficiaries of insurance companies, investment managers and sponsoring organisations in contract-based schemes (i.e. where the pension provider does not have fiduciary or equivalent obligations to the beneficiary in the way that a trustee would in a trust-based scheme) is not yet fully defined. These examples highlight the importance of ensuring that regulatory and policy changes reflect the realities of investment markets and of the investment system. Regulation and policy need to apply to all relevant actors and to be sufficiently flexible to adapt in response to changes in actors, in institutions, in technology and in the wider societal context within which the investment system functions.

Fifth, we need to understand how and under what circumstances investors are responsible for the real-world outcomes of their investment activities. Integrating consideration of ESG issues into investment practices and processes is a necessary but not sufficient condition for delivering a financial sector that serves societies and people, within existing planetary boundaries. As currently defined, fiduciary duties do not require a fiduciary to account for the sustainability impact of their investment activity, beyond its financial performance. In other words, fiduciary duties require consideration of how sustainability issues affect the investment decision, but not how the investment decision affects sustainability issues. More fundamental changes – to incentives, to structures, to duties, to obligations and to the broader legal frameworks within which investors operate – are needed if the financial sector is to enable economic activities and societies to prosper in a sustainable manner. Wider public policy, more explicitly focussed on real economy outcomes, is the key next step in moving towards a more sustainable economy (see Box 8.6). In that context, the proposals set out in this chapter for a modern definition of fiduciary duty are best seen as a staging post rather than a final destination.

BOX 8.6   **A legal framework for impact**

In January 2019, UNEP FI, the PRI and The Generation Foundation launched the Legal Framework for Impact project,[10] with the aim of making assessing and accounting for the sustainability impact of investment decision-making a core part of investment activity. The project will explore questions such as whether there are legal impediments to investors adopting 'impact targets' (e.g. that an investor's investment activity is consistent with no more than 1.5°C of warming), whether investors are legally required to integrate the sustainability impacts of their investment activity in their decision-making processes and on what positive legal grounds could or should investors integrate the realisation of the SDGs into their investment decision-making.

The project will publish analysis of the legal framework for investors to consider sustainability impact in five major economies, propose practical recommendations for investors and policy makers on how

---

[10] www.unepfi.org/investment/legal-framework-for-impact.

BOX 8.6   (cont.)

policies, regulation and investment practice may evolve to achieve the systematic integration of sustainability impact in investment decision-making and support wider implementation of the recommendations through investor and policy-maker outreach.

REFERENCES

Cheng, B., Ioannou, I. and Serafeim, G. (2014), 'Corporate Social Responsibility and Access to Finance', *Strategic Management Journal* 35(1), 1–23.

Eccles, R., Ioannou, I. and Serafeim, G. (2014), 'The Impact of Corporate Sustainability on Organizational Processes and Performance', *Management Science* 60(11), 2835–2857.

El Ghoul, S., Guedhami, O., Kwok, C. and Mishra, D. (2011), 'Does Corporate Social Responsibility Affect the Cost of Capital?', *Journal of Banking and Finance* 35 (9), 2388–2406.

Freshfields Bruckhaus Deringer (2005), 'A Legal Framework for the Integration of Environmental, Social and Governance Issues into Institutional Investment'. Geneva: UNEP. www.unepfi.org/fileadmin/documents/freshfields_legal_resp_20051123.pdf.

Friede, G., Busch, T. and Bassen, A. (2015), 'ESG and Financial Performance: Aggregated Evidence from More than 2000 Empirical Studies', *Journal of Sustainable Finance & Investment* 5(4), 210–233.

Khan, M., Serafeim, G. and Yoon, A. (2016), 'Corporate Sustainability: First Evidence on Materiality', *The Accounting Review* 91(6), 1697–1724.

Nguyen-Taylor, K. and Martindale, M. (2018), 'Financial Performance of ESG Integration in US Investing'. www.unpri.org/download?ac=4218.

Nguyen-Taylor, K., Naranjo, A. and Roy, C. (2015), 'The ESG Advantage in Fixed Income Investing: An Empirical Analysis'. Bethesda, MD: Calvert Investments. www.environmental-finance.com/assets/files/WP10011.pdf.

Principles for Responsible Investment (PRI) (2016), 'How Asset Owners Can Drive Responsible Investment: Beliefs, Strategies and Mandates'. www.unpri.org/asset-owners/how-asset-owners-can-drive-responsible-investment-beliefs-strategies-and-mandates/277.article.

PRI (2019), 'Taking Stock: Sustainable Finance Policy Engagement and Policy Influence'. https://d8g8t13e9vf2o.cloudfront.net/Uploads/c/j/u/pripolicywhite papertakingstockfinal_335442.pdf.

PRI, UNEP FI and The Generation Foundation (2016), 'Investor Duties and Obligations in 6 Asian Markets'. www.unepfi.org/fileadmin/documents/ Investor_obligations_and_duties_in_six_asian_markets.pdf.

PRI, UNEP FI and The Generation Foundation (2019), 'Fiduciary Duty in the 21st Century'. www.unepfi.org/wordpress/wp-content/uploads/2019/10/Fiduciary-duty-21st-century-final-report.pdf.

PRI, UNEP FI, UN Global Compact and UNEP Inquiry into the Design of a Sustainable Financial System (2015), 'Fiduciary Duty in the 21st Century'. www.unepfi.org/fileadmin/documents/fiduciary_duty_21st_century.pdf.

Sparkes, R. (2002), *Socially Responsible Investment: A Global Revolution*. Chichester: Wiley.

Subramanian, S., Suzuki, D., Makedon, A. et al. (2017), 'ESG Part II: A Deeper Dive'. New York: Bank of America Merrill Lynch Global Research. www.iccr.org/sites/ default/files/page_attachments/esg_part_2_deeper_dive_bof_of_a_june_2017.pdf.

UN Commission on Trade and Development (UNCTAD) (2014), 'World Investment Report 2014 – Investing in SDGs'. Geneva: UNCTAD. https:// unctad.org/en/PublicationsLibrary/wir2014_en.pdf.

UNEP FI (2009), 'Fiduciary Responsibility: Legal and Practical Aspects of Integrating Environmental, Social and Governance Issues into Institutional Investment'. Geneva: UNEP FI. www.unepfi.org/publica tions/investment-publications/fiduciary-responsibility-legal-and-practical-aspects-of-integrating-environmental-social-and-governance-issues-into-institutional-investment.

University of Oxford and Arabesque Partners (2015), 'From the Stockholder to the Stakeholder: How Sustainability Can Drive Financial Outperformance', March. Oxford: University of Oxford. https://arabesque.com/research/From_the_stock holder_to_the_stakeholder_web.pdf.

9 Active and Responsible

A Cost-Efficient Model for Integrating Sustainability

Magnus Billing and Carina Silberg

9.1 INTRODUCTION

This chapter reviews what it means to be an active and responsible pension fund and asset owner and how the long-term perspective requires consideration of sustainability dimensions. It is based primarily on a case study of our experiences at *Alecta*, a Swedish mutual fund with €90bn of assets under management.[1] *Alecta* manages occupational pension plans for 2.5 million people and 35,000 businesses. Its strategy is to be an active investor making investment decisions based on fundamental analysis. With only a very few exceptions, all asset management is conducted in-house. Concluding the chapter, we reflect on what challenges investors alike *Alecta* face going forward and what capabilities and conditions are required.

9.2 WHAT DOES IT MEAN WHEN A PENSION FUND AND ASSET OWNER DEFINES ITSELF AS AN ACTIVE AND RESPONSIBLE INVESTOR?

In order to deliver the long-term perspective required of a sustainable investor, we are a strong proponent of the need to fully comprehend what one invests into, that is to base the investment decision on fundamental in-house analysis. It is furthermore of utmost importance to retain high cost-efficiency, that is to control costs to enhance efficiency and leverage scalability.

---

[1] *Alecta's* portfolio comprises equity (40 per cent), fixed income (50 per cent) and real estate (10 per cent). Its equity holdings comprise approximately 100 listed companies. It participates in the nomination committees of 22 Swedish listed companies and holds €3.5bn in green bonds, and €1bn in other impact investments.

The competitive edge of a large pension fund includes the capacity to manage assets with long-term perspective and scalability.

An asset managers' duty of loyalty to and care for its beneficiaries can be provided in many different ways. Regardless of differences in approach, the single common denominator is ultimately the fiduciary duty, which entails the principles of avoiding conflict of interests and always acting in the best interest of the beneficiaries. We make the claim that from an asset management point of view, the objective should always be to deliver maximum value for the beneficiaries. That claim should be uncontroversial but requires further considerations.

The equity portfolio managed by our fund has an aggregated value of €35bn, consisting of investments in only approximately 100 companies. As a result, with direct investments into a selected number of companies, any large fund can swiftly become one of the largest shareholders in each of its chosen companies.

Being one of the larger shareholders carries with it special responsibility. Being an active shareholder does not necessarily mean being an activist investor or believing that one should take operational responsibility. Rather, it is a necessity to be focussed and recognise the limits of ones' capabilities.

An investor can provide added value by being an active and engaged long-term shareholder focussed on supporting and challenging the board of directors to strive for excellency and to be a role model within the industry and across industries. The great Greek philosopher Plutarch understood that humans and their organisations observe their peers with the implicit intention of copying successful behaviours. To some extent, as owners we can act as a catalyst and impetus for the constant observation of peers.

We present our arguments at a time when there is an increasing proportion of capital being allocated in passive index mandates. A recent (Harvard) study (Bebchuk and Hirst, 2019) concluded that the three large index fund managers: BlackRock, Vanguard and State Street Global Investors together represented holdings of more than

20 per cent of S&P 500 companies in 2018, and in reality represented 25 per cent of the voting shares, because of non-voting shareholders. This development is expected to continue with scenarios of up to 40 per cent voting power in the next twenty years. Combined with observations that incentives of the larger index funds are 'excessively deferential toward corporate managers', this risk increases the principal–agent conflict and can be detrimental to fostering an owner-ship culture of stewardship and active owners, that challenge the board and impose strong accountability on corporate executives.

Being an active and responsible investor can take many different shapes and forms and that is particularly the case looking across different asset classes. In this chapter, our focus is on active and responsible investors within (listed) equities. Hence, we ask: what are the characteristics of an active and responsible shareholder and what characteristics are more likely to be successful? Success in this context encompasses significant shareholder value creation over time.

The above raises the following questions: (i) how can significant shareholder value creation over time be measured? And (ii) what are the indicators showing that such shareholder value is being delivered?

Shareholder value is based on the company's ability to sustain and grow profits over time. A narrow definition of shareholder value creation is basically the company's ability to efficiently allocate capital towards investments generating a positive free cash flow that investors, based on cost of capital, find adequately attractive. Hence, appreciation of share price and dividends to shareholders provides clear and focussed measurements of total shareholder value creation.

This narrow definition of shareholder value was not top priority among executive management teams during the 1980s. However, it subsequently became the focus for executive managements operating within the public markets because of the leveraged M&A market seeking to capture the perceived value gap between market value and potential shareholder value.

This development has led to the establishment of a narrow shareholder value concept as an undisputed guiding star for day-to-day operations in many investment firms. Albeit, that many arguments about the scope of the shareholder value concept have always been present, with degrees of intensity and with regional differences. In the past few years, we have seen an intensified debate on shareholder value creation and how it relates to a company's social responsibility and from there towards Environmental, Social and Governance responsibility ('ESG factors').

Despite the globalisation of the industry and the capital markets, the regional differences are notable. Anglo-Saxon countries, like the United States and the United Kingdom, appear to us to be still leaning more towards the narrow interpretation of shareholder value creation emphasising the generation of short-term positive free cash flow. However, certain parts of continental Europe and Scandinavia are expanding the interpretation of positive free cash flow to 'a long-term sustainable positive free cash flow' that includes ESG factors to account for the transition process of externalities being internalised at some point in time. In contrast to a moral or ethical stance on corporate responsibility, the idea of externalities is based on economic rationale, that is current costs or benefits not accounted for or calculated in the income statement such as pollution – a common example of a negative externality. With carbon emissions, we have seen how some regional policy efforts have resulted in a price on carbon emissions, while in most parts it is still an externality. We are inclined to argue that the discussion on externalities holds up also for positive externalities or benefits, that is a company that creates favourable conditions for diversity, education and skills development can capitalise in terms of better dynamics and productivity which eventually will manifest over time in the company's capacity to sustain or grow profits.

As long-term investors, it is our responsibility and opportunity to look beyond short-term returns as long as we have confidence in the company's vision, its strategy to get there and the capacity of the organisation to lead accordingly – adapting, innovating, transitioning. Profitability and returns are necessities but not the purpose of the company. In plain words, profits and returns are the products of the company's ability to create an offer that is relevant for the market and to produce it in a responsible and efficient manner.

A key driver for long-term shareholders' ambition to integrate ESG factors with a material financial impact into the investment process is the market shift, whereby ESG factors have become a key component of the actual business model's value proposition. This is happening across sectors. Two concrete cases demonstrate business models that to different extents have efficiently integrated ESG factors to procure value creation. Hence, shareholders and investors must become literate in identifying and analysing how ESG factors impact future shareholder value creation.

CASE STUDY 9.1 **Electrolux**

Swedish appliance company Electrolux attributes its competitive advantage to having a sustainability leadership position in the industry. Electrolux is committed to science-based targets to reduce its carbon emissions, including from product use. Having a sustainability lens in product development and innovation, Electrolux's most resource-efficient products represented 21 per cent of products sold and 29 per cent of gross profit in 2018. Its innovation process allows it to constantly improve product performance and raise sustainability performance across the segments. Through more efficient products and operations, the Group aims to cut the CO_2 impact by 50 per cent by 2020 relative to 2005 levels. Sustainability permeates the strategic development – Electrolux is constantly making production and processes more resource efficient, developing sourcing and supply chain responsibly and sustainably – to ensure long-term profitable growth.

CASE STUDY 9.2   **AAK**

AAK is a global leader in production of speciality and semi-speciality vegetable oils and fats. AAK sources shea kernels from West Africa, to produce oil used in the chocolate and confectionary as well as the cosmetic industry. Women collect and process the shea kernels in a period when nearly no crops are being harvested, presenting an important nutrition source while parts can be sold and provide income. Disrupting parts of the traditional complex supply chain, AAK cooperates with (shea traders and) women's groups to build a solid and durable sourcing set-up across the shea production areas (as well as logistical hubs in the coastal areas). In 2009, AAK introduced a direct sourcing programme in Burkina Faso, and later in Ghana in 2015. Based on fair trade principles, the programme allows participants access to pre-financing and micro-credits, training and logistical support. Monitoring support evidence that women are investing in community development and other income-generating activities. Currently involving over 130,000 women, the programme is growing gradually and has become an integrated way of doing business for AAK, with benefits such as better quality, full traceability and stronger local infrastructure. With a genuine understanding for stakeholder relations, part of the S in ESG, AAK identify development opportunities of their business model which over time can be reflected in shareholder value.

These case studies serve as examples of a market trend towards a more commonly accepted concept of shareholder value creation entailing ESG factors integrated in their business models, representing a broader perspective to identify risks and opportunities. We acknowledge the importance of short-term positive free cash flows to allow for implementation of a business model integrating ESG factors, and thereby adjusting for externalities being internalised via, for example, technology innovation or policy shifts.

In conclusion we argue that an asset owner's and asset manager's fiduciary duty must entail an approach encompassing a wider take on shareholder value than just short-term positive free cash flow, share price appreciation and dividend. ESG factors may well materialise in financial results short-term, but increasingly will do so with a longer time horizon. A pension service provider with pension liabilities stretching out for a period of thirty to forty years combined with contractually committed guarantees must be able to manage ESG risks and opportunities adequately in the investment process when maximising return for the customers' future retirements.

Our preferred approach is to fulfil the fiduciary duty of maximising value by applying an investment model based on fundamental analysis and portfolio management conducted in-house and with focus on absolute returns. The focus on absolute returns is important for allowing contrarian investment decisions. It furthermore provides impetus for investing in assets with transition potential if combined with persistent engagement to safeguard proper transition.

Yet another dimension of being a responsible investor is the focus on cost-efficiency in the chosen investment model, which is of extraordinary importance given the wonder of compound interest. A fee of 1 per cent on the assets under management could lead to a 25 per cent depletion of the customer's pension capital during an accumulation period of forty years.

9.3   WHAT IS THE POTENTIAL VALUE ADDED AND WHAT MOTIVATES AN ACTIVE AND RESPONSIBLE INVESTMENT MODEL WITH INTEGRATION OF ESG FACTORS?

The Organisation for Economic Co-operation and Development (OECD, 2017, p. 13) describes the relationship between investor and investee company as 'a business relationship', which establishes a risk and reward relationship. Hence, investors may suffer substantial adverse results caused by direct or indirect actions, or non-actions, by the investee company.

As an example, Facebook's failure to protect user integrity was disclosed in the Cambridge Analytica scandal. That led to a US$119bn reduction in Facebook's market value, which was then followed thereafter by disclosure of slowed growth. This is a case of responsible business conduct failure directly impacting shareholder value, and thereby immediately causing asset owners and asset managers to adopt consequent measures as part of their fiduciary duty towards their beneficiaries.

Other recent concrete examples concern money laundering cases related to Nordic banks, which, as events have caused significant share price drops. In fact, there are numerous cases where a failure to uphold responsible business conduct causes damages to shareholders and other stakeholders. Wells Fargo's aggressive cross-selling practices damaged its standing and led to a significant governance reshuffle. And the Volkswagen diesel emission scandal led to a 20 per cent share price drop the first business day after the news of Volkswagen's admission of deception. That scandal also materially negatively affected the ownership value for the end customer.

There is a growing body of academic research that has shown correlation between strong ESG performance and financial performance, but not necessarily evidencing causation. However, recent studies based on MSCI data of ESG indicators have supported the notion of causality and financially significant effects, both in terms of lower risk and as a potential leading indicator for changes in risk profile (Giese et al., 2019).

A key success factor for any investment activity is correct and timely information forming part of the pricing mechanism for the investable asset. With engagement, an investor has the opportunity to seek more detailed, accurate and timely information, including information about ESG factors that may have a material significance for the valuation.

Based on the examples discussed previously, it can be argued that responsible business conduct cannot, at any given time, be taken for granted and that it is a risk for the investor to properly manage when seeking risk-adjusted return. We are of the view that an investor's risk management is well served by proper due diligence, adequate transparency and a good business relationship with the management and board of directors. The aforementioned can be achieved in many different manners. Subsequently we will elaborate on how an active and responsible asset owner can manage this without having to build up a complex and expensive asset management structure.

The investor's engagement with the investee company provides a tool for the investors to enhance its information pool. In particular, it can increase the detail, accuracy and quality of data. The engagement can also serve as a basis for building trust and a relationship between investor and the investee's management and board of directors. Such trust and relationship are of significant importance in adequately understanding and assessing the business model and strategy of the investee, along with its capacity to execute it to generate long-term shareholder value.

The above-mentioned trust and relationship created through engagement is of significant importance to changing behaviour by the investee company. To produce such impact, engagement will be reliant upon the power of the investors, the legitimacy of the investor and a sense of urgency. There seems to be a consensus within academic research that the above-mentioned conditions are essential for successful engagements (Gifford, 2010).

These conditions can present themselves in many different shapes and forms, however. The condition of legitimacy can present itself loud and clear for the investee company, not only through the share size of the investor, but also through the strength and substance of the arguments put forward. It is our experience that a long-term engagement tends to support legitimacy. The sense of urgency is impacted by investors' intensity of engagement and persistence, characteristics that are more evident for an investee company when dealing with an active investor relative to a passive index tracker investor.

The condition of power refers to tools such as voting and other shareholder rights, lobbying on regulation and so forth. We argue that an active investor generally regards power to be a tool of last resort, if and when it can be concluded that the investee company is not adjusting its behaviour in line with the investor objectives of the engagement, thus having (fundamentally) different views on what will serve the long-term interest of the investee company.

The quality and success of the engagement with the investee requires the investor being relevant and respected for their knowledge and professionalism, both about the business sector the investee is operating within and the financial industry sector the investor is operating in. Such credibility builds the trust necessary for the engagement, and it must be a two-way street. For the engagement to be successful over time, it will have to benefit not just the investor but also the investee. Such benefits can manifest themselves for the investee by, for example, providing benchmarks, clarifications and enhanced knowledge about shareholder preferences and/or expectations.

Potentially, the most important benefit for an investee to embrace engagement is the consequence it may have on the investee's cost of capital. A low investee acceptance and openness for investor engagements could potentially lead to uncertainty among investors. A high level of uncertainty will lead to demands for a higher risk premium by the investor, and thereby the cost of capital will increase for the investee.

It is our experience, within the field of ESG factors and their integration into the investee's business models, that due to the ever-growing demand for allocating capital to sustainable investments the investees are facing a material risk of higher cost of capital if they are unwilling to actively engage with investors on the subject of integration of ESG factors into their business models. It should be underlined that all engagements referred to are, of course, always within the bounds of applicable rules and regulations on matters such as confidentiality and competition.

The engagements with an investee should be conducted at different levels, inter alia, the board of directors, CEO, CFO, investor relation, for the investor to procure deep understanding of the investee's business risks and opportunities. That provides valuable input from different perspectives enabling the assessment of the investment and its long-term value creation capacity. It furthermore allows the investor to engage different areas of expertise in the investment process by adding to the traditional financial analysis expertise know-how in areas such as for example climate management, board composition, governance, privacy and human rights.

We have observed that the value added of long-term engagement manifests itself clearly in a crisis. When an investee company is facing a crisis, the market tends to overreact in the short term. The market reaction shows characteristics of being rather single-minded risk adverse. But an investor that has had the long-term commitment and discipline to focus on engagement with the objective of establishing a more in-depth understanding of the business model, the managements' capacity to deliver on the strategy and the underlying culture of the company is better positioned to adopt a less binary investment approach towards the investee company.

The investor should, if the engagement has been done in an adequate manner, have acquired the knowledge and the investment confidence that an enhanced knowledge base carries to be able to act contrarian to the market if its analysis supports such decision. As an active investor, believing in fundamental analysis, you seek to put yourself into a position where you have a possibility to act contrarian.

The long-term engagement with an investee company furthermore strengthens the investor's internal knowledge and experience, that is its 'structural capital'. Such structural capital, if it is properly managed within the investor organisation, can provide impetus not only for lower transaction costs, but also for an ability to be a successful investor. In our own portfolios, for example, there are some substantial holdings in the auto industry. Fundamentally understanding the challenges with respect to the technical disruption caused by electric vehicles has increased the attention on how holding companies in the auto industry value chain develops capacity to capitalise on that very shift.

For an investor to be able to fully leverage structural capital, it is our view that the investor is well served by predominantly doing the investment with in-house resources. If an investor to a large extent is utilising external resources in the investment decision process, structural capital is potentially built up with the external party's organisation, often an investment consultant or asset manager. That structural capital has the characteristics of being highly scalable, in particular with regard to investment in the asset classes equities and fixed income. The asset class 'alternatives' do not, in our opinion, allow the same evident ability to build scalable structural capital.

9.4 WHAT CHALLENGES DOES AN ACTIVE AND RESPONSIBLE INVESTOR FACE AND WHAT ARE THE HURDLES FOR TRANSFORMING INTO A TRULY SUSTAINABLE INVESTOR?

A key challenge that should be mentioned first is the restrictions of the financial product offered, in this case a pension product. While the offered product clearly meets conditions that enable active and responsible investments, in fact benefitting from such, in this section we will focus on the challenges faced. A pension company offering a defined benefit or a defined contribution scheme entailing a traditional insurance with guarantees to its beneficiaries has to accept that the exposure to risk assets must be limited.

In the case of our own fund, the defined contribution plan offers a risk asset exposure of around 70 per cent. In a European context this is a high level of exposure. The guarantee offered to beneficiaries is a repayment of contributions or 70 per cent of the capital at the time of retirement, whichever is higher. Furthermore, traditional pension companies within the second pillar of the pension system are compelled to allocate quite meaningful capital to government bonds, municipalities bonds and mortgage bonds.

Clearly, the value added by being an active and responsible investor creates less marginal value add, within the fixed income asset class compared to the risk asset classes of equities and real estate. Hence, with a traditional 60 per cent equity and 40 per cent bonds portfolio, the value added for pursuing an active and responsible investment approach is to a significant extent limited to the capital allocated towards risk assets.

An additional challenge for an active and responsible investor is the limitation of the investment universe. An active and responsible investor that relies upon fundamental analysis and strives to build up its structural capital is most likely not able to cover all regions and all segments within the asset classes of real estate and equities.

Such challenges can be overcome. However, they tend to come with fairly high costs and can be unreasonably time-consuming, thereby adding operational complexity for the pension company. The importance of the cost should at no point in time be underestimated given the operating environment for the pension company, that is liabilities falling due in twenty-five to thirty-five years combined with the power of compound interest. As mentioned earlier, an investment fee of 1 per cent can deplete the pension capital for a beneficiary by approximately 25 per cent over an investment horizon of forty years. Since no investor can predict future return, cost discipline and caution should be part of the DNA for any investor.

Some would now argue that this is a key argument for index investment, since active investment usually carries a high cost basis. Based on our experience, we argue that it is possible to be a successful investor with a low-cost operating basis: in our case approximately US$90bn is actively managed at a cost of just two basis points.

A third and key challenge is related to the availability and quality of the data provided by issuers. By that we imply that we need to continually require actual disclosures across the investment universe as there are still companies that lag. In addition, the ESG data that is being disclosed often represents a partial scope as opposed to being comprehensive, or its reliability can be put to question. And to a large extent financial markets and the investment environment rely upon historical financial data disclosed by the issuers. A well-functioning financial market supports efficient capital allocation by procuring a solid price mechanism with symmetric, concrete and relevant information.

This means that the perfect market can price all financially material risks. For a pension company, managing the mismatching risk vested in the duration discrepancy between its assets and liabilities, it is evident that certain externalities today will become internalised during a time horizon in parity with its liabilities. Now, this internalisation requires to a certain extent an ability to properly understand the governance and risk management context in which financial results are achieved by the issuers over time.

The recommendations from the G20 Task Force on Climate-related Disclosures (TCFD), in its final report from June 2017 (TCFD, 2017), provide an essential framework for how reporting entities should assess climate-related risks and opportunities, making it relevant for investors. It furthermore supports reporting companies in developing forward-looking financial disclosures. Perhaps most importantly, the TCFD recommends the issuer disclose the resilience of its strategy in relation to climate scenarios including a two degree or lower scenario. The TCFD recommendations are not limited to the climate scenarios. They could be a useful tool for inter alia biodiversity and freshwater scenarios.

Such disclosure is a necessity for an investor to be able to internalise risks that in the short-to-mid-term are externalities. Such externalities may be internalised due to the transformation currently taking place across societies and industries, or that will take place within a reasonably short period of time. Meaningful drivers for this transformation are policy decisions, innovations and connected learning curve forces.

The implementation of the TCFD recommendations in national legislation, as described in the EU Action Plan (European

Commission, 2018), will provide impetus for meaningful re-allocation of mainstream capital to sustainable investments. The investors that are able to adapt to a more forward-looking data and scenario disclosure environment and able to integrate it into their investment process will most likely have a competitive edge.

The integration of the forward-looking scenario disclosure will force the investors to develop their investment organisations, as well as incentivise it, to an extent where the investment process is more focussed on internalising the externalities identified today.

Academics have observed that shareholder engagement on climate change has been notably effective when it comes to lowering downside risk (Hoepener et al., 2019). Given the importance of the transition to a low carbon society, it is our belief that this will show an even stronger foundation going forward.

Furthermore, forward-looking disclosure is in conformity with the foundation of the fiduciary duty for a long-term investor. As such it motivates an active and responsible investment approach for a pension company serving beneficiaries with an investment horizon of around twenty-five to thirty-five years. The beneficiaries are rightfully expecting the pension company to manage their assets in such a manner that opportunities in the long-term are maximised and risks managed.

This means, in our opinion, the necessity to integrate forward-looking climate scenarios into the investment process in order to understand and adequately internalise the externalities that have a material financial impact. Hence, it is to be welcomed that the EU Action Plan has led to mandatory disclosures for investors, including asset managers and assets owners, on how ESG factors are integrated in their investment process, and that the TCFD framework is a central reference point in giving guidance to climate scenarios. This will provide necessary clarification and codification of the legal term fiduciary duty, and thereby give impetus for meaningful re-allocation of mainstream capital towards sustainable investments.

As a consequence of the regulatory development, any investor positioning itself as an active and responsible investor and an engaged shareholder leveraging the potential competitive edge offered by the regulatory development will have to be able to stress test its portfolio based on relevant climate scenarios.

In 2018, *Alecta* conducted its first stress testing of the portfolio assets with a few different climate scenarios, and it is evident that the quality of the data is not good enough. For Scope 3 emissions (upstream and downstream) it is extremely poor. Hence, we believe that significant progress with regard to data availability, quality and a standardisation of methods needs to happen before investors are able to claim to be in a situation where we can assure our beneficiaries and are adequately equipped to financially evaluate climate and other current externalities. This is an area where policy makers and concerned market participants need to work together in order to achieve progress.

9.5 CONCLUDING REFLECTIONS

It is possible to successfully combine an active and responsible investment approach with a cost-efficient operation, allowing for maximisation of beneficiary value – financially and from a broader perspective.

Based on our observations and going forward, we conclude that several aspects will become increasingly important in order for investors to contribute to a more sustainable development while at the same time being able to track our progress for our beneficiaries. Several of these are subject to actions in the EU Action Plan on Financing Sustainable Growth or will benefit from such actions.

Moreover, the pace at which the EU is moving forward on sustainable finance reflects the momentum that we are seeing in the investment and business sector, but we need to take this development beyond the EU and inspire and engage beyond our region to achieve the following:

• Enhanced ESG information quality – disclosures need to improve, climate is an urgent example, and this can be enabled through regulatory initiatives and/or market collaboration, including shareholder engagement. The ongoing exchange between investors of experiences and methodology for scenario analysis methods will emphasise the need for quality data and shed light on potential areas for standardisations.

- Competence development and new structural (ESG) capital – new data and information dimensions require a rapid learning curve in asset owner and asset management organisations. ESG or an expert area analyst can catalyse and enable a faster transition and interpretation, bridging ESG and traditional financial analysis. This development also needs to pick up pace on the sell side (Setterberg et al., 2019) and issuer side (bridging gaps between investor relations and sustainability departments) allowing for broader and more long-term strategies and financial market disclosure. Naturally, there are increased expectations among board members to inform themselves of the strategic ESG matters of the firm, again – both on the investor and investee side.

- More sophisticated ESG engagement and investor collaboration requires engagement with better articulated arguments and defined objectives that emphasise the alignment of corporate and investor objectives of long-term prosperity. We have recently seen studies trying to better analyse and understand investor influence through engagement, what distinguishes strong alliances that efficiently engage with companies – home bias, resources and so forth. There is a growing interest in not only understanding shareholder engagement's effect on a firms ESG rating or performance, but also how it links to financial value development.

REFERENCES

Bebchuk, L. A. and Hirst, S. (2019), 'The Specter of the Giant Three', *Boston University Law Review* 99, 721–741. www.bu.edu/bulawreview/files/2019/06/BEBCHUK-HIRST-1.pdf.

European Commission (2018), 'Action Plan: Financing Sustainable Growth'. Brussels, March. https://eur-lex.europa.eu/legal-content/EN/TXT/PDF/?uri=CELEX:52018DC0097&from=EN.

Giese, G., Lee, L.-E., Melas, D., Nagy, Z. and Nishikawa, L. (July 2019), 'Foundations of ESG Investing: How ESG Affects Equity Valuation, Risk, and Performance', *The Journal of Portfolio Management* 45(5), 69–83.

Gifford, J. M. (2010), 'Effective Shareholder Engagement: The Factors that Contribute to Shareholder Salience', *Journal of Business Ethics* 92, 79–97. https://philpapers.org/rec/JAMESE.

Hoepener, A. G. F., Oikonomou, I., Sautner, Z., Starks, L. T. and Xiaoyan, Z. (2019), 'ESG Shareholder Engagement and Downside Risk', *SSRN Electronic Journal*. doi: 10.2139/ssrn.2874252. https://papers.ssrn.com/sol3/papers.cfm?abstract_id=2874252.

OECD (2017), 'Responsible Business Conduct for Institutional Investors: Key Considerations for Due Diligence under the OECD Guidelines for Multinational Enterprises', OECD. https://mneguidelines.oecd.org/RBC-for-Institutional-Investors.pdf.

Setterberg, H., Sjöström, E. and Vulturius, G. (2019), 'Long-Term Perspectives in Investment Analysis', Stockholm Sustainable Finance Centre in collaboration with SWESIF. www.stockholmsustainablefinance.com/report-longterm-analysis.

TCFD (2017), 'Final Report: Recommendations of the Task Force on Climate-related Financial Disclosures', June. www.fsb-tcfd.org/publications/final-recommendations-report.

10 Passive-Aggressive or Just Engaged

New Active Ownership Approaches through Benchmarks

David E. Harris

10.1 INTRODUCTION

Far from their image as a boring technical tool of the financial world, indexes are becoming a critical lever for investors to raise market-wide standards and to catalyse sustainable corporate business models. Investors can choose from a wide spectrum of benchmarks to suit their precise needs. The rise of benchmarks and passive investments, then 'smart beta' and now the emergence of 'smart sustainability' has been a global phenomenon, and the stage is now set for their powerful application in active ownership strategies.

This chapter first outlines the rise in the use of benchmarks, in particular as a measure of active fund performance, and as a basis for investing. Second, it explains some important concerns regarding the use of indexes, including incentivising short-termism among active fund managers. Third, the rise of smart beta strategies is explained and how these approaches are now coming together with climate and other sustainability considerations to give rise to 'smart sustainability'. Fourth and finally, active ownership strategies are considered with respect to investor–corporate engagement. This important final section considers the role of universal investors, such as pension funds and sovereign wealth funds that are invested across the whole market, who may seek market-wide enhancements in corporate performance and standards, and a potentially important role of indexes in supporting them to drive this agenda.

10.1.1 *Definitions*

We note that the terms 'benchmark' and 'index' are sometimes used interchangeably in common parlance. To be precise an 'index' is simply a way of measuring market changes across more than one underlying security or financial instrument selected or weighted according to objective rules. It includes what are referred to as 'benchmark indexes', sometimes abbreviated to 'benchmarks',[1] that are typically used to provide a measure of broad market performance and to measure relative returns of active funds. An active fund is an investment portfolio where a fund manager decides on the underlying investment holdings by selecting specific shares or securities. This is in contrast with a passive fund where the fund manager needs to closely match the investment returns of a specified index; classically this can be done by holding the underlying securities according to their weights in the index, although there are other approaches to replicating the index returns.

The capital asset pricing model (CAPM) was developed by financial economist and Nobel laureate William Sharpe (1970), where he set out that investment portfolios have two types of risk; first specific risk, form specific securities which is reduced by diversification, and second systematic risks, for example from recessions, interest rates and wars, that cannot be diversified away. The market portfolio, epitomised by index investing, maximises diversification and reduces specific risk.

---

[1] Strictly, a benchmark is just a reference rate of return, it doesn't have to be calculated from an index, although it normally is. Note that precise definitions of Indexes and Benchmarks can be found in the EU Benchmark Regulations: EU Benchmarks Regulation (2016) 1011, 'BMR'. https://eur-lex.europa.eu/legal-content/EN/TXT/PDF/?uri=CELEX:32016R1011&from=EN. The International Organisation of Securities Commissions (IOSCO) defines a benchmark as indices or values that are available to the public, calculated by the application of a formula and used for reference for purposes including measuring the price or performance of a financial instrument.

10.2 THE RISE OF PASSIVE INVESTMENT: PERFORMANCE BENCHMARK TO INVESTMENT STRUCTURE

In 1975 John 'Jack' Bogle started a revolution when he invented what has become known as passive or index investing with the first index mutual fund[2] and set up Vanguard, now one of the largest fund managers in the world, that pioneered this new concept. Before Bogle, indexes had been used only as performance benchmarks, for measuring market return averages.

The first index is thought to be the Dow Jones Transportation Index launched in 1886. It had just eleven transportation stocks including nine railway companies. The index still exists today, now with twenty stocks but containing only one of the original constituents, Union Pacific Corporation. The Dow Jones Industrial Average followed in 1895. Its calculation method is more simplistic than most modern indexes. It takes a simple average of the stock prices whilst modern indexes usually account for the size (total market valuation) of each stock as well as other investability[3] considerations.

The oldest UK stock index that is still in use today is the FTSE All-Share, launched in 1962 as the FT Actuaries All-Share. The index was originally calculated by the Institute and Faculty of Actuaries and published by the *Financial Times* until 1984, when FTSE was set up as a joint venture between the *Financial Times* and the London Stock Exchange;[4] it was then that the FTSE 100 was launched.

The idea that Bogle pioneered was an alternative to stock picking fund managers who would carefully select a portfolio of companies on your behalf. Instead, Bogle's idea was to replicate the

---

[2] It is worth noting the very first index funds were actually set up two years earlier in 1973 by Wells Fargo and American National Bank, but these were only for private institutional clients.

[3] For example, 'free float' that considers the proportion of the company that is available to global investors and 'liquidity' which reflects how easily the stock can be traded.

[4] Hence FTSE: 'FT' for *Financial Times* and 'SE' for Stock Exchange.

average return performance of the equity market. These benchmark indexes were actually quite hard to beat, especially when one accounted for the fees paid to 'active' managers. Bogle's idea was therefore to be 'passive', to invest in an average way across the whole market and to pay the lowest fees possible.

Passive investing over the last forty years has become commonplace amongst pension fund and other large investors. For individual investors in the United States it is also quite common, but it is suggested[5] that this is less so among European investors where financial advisors were more likely, until recent regulatory changes, to recommend active funds which typically paid higher commissions to the advisors.

For many, Bogle is a hero who helped usher in a new way to invest, enabling many people to grow their retirement savings whilst paying lower management fees, giving retirees a potentially better standard of living. For others the growth of passive investing is a worrying development. An argument is made that these investments which neutrally follow the market also follow its more extreme movements – potentially amplifying its bubbles and its crashes.[6]

A further sustainability and climate concern, sometimes raised by environmentalists and others, is that traditional passive investing, based on the broadest standard indexes, gives investment exposure to an economy that still highly values polluting and carbon-intensive industries. Because these indexes neutrally follow the market, they will reflect average price consensus on the value of all companies and, unless explicitly designed to do so, will not discriminate against polluting companies or those in so-called sin sectors such as tobacco and weapons.

---

[5] A new Dawn for Europe's retail ETFs, Euroclear; January 2018, https://www.euroclear.com/newsandinsights/en/Format/Articles/RetailETFs.html.
[6] 'The Future of Asset Management in Europe', Vanguard, 27 September 2018.

10.3   TYRANNY OF THE BENCHMARK:
FREQUENT MEASUREMENT CAN MEAN
A FOCUS ON SHORT-TERM MEASURES

'The tyranny of the benchmark has created an environment where fund managers are less inclined to back businesses or industries for the long-term because they are concerned with the career risk of moving too far away from their benchmark index over shorter time periods' stated Professor John Kay in a report commissioned by the UK government (Kay, 2012).

The concern expressed by Kay reflects a view that in an effort to deliver the best possible returns, asset managers have put an overt focus on the short-term to the potential detriment of long-term returns. This, it is argued, leads to an emphasis on corporate quarterly reporting and short-term financial performance leading to less focus on longer-term strategic considerations. There is also a concern regarding potential trade-offs of short-term financial priorities, over longer-term strategic priorities, which may take more investment and patience before substantive long-term benefits accrue. This applies for the asset manager and the investee company. There is follow-through investor pressure on the management teams of the companies who themselves then prioritise short-term financial management, over longer-term investment and strategy execution. The pressure corporate management teams feel under from their investors for short-term results is well documented (Graham et al., 2005, 2006; Barton et al., 2017).

The rationale for this predicament is that to ensure they (the asset owners e.g. pension funds) are using the best possible investment managers and investment strategies, the asset owners frequently re-assess the asset managers against average market returns, reflected in the selected performance benchmark. The psychology is that if the fund is performing badly, they can make a decision to get out sooner rather than later. However, the academic evidence and retrospective performance statistics[7] suggest otherwise, that even the best asset managers may have long periods of underperformance.

The debate over how to incentivise long-term investment is closely aligned with sustainable investment. ESG considerations typically play out over longer time periods. For example; investing in staff training and development, redesigning industrial processes to be less polluting and more carbon-efficient, or even implementing better governance controls and changing corporate culture, all require upfront capital costs and take time before they deliver business benefits.

These concerns are very serious, but blaming benchmark indexes for the woes of short-termism would be akin to the bad workman blaming his tools.[8] Benchmarks are informational constructs aiming to mirror the market; they provide a ruler that can approximate what the total market returns have been over a specified period. How frequently they are used to measure relative fund performance, and how that information is used, is down to the investor.

Some asset owners are experimenting with new ways of assigning and incentivising longer-term-orientated asset manager mandates. This can include less frequent performance reviews with more focus on investment rationale/philosophy with the managers explaining how they expect their investment strategies to play out in different market cycles, conditions and scenarios.

---

[7] Kaplan and Kowara (2019), Harvey and Liu (2016), and Morningstar; Even the Best Funds Underperform. 23 March 2019. www.morningstar.co.uk/uk/news/166104/even-the-best-funds-underperform.aspx.

[8] It is perhaps also worth noting that before indexes became popular, fund managers were measured against the 'consensus', or fund manager average performance. This suggests that the indexes are not the issue, more an embedded desire by managers not to deviate too far from consensus. Further, any overemphasis of short-term financial management over long-term considerations would be driven by active managers deciding whether to buy or sell securities in particular companies. Traditional passive index funds would simply aim to mirror the market which was not pricing long-term sustainability measures effectively.

Some investors are moving to absolute return benchmarks[9] and there is also a growing use of either alternative or 'secondary' benchmarks which are designed to better reflect the investment strategy of the fund manager. An example could be an active fund manager focussing on 'clean tech' or environmental solution companies. Comparison with a usual market benchmark would mainly show how clean tech companies are performing, whilst being benchmarked against a more specialist environmental technology index[10] would assess the manager's skill at beating the performance of the clean tech market. A simpler approach is that, if certain companies or sectors (e.g. fossil fuel companies) are to be excluded by the active manager, they could also be excluded from the performance benchmark (it is nowadays relatively straightforward to select such benchmarks or have custom ones created).

Whatever the choice of performance benchmark, it is important to consider what approach to using it, including frequency of reference, is best reflective of the investment beliefs and strategy of the investor and the underlying asset owners. A benchmark itself does not in itself promote 'short-termism', it's just a measurement tool. But how it is selected and applied needs careful consideration.

10.4 SMART BETA AND SUSTAINABILITY TO ENHANCE INVESTING

10.4.1 The Rise of Smart Beta

The dot-com bubble spectacularly burst in 2000 and investors were hit hard including those in passive funds. The previous valuation of technology stocks became untenable and the market exuberance pushing the value of these companies ever higher came to a sudden end. Passive index funds, by representing the market value of the

---

[9] An absolute return benchmark would typically be just a fixed figure, for example, 5 per cent return per annum.

[10] An example is the Jupiter Ecology fund which invests in environmental solution companies and uses two benchmarks: both the FTSE Environmental Technology 100 index as a benchmark for its investment strategy and the IA Global as its broader market-wide benchmark.

companies, simply followed the bubble up then down. Passive investors in broad market index funds such as the S&P 500, FTSE All-World or MSCI World initially benefitted by generating high returns from their growing exposure to technology firms, but faced losses for three years after the bubble burst. For example, the S&P 500 lost 10 per cent in 2000, a further 13 per cent in 2001 and another 23 per cent in 2002.[11] This experience was important in the rise of a new investment approach, that now encompasses a range of different methodologies, referred to as 'smart beta'[12] and 'factor-investing'.

Active managers have always carefully considered certain financial ratios to inform their investment decisions such as price-to-earnings (P/E). At the height of the dot-com bubble, some active investors had avoided the most overvalued stocks because their P/E ratios were so spectacularly high. This meant that as markets went up, cautious active investors may not have captured as high a return as passive investors or indeed less-discerning active asset managers, but they were later rewarded when markets crashed because they had fewer investments in the most overvalued stocks that fell the furthest. Because the avoidance of investments in potentially overvalued stocks could be based on the application of financial ratios, such as P/E, there was a potentially neat fit with index investing which is essentially the application of clear rules to select and weight securities.[13] This gave support to the rise of new types of indexes using company financials and 'fundamentals' – giving a selection or weight preference to certain companies. These fundamentals could include, for example, 'value' stocks which can be determined by lower P/E or other financial ratios and fundamentals. An early example of such an

---

[11] www.macrotrends.net/2324/sp-500-historical-chart-data.

[12] Beta is generally used to refer to the returns on the market as a whole, whilst Alpha applies to uncorrelated returns which can potentially be associated with active manager skill. Smart beta implies improving on the market return through application of factors, but not going fully active in search of Alpha.

[13] As the application of standard market capitalisation benchmarks as passive structures can amplify the herding of the market, the application of anything that moves the company weights away from price or market cap will reduce this.

index was FTSE RAFI, a joint partnership, starting in 2005, between the index company FTSE and the firm Research Affiliates who designed certain formulas based on consistent application of each stock's fundamental and financial data.

A huge variety of other indexes followed, using other financial and fundamental stock ratios. Initially these modified company weights to address perceived concentration and herding concerns and a second wave then aimed to more explicitly target exposure to specific 'risk-premia' factors such as volatility, momentum, quality and yield, sometimes in combination. This is what is loosely referred to as 'smart beta', ultimately aiming to achieve better risk-adjusted investment returns building on Harry Markowitz's modern portfolio theory and the efficient market hypothesis (Markowitz, 1952).

10.4.2   The Rise of ESG Indexes

With entirely separate origins to the rise of smart beta there was also a parallel rise of ethical, sustainable and green-themed indexes; also known as 'ESG' indexes standing for environmental, social and governance. These started in the United States with the Domini 400 Social Index launched in 1990 by the investment advisor Amy Domini. It captures 400 of the most socially responsible US-listed companies (now the MSCI KLD 400 Index). There followed in 1999 the ET50 capturing the stock price performance of the fifty largest environmental technology companies globally. This index was created by UK-based Impax Asset Management and is now the FTSE ET50. Also, in 1999, there was the launch of the Dow Jones Sustainability Index and shortly after that the FTSE4Good Global Index Series in 2001.

The origins and data for these early ESG indexes were from specialist fund managers and boutique research providers, sometimes in partnership with large index players. These indexes now, however, are frequently calculated by the major index providers. The three largest[14] global index companies FTSE Russell, MSCI and S&P Dow

---

[14] *Financial Times*, 19 May 2019, 'Index companies to feel the chill of asset managers' fund war'.

Jones now each calculate a wide variety of different types of ESG indexes and each has acquired specialist boutique ESG research providers.

The first ESG indexes were used to create ethical funds targeting retail clients but were rarely used by institutional investors. In 2006 when the UN-backed Principles for Responsible Investment (PRI) was set up,[15] the market for ESG data and indexes was minimal, and consequently only one of the index companies, FTSE, was a founding member. MSCI joined four years later in 2010 and S&P Global in 2012. The PRI is a global investor association and has promoted the concept of integrating ESG into institutional investment through asset owners like pension funds requiring this of their asset managers and service providers. At first the integration of ESG considerations into investment was through active asset management where ESG insights were used to influence the selection of securities. The incorporation, or integration of ESG considerations into passive asset management, until recently, was focussed only on how effectively the asset manager voted the stocks in the index funds (in relation on ESG topics) and how they engaged with the management of investee companies on these issues. The actual indexes used for these funds were standard (non-ESG) index funds. The incorporation of detailed ESG methodologies into the design of indexes, for use by large institutional investors, as part of their main passive equity portfolios started from the mid-2010s onwards.[16]

The range of ESG methodologies applied to indexes is not dissimilar to those used in active funds too. It is important to consider (a) the type of ESG data being used and (b) how it is being applied to determine, or weight, the securities in the index. More information on

---

[15] The PRI is a United Nations-backed global investor association that promotes the integration of ESG into investments.

[16] It is worth noting that more simple exclusions, most obviously tobacco, but also others, had been applied as negative screens in index funds by large pension funds like CalPERS (California Public Employees' Retirement System) from a much earlier period, for CalPERS since 2001.

ESG methodologies is given in Boxes 10.1 and 10.2. A further area worth exploring, at least briefly, is the role of regulation which is covered in Box 10.3.

BOX 10.1   **ESG data types**

For simplicity we will focus on corporate data, relevant for both equities and corporate bonds, rather than, for example, country-level data relevant for government bonds. The type of corporate data being used can include both what the company sells and the company's conduct.

Some products or services that a company produces can have negative societal impacts such as tobacco, gambling, weapons, fossil fuels, whilst others can have positive societal/environmental impacts such as 'clean tech' companies. This type of data can be simple binary information covering any involvement/non-involvement, or can cover percentage of total revenues derived from those products.

Corporate conduct and operational practices need to be assessed in a different manner. This includes a broad variety of ESG themes such as corporate governance, labour standards with respect to direct staff and in suppliers and environmental performance of factories and supply chains. Further operational conduct areas also include health and safety, relations with local communities, anti-corruption, risk management and tax transparency. This data can also be binary, for example an anti-corruption indicator could be whether the company has a public whistle-blowing policy, whilst other conduct data can be quantitative annual data such as number of staff and contractor fatalities or tonnes of CO_2 equivalent greenhouse gas emissions.

Given the breadth of different themes, types of data used and of course how they are aggregated including which specific issues are considered most material for a given company, it is unsurprising that overall ESG ratings or scores vary considerably by ESG data provider.

i Inside-out versus Outside-in Data
The sources of the data also vary. Much corporate ESG data comes from publicly reported sources such as corporate annual reports and

BOX 10.1   **(cont.)**

sustainability reports. This can sometimes be called 'inside-out' data, meaning this is the inside data being provided by the companies for external use. There are inevitable questions on the quality and bias in information reported, although some companies do apply external verification to certain data points they report. Some companies, however, do not report relevant data or information at all and this can be treated in different ways. There can be a reduction in score for lack of transparency and/or because there is a doubt over whether appropriate policies exist. Another approach is to estimate the missing data. For some variables like carbon equivalent greenhouse gas emissions data, a whole market exists in different methodologies to estimate this missing data.

Outside-in data is information about a company gleaned from external sources. This can cover information on controversies from the media, regulators and non-governmental organisations including actual, potential and alleged breaches of national laws, and international standards or treaties. There are also increasing numbers of so-called big-data or artificial intelligence approaches that search for online sentiments about a company from a variety of external sources.

ii Raw versus Modelled and Processed Data
Raw data can be considered here to be the direct information collected related to individually defined data points that may be binary, discrete or continuous variables. To make the data set more meaningful, useful to apply or to provide investment insights, they can be modelled or processed together with other data types. This can include modelling to complete missing data, as outlined above. Aggregated ESG scores or ratings apply models in their calculation as they require a variety of different data types to be combined which will require the consideration of the relative importance of different raw data types (often referred to as indicators). This can also include scoring companies against relevant peers, for example industry, regional or country peer groups.

BOX 10.1 **(cont.)**

There can also be the application of ratios using ESG indicators and
financial measures, for example, when considering the 'carbon
intensity' of a company then a common measure is the company's
revenues divided by tonnes of carbon emissions[17] to give the number of
tonnes of emissions per million dollars of revenue generated. More
complex models can also be generated, for example, to estimate how
much of the company's market value may be at risk from potential
future costs associated with certain ESG attributes, such as higher
carbon costs under different climate scenarios. There are also a variety
of models being developed to calculate the carbon performance
associated with a specific company, and its industrial sector, relative to
what is required to achieve keeping average increases in global
temperatures to below 2°C; however depending on a variety of
assumptions applied in these models the results will be highly variable.

iii Debate over Variation between Different ESG Ratings and Scores
There has been concern raised in the media and in publications (e.g.
Mackintosh, 2019) over the variations in ESG ratings by different
providers. Given the vast variety of different data types, and differing
views on the relative importance of different ESG themes when
assessing different companies, it is natural to find widely differing
outcomes from different ESG providers. Those wanting simple
methods or just answers can find the variation in ESG ratings and
scores bewildering. Instead of considering companies as simply
'sustainable' or 'unsustainable' the focus needs to be on the underlying
data so as to be able to judge corporate performance in multiple
dimensions and this requires full transparency of assessment
methodologies. It is important to understand the underlying rationale
for differing assessments – these differences add richness, depth and
provision of choice for the investment community, in the same way
that the range of indexes and funds do.

---

[17] 'Carbon emissions' is shorthand for carbon dioxide equivalent greenhouse gas
(GHG) emissions. There are three different Scopes defined under the GHG Protocol,
first published by the WRI and WBCSD in 2001.

BOX 10.2 **How ESG data is applied in the index design**

Depending on the objectives of the index, ESG data can be applied into the design in a variety of ways.

i Exclusion or Inclusion Applying 'Standard' Index Constituent Weights
The approach can be a very simple one, in which certain defined thresholds lead to exclusion or addition in the index of constituent stocks, bonds or other securities as appropriate. This could include exclusionary indexes applying negative screens, where for example tobacco companies are excluded. It also includes indexes where inclusion rules were applied, for example where companies with high ESG ratings are included. The Dow Jones Sustainability World Index includes the top 10 per cent of companies within a sector and country peer group. The FTSE4Good Global index includes companies with an ESG rating above a specified threshold. Both these latter two indexes apply weights to each stock according to their market capitalisation as applied to the equivalent standard underlying indexes such as the FTSE All-World.

ii Tilting the Index Constituent Weights
Another approach is to tilt individual security weights (i.e. at company level for stock indexes) based on their ESG data. There is normally a starting or standard index such as the MSCI World or FTSE All-World Index and the weight changes are applied to its constituent parts. The starting weight will typically be the market capitalisation basis that would be applied in the underlying index. The weight of that company would then be increased if the ESG data are positive, and the weight of stock would be decreased if the ESG data are negative (this could be on a relative or absolute basis). The term overweight would be used if the stock has a higher weight than in the starting index and underweight if it has a lower weight than in the starting index.

BOX 10.2   **(cont.)**

The most common tilted indexes have been climate adjusted where factors such as emissions over revenue, on a sector–peer basis, are used as the tilt factor. The concept is that the more carbon-efficient companies in each peer group are overweighted, whilst those that are more inefficient are underweighted.

iii Optimisation Approaches (Instead of Peer Group Tilting)
Instead of applying tilts, another option is 'optimisation', in which a statistical model is applied that seeks to achieve the desired exposure to a particular characteristic, which could be an ESG or risk-premia characteristic, whilst generating as similar returns as possible to the starting index, which is described as low-tracking error versus returns of the starting index. This can be attractive for some investors, but a criticism has been the 'black box' of optimisation, that is the lack of transparency on why particular stocks are over- or underweighted. The type of engagement described in the last section of this chapter is potentially more difficult with optimisation as it is hard to explain to constituent companies in the index why they are over- or underweighted.

BOX 10.3   **Index regulation**

Much of the relevant regulatory developments have been focussed on sources of ESG data and reporting, with regulators around the world introducing different forms of corporate reporting requirements. As the inputs for ESG and climate indexes this is of significant importance. The quality of the indexes is directly proportional to the quality of the input data. Efforts to improve the availability, reliability and consistency of such data improves the quality of data, analytics and indexes available to investors.

There is a balance to be struck in relation to corporate reporting burdens, although efforts to make reporting frameworks more

BOX 10.3   (cont.)

consistent globally helps both investors and companies; investors have comparable data from companies operating in different countries, and companies operating globally don't have multiple different requirements.

The EU's High-Level Expert Group (HLEG) on Sustainable Finance made recommendations (European Commission (2018a)) to the EU across a number of areas including benchmarks, particularly including a call for improved transparency on sustainability across active and passive funds to aid investor ability to distinguish between them.

Given the level of innovation and change going on in the design of such indexes, it is important that the market can compare index methodologies, the resulting index designs and the constituents. Climate indexes, in particular due to the market focus on this theme, are changing and evolving, becoming increasingly sophisticated over time. They vary considerably in both data types and how the data is applied in the index design.

Through the European Union's Action Plan on Financing Sustainable Growth (European Commission (2018b) there has been much work including on disclosure, taxonomy, investor duties and benchmarks that was inspired by the 2018 HLEG recommendations. As this chapter is being written, benchmark regulations are being finalised that include prescriptive methodological designs for 'EU Climate Transition Benchmarks' and 'EU Paris Aligned Benchmarks', as well as ESG disclosure requirements. Given the rapid evolutionary trajectory of these indexes, and the fierce competition between providers, it will be interesting to see how the introduction of the new EU-designated indexes will affect the market.

10.4.3   *The Rise of Smart Sustainability Indexes*

As ESG data, especially carbon data from around 2010,[18] started to get used in tilt or optimisation indexes (see Box 10.2) in a similar manner

---

[18] In 2010, FTSE and Trucost (now part of S&P Global) created a carbon-efficient index that was tracked by Legal and General Investment Management in which BT

to risk-premia factors, it was perhaps just a matter of time before these data types started to be used in combination.

Two growing trends in passive investing – smart beta and ESG – with completely separate origins began to come together, particularly as institutional investors started to see applying ESG as being consistent with fiduciary duty (see Chapter 8).

The main motivation among investors for integrating ESG is 'risk management':[19] investment risk linked to climate change is the core rationale for applying climate considerations into passive portfolio index design. At the same time different smart beta strategies are also being selected by institutional investors that align with their investment beliefs on what will give them the best risk-adjusted returns over relevant periods of time, which can be very long-term. They may, for example, prefer strategies that focus on value, quality, smaller size or low volatility. These preferences can easily be combined with ESG preferences and there can be a natural fit.

An example could be combining measures of ESG including climate alongside measures of value. A company would be treated as a 'value' stock if it appears undervalued by the market given relatively strong fundamental financials (e.g. low P/E ratio), but if it has high carbon exposure[20] then part of its lower valuation may be reflecting this. A smart beta value investment approach in this scenario would lead an increased weights of high carbon stocks. This can be reversed by applying climate factors alongside value, whereby companies in the index get overweighted or underweighted according to

Pension Fund made a £100mn allocation. More substantial allocations were later made to such carbon-tilted indexes later around 2014 when MSCI launched a range of low carbon indexes.

[19]   CFA Institute Survey 2017 and 2015. www.cfainstitute.org/-/media/documents/ survey/esg-survey-report-2017.ashx.

[20]   For example, in terms of fossil fuel reserves or coal-powered energy generation, or through being a heavy energy consumer; potentially exposed to high energy and carbon costs in future scenarios where governments introduce increasing carbon penalties, and through consumer and market demand becoming more climate aware and discerning.

BOX 10.4   **Smart sustainability case study**

HSBC UK Pension Fund had investment beliefs on certain risk-premia factors, namely value, quality, size and volatility and at the same time also had investment beliefs on climate risk. They felt that for the youngest members in their pension fund, who had the longest time period to go before they would access the pension, climate risk was particularly pertinent. Therefore they chose the default option for their defined benefit equity portfolio to be a smart sustainability index that combined four of the usual smart beta factors, with three climate parameters: carbon intensity (which was industry neutral, and normalised by revenues), carbon reserves (future emissions from fossil fuel reserves normalised by market value) and green revenues (i.e. revenues from green products and services as a percentage of total revenues). Note that the latter two of these applied only to a subset of the companies as most companies had no carbon reserves and no green revenues. Company weights in the starting index were tilted up and down by these seven parameters. Shortly later, Merseyside Pension Fund and then LGPS Central funds also allocated core equity portfolios to very similar index funds, the only difference being that they added one other additional factor, momentum.

both of these themes.[21] In such a case, companies that are the most carbon efficient[22] and highest value would be most overweighted, whilst the reverse would be most underweighted. See Box 10.4 for

---

[21] In this scenario, the investor may want to go further than just reversing the potential overweighting of carbon stocks from the value tilt. If the investor's belief was that the market was not adequately pricing in the risk of escalating future carbon costs, then the tilts applied could be stronger in order to reduce the total index carbon exposure. This would tilt further away from high carbon stocks than the standard market-weighted index.

[22] Carbon efficiency can be defined in a number of ways including, but not limited to, annual operational carbon emissions normalised by annual revenues (or other normalising factor) or for fossil fuel companies then the total theoretical emissions if all of the companies coal, oil or gas reserves were combusted, normalised by a valuation statistic, such as market capitalisation.

the example of HSBC Pension Fund, Merseyside and LGPS Central pension funds and how they have approached this.

This concept of 'smart sustainability' demonstrates how ESG integration can be applied to passive investments in a manner that is consistent with active asset management. The next section will explore the frontier at which ESG indexes may help asset owners to catalyse powerful changes in corporate practices globally.

10.5   THEORY OF CHANGE; UNIVERSAL OWNERS AND THE POWER OF ALIGNING ASSET RE-ALLOCATION AND SHAREHOLDER ENGAGEMENT

Many of the world's largest asset owners are realising that, as universal investors, they can play a powerful stewardship role and may be able to positively influence the trajectory of the global economy. The following is a quote from Hiro Mizuno, the former Chief Investment Officer of GPIF, the Japanese government pension fund which owns around 8 per cent of all Japanese-listed companies and has $1.3trn in assets, making it the largest pension fund in the world.

> What are the fundamental traits of an asset owner? One is universal ownership. The second one, at least for us, is cross-generational investment. Those that are sceptical about the investment relevance of ESG are probably not thinking long-term enough. Passive [investment] is the most important for engaging on long-term issues. We really count on the use of benchmark; we try to affect the whole system, so we need to affect the benchmark. We are shifting the money from the conventional market-based benchmarks to these ESG weighted indexes.[23]

GPIF is not alone in moving assets from conventional benchmarks towards those that capture climate and other ESG

---

[23] Hiro Mizuno, CIO GPIF, speaking at the London Stock Exchange Group 'Climate and Sustainability Summit' during New York Climate Week in September 2019.

characteristics. Part of the rationale is how these types of indexes can support stewardship and issuer engagement.

In many asset managers, there is a team that conducts engagement and voting that are separate from the portfolio management teams that select and invest in securities for the funds. Although there is interaction between the teams, the experience from investee companies is that there can be a disconnect, and it's unclear how their performance in ESG areas will lead to greater investment in their company.

Transparent climate or ESG indexes, when there is associated dialogue and engagement with issuers, enables investment and engagement to be entirely aligned. As a company's performance in relevant ESG areas improve they achieve inclusion in the index, or for tilted indexes, their weight in the index increases. This means an improvement in ESG practices leads directly and transparently to increased investment flows into the company's securities. This provides a very impactful way to engage companies at scale across the whole market in a consistent manner. They can see the very direct implications of achieving the changes desired by investors in terms of their index inclusion, index weight and ultimately through investment flows.

This is a growing trend across many pension funds worldwide. There is also increasing collaboration between asset owners and index providers to create potentially powerful tools for corporate engagement.

To better understand this approach two examples are worth exploring. The first examines GPIF's approach, and the second considers the Transition Pathway Initiative, which forms part of a mammoth-scale collaborative engagement effort called 'Climate Action 100+'.

GPIF, as noted in the quote above, has been slowly moving away from standard market benchmarks to follow ESG indexes. As universal investors they wish to influence corporate standards across the whole market, as their investment belief is that higher corporate sustainability standards will lead to more stable global economic development and growth, which in turn will lead to better long-term (inter-generational) investment returns. The ESG indexes they have chosen are a tool to achieve this, and they therefore also carefully monitor and report on the progress being made in catalysing improvements in corporate standards[24] linked to the changes companies are making to achieve inclusion or increased weight in these indexes.

The Transition Pathway Initiative is a global asset owner-led initiative which assesses company preparedness for the low carbon economy. It categorises companies in a very simple and transparent manner based on their climate strategies and management quality from zero (unaware) to level four (strategic assessment), and on their climate performance in relation to what is required to achieve the goals of the Paris climate agreement, and how they stack up against competitors. Part of the concept is that investors have a consistent basis on which they can all positively engage the management and boards of companies to encourage them to take relevant steps to improve their practices in relation to climate change. This forms a core part of Climate Action 100+ which by summer 2020 was already backed by 450 investors with US$40trn in assets under management. They describe themselves as 'an investor initiative to ensure the world's largest corporate greenhouse gas emitters take necessary action on climate change. The companies include 100 "systemically important emitters", accounting for two-thirds of annual global industrial emissions, alongside more than 60 others with significant opportunity to drive the clean energy transition.'[25]

For the mining and for the oil and gas sectors, climate change is now a core part of their engagement with the investment community. TPI and CA 100+ have been credited with catalysing changes at some of the largest companies in the world: Shell, where the boards agreed to tie climate strategy to executive remuneration,[26] and Glencore, which agreed to cap its coal production and disclose its long-term

[24] GPIF ESG Report (2018).   [25] www.climateaction100.org.
[26] BBC, 3 December 2018, www.bbc.co.uk/news/business-46424830.

trajectory for emission reductions.[27] These changes lead directly to improved climate scores for the companies based on defined criteria; this creates milestones and a clear basis for collaborative engagement.

Already TPI has been used extensively to inform investor engagement with companies but the next stage is to bring this into the design of indexes for passive investment strategies. The Church of England Pensions Board has announced[28] that it intends to build the TPI data into its equity index design. They see this as a powerful way to align their investment priorities and their corporate engagement strategy to drive and catalyse change in corporate practices. Companies can understand that if they respond to engagement and improve their TPI scores, the investment will follow because their weight in the index fund increases as a direct consequence.

This is true impact investing: helping achieve the goals of the Paris agreement on climate change through supporting change in those companies who have the greatest contributions to make in achieving the large-scale emission reductions needed.

Indexes, like other tools, can be used poorly, or in a manner that is short-sighted. However, in the right hands, and if used in an effective way, indexes can be an enabler for investors wishing to invest more sustainably. They represent one of the most powerful and potent levers available to investors to catalyse market-wide changes across the economy to achieve sustainable economic development: Passive investors can deliver real world impact through embedded engagement with market-wide scale.

REFERENCES

Barton, B., Manyika, J., Koller, T., Palter, R. and Godsall, J. (2017), 'Measuring the Economic Impact of Short-Termism'. McKinsey Global Institute Discussion

---

[27] Pensions and Investments, 20 February 2019, www.pionline.com/article/20190220/ONLINE/190229981/glencore-agrees-to-investor-demands-for-climate-change-action.

[28] Pensions Age, 4 July 2018, www.pensionsage.com/pa/Church-of-England-Pensions-Board-calls-for-low-carbon-index.php.

Paper. www.mckinsey.com/~/media/mckinsey/featured insights/Long term Capitalism/Where companies with a long term view outperform their peers/ MGI-Measuring-the-economic-impact-of-short-termism.ashx.

European Commission (2018a), 'Final Report of the High-Level Expert Group on Sustainable Finance'. https://ec.europa.eu/info/publications/180131-sustain able-finance-report_en.

European Commission (2018b), 'Action Plan: Financing Sustainable Growth'. https:// eur-lex.europa.eu/legal-content/EN/TXT/PDF/?uri=CELEX:52018DC0097&from= EN.

GPIF ESG Report (2018), 'For All Generations'. www.gpif.go.jp/en/investment/ 190905_Esg_Report.pdf.

Graham, J. R., Harvey, C. and Rajgopal, S. (2005), 'The Economic Implications of Corporate Financial Reporting', *Journal of Accounting and Economics* 40(1–3) 3–73. https://EconPapers.repec.org/RePEc:eee:jaecon:v:40:y:2005:i:1-3:p:3-73.

Graham, J. R., Harvey, C. and Rajgopal, S. (2006), 'Value Destruction and the Financial Reporting Decisions', *Financial Analysts Journal* 62(6), 27–39.

Harvey, R. H. and Liu, Y. (2016) 'Does Scale Impact Skill?', Duke I&E Research Paper No. 2016-46. https://papers.ssrn.com/sol3/papers.cfm?abstract_id=2872385.

Kaplan, P. and Kowara, M. (2019) 'Are Relative Performance Measures Useless?', *The Journal of Investing* 28(4), 83–93.

Kay, J. (2012) 'The Kay Review of UK Equity Markets and Long-Term Decision Making', Interim Report. Department for Business, Innovation and Skills. https:// assets.publishing.service.gov.uk/government/uploads/system/uploads/attachment_ data/file/31544/12-631-kay-review-of-equity-markets-interim-report.pdf and Final Report: https://assets.publishing.service.gov.uk/government/uploads/system/ uploads/attachment_data/file/253454/bis-12-917-kay-review-of-equity-markets-final-report.pdf.

Mackintosh, J. (2019) 'A Users Guide to the ESG Confusion', *Wall Street Journal*, 19 November 2019. www.wsj.com/articles/a-users-guide-to-the-esg-confusion-11573563604.

Markowitz, Harry M. (1952), 'Portfolio Selection', *Journal of Finance*, March, 7(1), 77–91.

Sharpe, S. (1970), *Portfolio Theory and Capital Markets*. New York: McGraw-Hill Education.

11 Financing a Just Transition

How to Connect the Environmental and Social Dimensions of Structural Change

Nick Robins

11.1 INTRODUCTION[1]

Climate change is arguably one of the greatest injustices in history, given the projected extent and duration of its negative impacts on current and future generations. Climate disruption already harms the lives of billions and these impacts will intensify and extend for centuries into the future, particularly if the rise in temperature is not capped at well below 2°C and ideally 1.5°C above pre-industrial levels, the goal of the Paris Agreement. Many of those most affected by climate change live in poverty and have contributed least to its causation. It is therefore a matter of fundamental global justice to deliver the goals of the Paris Agreement and protect current and future generations. More than this, the activities that contribute to climate change can lead to many other injustices, notably the immense health implications of air pollution from fossil fuel combustion as well as the impacts on vulnerable communities from deforestation and unsustainable land use. For Pope Francis, it is clear that when faced with the climate emergency, 'we must take action accordingly, in order to avoid perpetrating a brutal act of injustice towards the poor and future generations' (O'Kane, 2019).

As a result, the transition to a climate-resilient, net zero economy is essential for the delivery of inclusive economic development

[1] This chapter draws on the findings of the Investing in a Just Transition initiative at the Grantham Research Institute, which involves a number of partner organisations. The author would like to particularly thank the following for their insights and contributions which have informed this chapter: Sharan Burrow, Vonda Brunsting, William Irwin, Fiona Reynolds, Bettina Reinboth, James Rydge, Alison Tait, Sophia Tickell and David Wood.

in the twenty-first century. The prize is not just to minimise the human damage of climate change, but also to design the transition so that it tackles entrenched poverty and rising inequality. To do this, the transition itself needs to be just and achieved in ways that are fair for all. It is in this context that the 2015 Paris Agreement states that governments should 'take into account the imperatives of a just transition of the workforce and the creation of decent work and quality jobs in accordance with nationally defined development priorities' (United Nations, 2015). Three years later at the COP24 UN climate conference in 2018, fifty-three countries (including all of the members of the European Union) signed the Just Transition Declaration, which recognised the need to factor in the needs of workers and communities to build public support for a rapid shift to a zero-carbon economy.

The just transition is no longer simply an issue for international climate negotiations, however. Fears about the downside consequences for workers and consumers of the transition have risen to the top of the political agenda in a number of countries. In 2017, among the many reasons given by President Trump for withdrawing from the Paris Agreement was a claim that compliance would cost the US millions of jobs, including in the coal industry. According to a fact-check conducted by Germany's Environment Ministry, President Trump's assertions on job losses were 'doubtful and misleading' (Federal Ministry for the Environment, Nature Conservation and Nuclear Safety, 2017). In November 2018, the Gilets Jaunes ('yellow vest') protests started in response to fuel tax increases designed to tackle climate change on account of the impact on middle- and low-income consumers.

Yet, the just transition is also a key demand of the youth climate strikers led by Greta Thunberg as well as the Extinction Rebellion movement. It is a core feature of plans for a radical Green New Deal on both sides of the Atlantic (Pettifor, 2019). And it is rising up the sustainable finance agenda, with institutional investors, commercial banks and development banks as well as policy makers and regulators recognising the importance of connecting the environmental and social dimensions of the transition. Indeed, it was the EU's High-Level Expert Group (HLEG) which was one of the first to make the links between responses to climate change and the societal consequences, arguing in its final report that:

> Sustainable finance has a key role to play in delivering a 'just transition', and in making sure that the shift away from high-carbon, resource-intensive and polluting sectors produces net benefits for workers and communities. This could be achieved, for example, by working with local authorities, communities and others to develop investable pipelines of green assets (such as property and infrastructure) in vulnerable regions.
>
> *(European Commission, 2018)*

This chapter explores how financial institutions and policy makers can support the just transition. It first sets out the scope of the just transition and then looks at the implications for different financial actors. It concludes by identifying key priorities for the EU's sustainable finance strategy to make the just transition a reality in the 2020s.

11.2 SCOPING THE JUST TRANSITION

It is increasingly clear that the twin crises of climate change and inequality need to be managed and resolved as one. This is the agenda of the just transition, which is included in the Paris Agreement to ensure that the interests of workers and communities are respected in the shift to a net zero and resilient economy. This fits as part of the wider climate justice agenda, which places the human rights of current and future generations at the heart of actions needed to overcome the climate and environmental emergency. Without a just transition, efforts to accelerate climate action could stall or fall short of their potential.

This agenda is of core relevance to banks and institutional investors, who manage the savings of hundreds of millions of citizens across the world. The integration of ESG factors is being mainstreamed across the banking and investment sectors to manage risk, respond to customer demand and align portfolios with societal goals. The just transition provides connective tissue between the environmental and social dimensions of the climate crisis – and helps to place a spotlight on the human aspects of this structural shift, aspects which have often been missing in climate policy and financial sector responses to date. For example, the disclosure recommendations of the TCFD contains little on the workplace dimensions of corporate strategy, such as human capital formation and skills, employee engagement, corporate restructuring and labour rights.

Managed well, the net zero transition will not only help to mitigate and largely prevent the immense human and economic costs of climate disruption, it could also generate net new jobs and sustainable, inclusive growth now and in the future. This could help to maintain decent employment and thriving communities over the coming decades. 'Earlier episodes of innovation-led structural change teach us that it can be a powerful engine for job creation, productivity improvements and growth,' argued Sam Fankhauser, Friedel Sehlleier and Nick Stern a decade ago, concluding that 'if this evidence is right, climate change has the potential to create many more jobs than it destroys in the long run' (Fankhauser et al., 2008; see also Bowen, 2012). More recent assessments have confirmed this. In its 2017 Investing in Climate, Investing in Growth report, the OECD estimated that a decisive transition package that avoids climate damage could boost long-run output by 5 per cent on average across the G20 economies by 2050 (OECD, 2017). However, these benefits will not happen automatically. Policies are needed to ensure that jobs and workers in the new low-carbon economy have working conditions that are at least as good, or better, as those in the old high-carbon industries.

Managed poorly, however, countries and regions could see not only 'stranded assets' but also 'stranded workers' and 'stranded communities' to use the words of Sharan Burrow, General Secretary of the International Trade Union Confederation (see Burrow, 2017). Trade unions were among the first to call for a just transition: one that involves environmental regeneration as well as decent work, social inclusion and poverty eradication. The term originates from the US chemical industry which was facing in the 1990s the challenge of overcoming toxic pollution. 'The basis for just transition is the simple principle of equity', argued Les Leopold of the Labor Institute at the time (Labor Network for Sustainability and Strategic Practice, 2016). Past experience of deindustrialisation in many parts of the world highlights the importance of looking beyond the direct employment impacts to understand the wider ecosystem of prosperity in affected regions. Failing to do so could slow or even stall climate progress, while contributing to economic stagnation and political instability.

Economic and climate policies are often assessed against the three principles of effectiveness, efficiency and equity (fairness). By 'effective', we mean that they achieve their aim. By 'efficiency', we mean that they are implemented in the most cost-effective way. And by 'equity', we mean that the costs and benefits are shared fairly across society. This means both shaping the transition, so it brings positive benefits to underserved groups (e.g. by extending access to energy) and also ensuring that those less well-off do not bear a disproportionate share of policy costs (Stern, 2008). In a globalised world, it also means that countries need to consider the cross-border impact of their climate policies. The depth, speed and scale of the global economic transformation needed to meet the Paris climate change targets mean that these issues need to be addressed with foresight. Until the last five years, however, the equity dimension of climate policy lagged far behind.

In the run-up to the Paris Agreement, the International Labour Organization (ILO) released a consensus set of guidelines in 2015 which show how this shift can support the goals of decent work and quality jobs across the full spectrum of government policies, including macro-economic strategy, industrial and regional policy as well as employment, skills and education policies; specific guidelines for financial policy were not included (ILO, 2015). For the ILO, the just transition thus captures a holistic approach:

it is a bridge from where we are today to a future where all jobs are green and decent, poverty is eradicated, and communities are thriving and resilient. More precisely, it is a systemic and whole of economy approach to sustainability. It includes both measures to reduce the impact of job losses and industry phase-out on workers and communities, and measures to produce new, green and decent jobs, sectors and healthy communities.

(quoted in Smith, 2017).

The just transition starts from the perspective of how workers are affected, positively and negatively, by the transition. Numerous studies have been undertaken to evaluate the aggregate implications on job numbers. These are summarised in Table 11.1: the conclusion of the most recent studies is that the transition will deliver a net boost for job creation.

These assessments have little to say, however, about the quality of low-carbon jobs compared with today's existing jobs. Crucially, job losses and change are likely to be concentrated in particular places, not least for resource-intensive sectors such as energy. In addition, the scope of the just transition extends beyond the world of work. Communities will be affected by indirect implications of economic change on local businesses and supply chains. For example, renewable energy may be more decentralised than large fossil fuel power stations. Consumers also face the distributional impacts of climate policies, such as carbon prices. Ultimately, all citizens are affected in terms of the distributional and procedural aspects of the transition.

The just transition is also a whole economy agenda, addressing the upside potential from clean growth as well as managing the downside risks of decarbonisation. It is key that the new 'green jobs' in the renewable sector, for example, deliver decent work and also respect human rights of communities. In addition, many argue that the resilience to the physical shocks of climate change should also be included in the just transition agenda. This is particularly relevant for developing countries, where most of the world's one billion

Table 11.1 *Employment implications of the transition: key findings*

Global Assessments	Region/ Country/ Sector	Low-Carbon Transition Policies	Employment Change
Chateau et al., (2011)	OECD countries	With just transition policies	−0.32% in 2030
Chateau et al., (2011)	OECD countries	No just transition policies	−2.00% in 2030
IRENA (2019)	Global/ energy sector	Energy transition policies only	+2.00% in 2050
New Climate Economy (2018)	Global	Carbon pricing and sector policies only	65 million additional low-carbon jobs, 37 million net additional by 2030
EU (2018)	EU	Policies consistent with 2°C (1.5°C) path – carbon price with revenues used to reduce taxes	Up to 1.3 (2.1) million new jobs compared with baseline by 2050. 0.6% (0.9%) increase in total employment compared with baseline in 2050
Chateau et al., (2018)	OECD and non-OECD	Policies consistent with 2°C (1.5°C) path	0.3% (0.8%) reallocation of jobs (sum of jobs created and destroyed) compared with 20% past reallocation rates across OECD countries
ILO (2018)	Global/ energy, transport and construction sectors	Energy-related policies to achieve 2°C path	24 million additional jobs, 18 million net additional, by 2030

agricultural workers live. Without measures to boost resilience to increased heat stress and natural disasters, income, health and productivity will all fall. Table 11.2 sets out these interlocking relationships. Policy makers and financial institutions investors will need to consider all of these dimensions.

These just transition dimensions are not new: the economy is always in transition. What is striking about the climate transition is that it is largely policy-led – and therefore rightly open to public involvement – and is also on a scale not seen since reconstruction efforts after the Second World War. One of the ways of ensuring public acceptability and accelerating climate action is to ensure that it is inclusive. This means taking account of the distributional consequences so that no one is left behind.

Finally, it's important to recognize that the transition related to climate change is only one of many other transitions currently underway, notably the digital revolution and rise of artificial intelligence (AI). The just transition related to climate policy impacts also needs to simultaneously consider other disruptive economic transitions, as well as recognize the wider environmental emergency facing natural systems. As Nick Stern has remarked:

> We should see the just transition as part of the new story of inclusive, sustainable growth. This is a highly attractive economic model, with strong innovation and growth and able to overcome poverty in an effective and lasting way. But it requires us to manage the process of change in much better ways ... We need to be organising for transitions in the plural including technologies, economic structures, cities and the international division of labour. And we must accelerate the pace of decision-making if we are to respond to the urgency of climate change.

Failure to consider adequately the socio-economic dimensions of emissions reduction and sustainable growth policies is already hindering the pace of the transition. This is reflected at the ballot box, where anti-climate action politicians have come to power partly

Table 11.2 *Setting the scope of the just transition: initial illustrations*

	Workers	Communities	Consumers	Citizens
High-exposure, high-carbon sectors	Ensuring responsible decarbonisation in the fossil fuel energy sector, transport, industry etc.	Responding to the spillover impacts on industrial communities. Revitalising regional economies.	Tackling energy poverty in industrialised countries; ensuring fairness in carbon pricing.	Managing the distributional and participative issues of phasing out fossil fuels (e.g. those unfairly impacted by changes or excluded from decision-making).
Zero-carbon, green sectors	Delivering good green jobs in renewables, building efficiency, EVs and their supply chains (e.g. local jobs, gender dimension).	Building a strong license to operate, empowering community rights (e.g. land rights around renewable energy).	Delivering universal access to sustainable energy, promoting prosumers and citizen-investors.	Managing the distributional and participative issues of 100% zero-carbon energy (e.g. broadening the beneficiaries).
Resilience	Ensuring workers are resilient to heat stress and other physical impacts of climate change to protect well-being, incomes and productivity.	Ensuring communities have resilience plans, including trees, green space, adequate building codes, disaster recovery plans etc.	Ensuring households have access to affordable cooling, to prevent overheating/heat stress.	All citizens to have a voice on resilience measures, ensuring planning is not only directed by central governments and/or vested interests.

Source: Robins and Rydge (2019).

on the basis of claiming to protect vulnerable workers and communities from change. In the words of the UK's Committee on Climate Change (2019), 'if the impact of the move to net-zero emissions on employment and cost of living is not addressed and managed, and if those most affected are not engaged in the debate, there is a significant risk that there will be resistance to change, which could lead the transition to stall'. The Committee concluded that it is critical that the transition is 'fair and perceived to be fair', recommending that the UK government to adopt a strategy to ensure a just transition.

This rapid overview of the just transition agenda allows us to draw out some guiding principles for taking action.

- *Anticipation:* the economy-wide implications of the transition need to be anticipated through careful assessment and scenario planning, so that impacts can be identified ahead of time to enable adjustment. The more time there is to prepare, the more likely the transition will be just and the less disruptive to workers and communities.
- *Empowerment:* many stakeholders will need to be empowered so that they can be actively involved in decision-making that shapes the transition, whether in the workplace, in communities or in key local and national policy processes, making sure that this is open to all in terms of gender, ethnic group, age or income.
- *Capabilities:* The climate economy will involve new sets of skills and capabilities, and a dedicated effort is needed to equip individuals with the technical and other expertise needed to thrive in the transition. This involves fresh approaches to human capital formation by business, trade unions and investors as well as government.
- *Place:* The transition will have profound spatial and place-based dimensions, requiring development of anchor institutions – such as local universities, government agencies utilities and financial institutions – that can help to support community wealth-building at a time of disruption.
- *Investment:* The just transition will require investment from the public and private sectors, notably fiscal support from government and patient capital from development banks as well as targeted lending from commercial banks as well as forceful stewardship from institutional investors.

The next section looks in more detail at this financial dimension.

11.3 FINANCIAL SYSTEM ACTION TO SUPPORT THE JUST TRANSITION

Action to support green and sustainable finance have largely focussed to date on the environmental dimension, addressing issues such as climate risks and low-carbon investment opportunities. To address the just transition, financial strategies need to incorporate the full range of ESG factors. To date, investors, banks and financial policy makers have given insufficient attention to the social consequences of climate change. In a sense, this could be due to an unintended siloing of efforts. Climate change is clearly an environmental issue; the transition, however, is not. Rather it is a process of structural economic, technological and societal change that requires a similarly integrated response from the financial system.

Institutional investors have been the first to respond to this challenge. Launched in February 2018, the *Investing in a Just Transition* initiative is working to identify the role that institutional investors can play in connecting their action on climate change with inclusive development pathways. The initiative is led by the Grantham Research Institute on Climate Change and the Environment at the London School of Economics and Political Science (LSE) and the Initiative for Responsible Investment at the Harvard Kennedy School, working in collaboration with the Principles for Responsible Investment (PRI) and the International Trade Union Confederation (ITUC). The initiative has produced a global guide for investor action, and over 150 institutions with more than US$10trn in assets under management have signed an investor statement on the just transition (PRI, 2019). In addition, the latest Global Investor Statement to Governments on Climate Change, released in September 2019, also highlighted the need for a just transition. In this statement, 515 investors representing well over US$35trn in assets urged the full implementation of the Paris Agreement. Adding that 'it will be important that the benefits of gaining access to cleaner energy sources are shared by all, and that those workers and communities affected by the transition are supported' (Investor Agenda, 2019).

11.3.1 Strategic Motivations

As fiduciaries, investors can make an important contribution to achieving a just transition, as stewards of assets, allocators of capital and as influential voices in public policy. For investors, the just transition provides the framework for connecting climate action with the need for an inclusive economy and sustainable development. The case for investor action rests on five strategic motivations, set out in Figure 11.1.

i. *Broadening the understanding of systemic risks:* Climate change is well understood by investors as a systemic risk to the global economy, undermining the ability of the financial system to deliver long-term returns. There is also growing realisation among investors that they need to be concerned about the systemic risk posed by social inequality (Wood, 2016). One systemic concern raised by the just transition is that failing to take account of the social dimension will give rise to pressures to delay, dilute or abandon climate policy. This will make the shift to a low-carbon economy less likely, thereby placing investors at risk from rising climate costs. Another systemic concern is that the transition could go ahead in a partial and suboptimal fashion, achieved at high social cost, potentially deepening inequality and harming the sustainability of economic growth by increasing fiscal drag.

FIGURE 11.1 Reasons for investor action on the just transition
Source: Robins et al. (2018).

ii. *Reinvigorating fiduciary duty:* The just transition extends the core fiduciary case for action on climate change to include the social dimension. Fiduciaries will need to understand and consider the interests and sustainability preferences of savers and beneficiaries as they relate to both the environmental and social dimensions of the transition. Beneficiaries in specific corporate, sector- or geographically based funds may have additional reasons for seeking a just transition. For example, beneficiaries may need assurance that they will not be in 'stranded pensions', where solvency is put in question by reliance on high-carbon business models and asset allocation.

iii. *Recognising material value drivers:* Moving from the strategic to the portfolio level, the just transition highlights for investors that a siloed analysis of ESG factors is unlikely to generate a full picture of long-term performance. For investors, it will be essential that the assets they hold operate effective systems for human capital management at a time of transformational change in technologies, business models and market demand. To date, human capital management has been absent from most business responses to climate change. The way that companies manage the transition will also have important impacts on their social licence to operate in the wider community. Companies that do not engage with workers and communities or take into account their views face operational, consumer, client and regulatory repercussions. Conversely, companies that manage this well could benefit from better reputations as well as reduced transaction costs.

iv. *Uncovering investment opportunities:* The just transition provides a lens through which investors can identify new investment opportunities and develop investment products that connect environmental and social goals. By incorporating a social dimension, investors can better understand the way in which the transition is disrupting the traditional investment landscape. For example, the shift to decentralised renewables is bringing structural changes to the energy system, with a greater role for community involvement and ownership.

v. *Contributing to societal goals:* Investors clearly need to manage the just transition as it relates to their own beneficiaries, portfolios and systemic risks. But they are also social actors and the just transition provides a framework to contribute to societal ambitions, notably the Paris Agreement and the Sustainable Development Goals (SDGs). Indeed, the just transition provides connective tissue that brings together different SDGs, most notably the goals on climate change (SDG 13) and decent work (SDG 8), showing how the other SDGs support this process.

11.3.2 Areas for Action

Based on these strategic motivations, there are five areas for action through which investors can make the just transition part of their core operating practices. The good news is that investors do not need to reinvent the wheel to address the social dimension of climate change. There are a range of well-tested investor approaches that already exist, set out in Figure 11.2.

a. *Investment strategy:* A growing number of investors have extended their responsible investment and climate change strategies to include a focus on the just transition. In 2018, for example, Italian insurance company Generali released its climate strategy including targets to increase green assets and divest from coal. In addition, it has made a commitment to stakeholder dialogue, stating: 'in countries in which the economy and employment depend heavily on the coal sector, Generali will involve issuers, clients, and other stakeholders through dialogue, monitoring their plans to reduce environmental impacts, the strategy to transition to activities with low environmental impact, and measures envisaged for protecting the community and citizens' (Generali, 2018).

b. *Corporate engagement:* Investors are significantly ramping up their collective engagement with the businesses and assets they own to ensure

FIGURE 11.2 Priorities for investor action on the just transition
Source: Robins et al. (2018).

alignment with the Paris Agreement. The just transition is now emerging as a natural extension to this engagement strategy, notably in the construction, energy, industrial and transport sectors. The purpose of this engagement is to ensure that companies introduce high social standards as part of their climate strategies (including labour rights, skills and training, community well-being). These standards are not only the right policies for businesses to adopt, but can be a smart approach, strengthening resilience during a disruptive transition process.

c. *Capital allocation:* Investors can also shift their allocation of capital to specific assets aligned with the just transition, particularly through place-based strategies. Currently, however, investors face an inadequate supply of assets that meet the goals of the just transition. Today's policy and market frameworks still do not reward the development of sufficient equity- and debt-based assets that both drive a just transition and meet investors' risk–return requirements. Two areas stand out for further action to scale up capital flows into assets that can support a just transition. The first is to extend the green bond market to address social criteria for local, corporate and public issuers. The second is to mobilise the growing interest in impact investing to channel capital into unlisted assets that support the transition and deliver social inclusion.

d. *Policy advocacy and partnerships:* Market and policy failures lie at the root of the climate crisis. These failures need to be corrected through policy reform; policy is also required to create new markets that channel capital towards strategic public goods, as proposed by supporters of a Green New Deal. In addition, policy reform is equally important to address the social dimensions of climate change, not least because the just transition often involves changes to models of decision-making and questions of distribution that are best dealt with by public authorities. Investors have been active participants in climate policy and the just transition is a new area for constructive dialogue and partnership at the local, national and international levels.

e. *Learning and review:* As the just transition is still a relatively new dimension of the climate change agenda for investors, investors will need to build capacity to deliver experimentation at scale for the just transition with effective monitoring, evaluation and sharing of outcomes. This means establishing effective ways of listening to, learning from and partnering with key stakeholders affected by the transition. Results of investor activities can also be incorporated in their reporting using frameworks such as the TCFD.

Beyond the investment community, public sector institutions also have a key role to play in financing a just transition. They can provide patient, long-term capital that does not necessarily seek to maximise risk-adjusted returns. One example of leadership comes from the UK's development finance institution, CDC, which has included the just transition as one of three pillars of its climate change strategy alongside a commitment to net zero and resilience (CDC, 2020). CDC's new renewable energy company, Ayana, in India gives a sense of what this means in practice. As part of the Ayana investment, CDC identified a major skills gap in the solar sector which could hold back expansion. To help overcome this, Ayana is partnering with the UK's Department for International Development and SEWA Bharat (the All India Federation of Self-Employed Women's Association) to train the local community, with a particular focus on women, who face more challenges than men in entering the green jobs market. (Ayana, 2019).

The European Investment Bank (EIB) has also recognised the role it can play in delivering a just transition. As part of its new Energy Lending Policy, the EIB will provide extra support for EU member states and regions that have a more challenging transition path as part of broader EU solidarity and regional policy frameworks (EIB, 2019). This includes financing for economic development and job creation in regions transitioning away from fossil fuels.

11.4   AN AGENDA FOR EU LEADERSHIP ON FINANCING THE JUST TRANSITION

The new European Commission that commenced work in late 2019 has made a transformational Green Deal a centrepiece of its strategic programme for the next five years. In the words of Commission President Ursula Von Der Leyen, 'we will ensure a just transition for all' and 'support the people and regions most affected' through a new Just Transition Fund.

This new fund could have an important catalytic role, but it needs to be seen as one component of the next phase of Europe's Action Plan on Financing Sustainable Growth. Much has been achieved by the Plan in a very short time, particularly in terms of introducing the core policy and regulatory architecture for sustainable finance (such as the taxonomy). A priority for the next phase is to ensure that these frameworks lead to actual changes in flows of capital across the EU and beyond so that finance rapidly becomes aligned with environmental goals in ways that deliver an inclusive economy. To do this, the following four actions could help to make sure that Europe's Green Deal finances a just transition.

i. *Green Deal Strategy – assessment and standards:* To make sure that the just transition becomes a core part of the European Green Deal, the EU will need a powerful assessment capability to anticipate the potential impacts, both positive and negative, of the ecological transition. This needs to go beyond the energy sector to look across the whole economy and extend beyond the quantitative to the qualitative in terms of co-benefits, workplace conditions, well-being and spatial implications. In addition, further work is needed to make the EU's Sustainable Finance Taxonomy a powerful tool for the just transition. Currently the focus is on environmental goals, with the proviso that minimum social standards should be respected. Working with financial institutions and civil society, the Commission could develop a set of commonly accepted expectations of industrial practice to deliver a just transition which would be used alongside the taxonomy by banks and investors in their ESG analysis.

ii. *Investment Plan – public, private, local:* The Commission has already committed to introduce a Sustainable Europe Investment Plan, deploying €1trn over the next decade. Key to success will be structuring the different blends of grant funding from government, patient capital from development banks (such as the EIB) and private funding from commercial banks and institutional investors to scale up flows for a just transition. This will need to cover all sectors of the economy and be designed to ensure that positive social impacts are generated. For example, Europe's circa 300mn residential, public and commercial buildings will all need to be retrofitted for a carbon-neutral world, providing an opportunity to simultaneously end long-standing problems of fuel poverty, insufficient supply of social housing and homelessness. Many of Europe's member states have strong traditions of local and regional-level financing which can be drawn on to build up the anchor institutions needed for the just transition.

iii. *Financial System – innovation and mobilisation:* Delivering the Green Deal will require a refreshed financial system, one that is fully engaged with the societal task of long-term sustainable development. Pragmatic, incremental measures to improve disclosure and risk management will need to be supplemented by more systemic interventions in order to reallocate capital at the scale and speed required. Fiscal leadership will be critical, particularly to channel low-cost public finance at productivity-enhancing investments in infrastructure, innovation and inclusion. Here, Europe could step up the pace of green sovereign bond issuance, extending the scope from purely environmental goals to incorporate social objectives (such as skills development and enterprise development in disadvantaged regions). This new wave of 'just transition' sovereign bond issuance should also be coordinated with the asset purchase and balance sheet management programmes of the European Central Bank (ECB) so that its holdings are progressively brought into line with the EU's long-term climate goals.

iv. *International – leadership, ambition, transformational transactions:* The EU already plays a leadership role in many aspects of the sustainable finance agenda, not least in the work of central banks through the Network for Greening the Financial System and finance ministries through the new International Platform for Sustainable Finance. Geopolitically, effective measures to channel finance for the just transition could become important confidence-building measures between the EU and key emerging and developing economies. This could help to build the basis for more ambitious national climate strategies. As part of this, the EU could identify ways in which it could with its member states support transformational financing packages such as the *'Just Transition Transaction'* announced by South Africa's President Cyril Ramaphosa, which would wind down the country's troubled coal assets, scale up renewables and do the right thing by affected workers and communities (Ramaphosa, 2019).

The just transition is a relatively new priority for sustainable finance. But it speaks to the long-standing need to integrate environmental and social factors into the routine operations of financial institutions and policy makers. It is set to be an essential element of the next wave of sustainable finance in the 2020s, both in Europe and beyond.

REFERENCES

Ayana (2019), 'Skills for a Solarised Future'. www.ayanapower.com/news.html.

Bowen, A. (2012), 'Green Growth, Green Jobs and Labor Markets', Policy Research Paper 5990, World Bank, Washington, DC.

Burrow, S. (2017), 'Climate: Towards a Just Transition, with No Stranded Workers and No Stranded Communities', OECD Insights, May. http://oecdinsights .org/2017/05/23/climate-towards-a-just-transition-with-no-stranded-workers- and-no-stranded-communities.

CDC (2020), 'Investing for clean and inclusive growth: climate change strategy', July. https://assets.cdcgroup.com/wp-content/uploads/2020/07/01170324/CDC_Climate_ Change_Strategy_spreads.pdf.

Chateau, J., Rebolledo C. and Dellink, R. (2011), 'The Env-Linkages Economic Baseline Projections to 2050', OECD Environment Working Papers No. 41, Paris. www.oecd.org/officialdocuments/publicdisplaydocumentpdf/?cote= ENV/WKP(2011)11&docLanguage=En.

Chateau, J., Bibas, R. and Lanzi, E. (2018), 'Impacts of Green Growth Policies on Labour Markets and Wage Income Distribution: A General Equilibrium Application to Climate and Energy Policies', OECD Environment Working Papers, No. 137, Paris. https://doi.org/10.1787/ea3696f4-en.

Committee on Climate Change (2019), 'Phase Out Greenhouse Gas Emissions by 2050 to End UK Contribution to Global Warming'. www.theccc.org.uk/2019/ 05/02/phase-out-greenhouse-gas-emissions-by-2050-to-end-uk-contribution-to- global-warming.

European Commission (2018), 'Financing a European Economy: Final Report of the High-Level Expert Group on Sustainable Finance'. https://ec.europa.eu/info/ publications/180131-sustainable-finance-report_en.

European Investment Bank (2019), 'Energy Lending Policy', EIB, November. www .eib.org/en/publications/eib-energy-lending-policy.htm.

European Union (2018). 'In-depth Analysis in Support of the Commission Communication COM(2018) 773: A Clean Planet for All – A European Long- Term Strategic Vision for a Prosperous, Modern, Competitive and Climate Neutral Economy'. Brussels, November. Available at: https://ec.europa.eu/clima/ sites/clima/files/docs/pages/com_2018_733_analysis_in_support_en_0.pdf.

Fankhauser, S., Seheiler, F. and Stern, N. (2008), 'Climate Change, Innovation and Jobs', *Climate Policy* 8(4), 421–429. www.lse.ac.uk/GranthamInstitute/wp-con tent/uploads/2014/02/climate-change-innovation-jobs.pdf.

Federal Ministry for the Environment, Nature Conservation and Nuclear Safety (2017), 'The BMUB Fact-Checks Trump', Press release, 14 August. www.bmub .bund.de/en/topics/climate-energy/climate/international-climate-policy/paris-agreement/fact-check.

Generali (2018), 'Climate Change Strategy: Technical Note', November. www .generali.com/our-responsibilities/our-commitment-to-the-environment-and-climate.

International Labour Organization (2015), Guidelines for a Just Transition towards Environmentally Sustainable Economies and Societies for All. Geneva: ILO. www.ilo.org/global/topics/green-jobs/publications/WCMS_ 432859/lang–en/index.htm.

International Labour Organisation (2018). 'Greening with Jobs: World Employment Social Outlook, 2018', ILO. Available at: https://www.ilo.org/global/research/ global-reports/weso/greening-with-jobs/lang–en/index.htm.

International Renewable Energy Association (IRENA) (2019), 'Global Energy Transformation: A Roadmap to 2050'. www.irena.org//media/Files/IRENA/ Agency/Publication/2019/Apr/IRENA_Global_Energy_Transformation_2019.pdf.

Investor Agenda (2019), 'Global Investor Statement to Governments on Climate Change'. https://theinvestoragenda.org/wp-content/uploads/2019/09/190916-GISGCC-for-UNCAS.pdf.

Labor Network for Sustainability and Strategic Practice (2016), '"Just Transition" – Just What Is It? An Analysis of Language, Strategies, and Projects'. www .labor4sustainability.org/files/Just_Transition_Just_What_Is_It.pdf

The New Climate Economy (2018), 'Unlocking the Inclusive Growth Story of the 21st Century', The Global Commission on the Economy and Climate. https:// newclimateeconomy.report/2018/wp-content/uploads/sites/6/2018/09/NCE_ 2018_FULL-REPORT.pdf.

OECD (2017), 'Employment Implications of Green Growth: Linking Jobs, Growth, and Green Policies', OECD Report for the G7 Environment Ministers. www .oecd.org/environment/Employment-Implications-of-Green-Growth-OECD-Report-G7-Environment-Ministers.pdf.

O'Kane, L. (2019), 'Pope on Climate Crisis: Time Is Running Out, Decisive Action Needed', *Vatican News*, 14 June. www.vaticannews.va/en/pope/news/2019-06/ pope-declares-climate-emergency.html.

Pettifor, A. (2019), *The Case for the Green New Deal*. London: Verso.

Principles for responsible Investment (PRI) (2019), *Global Investor Statement to Governments on Climate Change*. London: Principles for Responsible Investment. https://theinvestoragenda.org/wp-content/uploads/2019/09/190916-GISGCC-for-UNCAS.pdf.

Ramaphosa, C. (2019), Statement by H.E. President Cyril Ramaphosa of South Africa to the United Nations Secretary-General's Climate Summit, 23 September 2019. www.dirco.gov.za/docs/speeches/2019/cram0923.htm.

Robins, N., Brunsting, V. and Wood, D. (2018), *Climate Change and the Just Transition: A Guide for Investor Action*. London: Grantham Research Institute on Climate Change and the Environment. www.lse.ac.uk/GranthamInstitute/publication/climate-change-and-the-just-transition-a-guide-for-investor-action.

Robins, N. and Rydge, J. (2019), 'Why a Just Transition Is Crucial for Effective Climate Action', Discussion paper for the Inevitable Policy Response project. London: Principles for Responsible Investment. www.unpri.org/download?ac=7092.

Smith, S. (2017), 'Just Transition: A Report for the OECD', Just Transition Centre, May. www.oecd.org/environment/cc/g20-climate/collapsecontents/Just-Transition-Centre-report-just-transition.pdf.

Stern, N. (2008), 'Key Elements of a Global Deal on Climate Change', London School of Economics and Political Science. http://eprints.lse.ac.uk/19617/1/Key_Elements_of_a_Global_Deal-Final_version%282%29_with_additional_edits_post_launch.pdf.

United Nations Framework Convention on Climate Change. (2015), 'Adoption of the Paris Agreement, 21st Conference of the Parties', Paris: United Nations. https://unfccc.int/resource/docs/2015/cop21/eng/l09r01.pdf

Wood, D. (2016), 'Why and How Might Investors Respond to Economic Inequality?', Discussion paper, Principles for Responsible Investment and Initiative for Responsible Investment, Harvard Kennedy School. https://iri.hks.harvard.edu/links/why-and-how-might-investors-respond-economic-inequality.

12 Sustainable Finance for Citizens

Anne-Catherine Husson-Traore

12.1 INTRODUCTION

Sustainable finance can be viewed as political in the original sense of the word: it not only enables to direct financial flows towards a low-carbon and inclusive economy aligned with Europe's environmental objectives, it also serves as an indicator for European citizens of how their personal savings are used. Additionally, it helps to re-legitimise the financial sector for those still outraged by the 2008 financial crisis and its ensuing consequences.

However, to gain back the public's trust, asset managers will have to do more than just stamp sustainable finance labels on traditional funds. They are going to have to explain their objectives and integration strategy for ESG criteria in financial management. They will also need to explain how they evaluate the financial impact of risks, such as climate change, as well as how they select environmental and social performance indicators alongside standard financial performance.

The European Commission launched its new Green Deal[1] to transform Europe's economy and shape it for a sustainable future and has included an Action Plan on Financing Sustainable Growth into this project for the implementation of a Just Transition. The main challenge now is to share this objective with citizens in clear words.

12.2 TRANSPARENCY, PEDAGOGY AND CREDIBILITY ARE REQUIRED

To convince citizens to gear their savings towards financing the ecological transition, a combination of transparency, pedagogy and

---

[1] https://ec.europa.eu/info/sites/info/files/european-green-deal-communication_en .pdf.

credibility is key. This is the model outlined by the EC's High-Level Expert Group on Sustainable Finance[2] (the HLEG) in a twofold approach: minimum standards for funds that claim to belong to sustainable finance and ecolabel criteria for 'green' investments. At the end of 2019, the first European regulations on sustainable finance echoed these approaches as concrete mechanisms to put in place by 2021.[3]

To engage with citizens on sustainable finance, one must first define sustainable activities. Europe has taken a big step in this direction with the adoption of its classification system (taxonomy) at the end of 2019. It also published a regulation on 'the publication of sustainability-related disclosures in the financial services sector' on 27 November 2019,[4] which effectively detailed the approach to be adopted.

The regulation's introductory note states: 'The absence of harmonised Union rules on sustainability-related disclosures to end investors creates divergent disclosure standards and market-based practices [that] make it very difficult to compare different financial products and such divergences could also be confusing for end investors and could distort their investment decisions.' The document also stressed that 'the lack of harmonised rules relating to transparency makes it difficult for end investors to effectively compare different financial products with respect to their environmental, social and governance risks and sustainable investment objectives'. Thus, the regulation's objective is to lift these obstacles, as they are some of the primary difficulties in discussing sustainable finance with individuals, especially in the French market, despite ongoing efforts.

In European countries like France and Germany, citizens save a significant amount of money with long-term purposes such as

[2] European Commission (2018), 'The Final Report of the High Level Expert Group on Sustainable Finance'. https://ec.europa.eu/info/publications/180131-sustainable-finance-report_en.

[3] https://eur-lex.europa.eu/eli/reg/2019/2088/oj.

[4] https://eur-lex.europa.eu/legal-content/EN/TXT/?uri=CELEX:32019R2088.

retirement. It appears crucial that they adopt sustainable finance to secure these savings so as to avoid major ESG risks like climate change and support a sustainable economy. For this to happen, however, there still must be a shift in the conversation between customers and advisors which typically has focussed only on financial performance.

The larger part of savers is aware of environmental and social challenges and will expect their financial products to have positive impacts in this respect. ESG integration into asset management is going to go mainstream but the path is not that easy. The 2019 HSBC survey on sustainable financing[5] showed that investors think that two-thirds of their clients have a positive perception about ESG considerations. They also consider that half of their clients expect them to develop skills in this area.

Confusion about sustainable finance is another major issue underlined by the survey. Half of investors get 'confused about the differences between terms such as responsible, socially responsible, ethical, environmental, social and governance, impact, sustainable, green investing'.

The lack of clear explanations on all types of practices is one of the main obstacles for savers. It is difficult for them to trust asset managers if these are not able to elaborate on the chosen approach and its impact on portfolios. But HSBC's survey also adds that 'for investors, impact is still only an emerging way of considering environmental and social issues. Less than 30% of investors globally use impact goals or metrics as part of their investment decision-making'.

This is one of the biggest mismatches about sustainable finance related to a portfolio. Clients expect environmental and social targets and metrics combined with financial performances, and asset managers are not able to deliver larger concepts such as better ESG performances than their usual benchmarks!

---

[5] www.gbm.hsbc.com/insights/sustainable-financing/sustainable-financing-and-investing-survey-2019.

12.3 CHANGING THE CONVERSATION BETWEEN CLIENTS AND ADVISORS

In France, the amount of general savings in its many forms including retirement funding and social security is estimated at €5trn. Of this, approximately €1.7trn is invested in market investment products, such as life insurance. But conversations between French citizens and their financial advisors are limited to a product's financial performance and evaluation of its risk adversity. The stronger the risk adversity, the more advisors recommend bond investments. The weaker the risk adversity, the more advisors direct clients towards equity investments.

Clearly conversations such as these are not focussed at all on the usage of capital, however modest, nor on its impact. Yet, a client concerned with climate change would no doubt limit their air travel. It is plausible to assume that the same client would also wish to invest their personal savings in financial products that have the same positive impact. This is to say that such a client would prefer to invest in a product that does not finance a high-carbon emission economy fuelled by fossil fuel energy. The easiest way to meet such a client's concerns consists in excluding not only coal companies but also the major oil and gas companies that are still dominating major stock markets. This is a dilemma for professionals who are used to giving advice based on financial figures while ignoring other considerations.

If we consider a client's sole concerns to be quality, security and financial performance, the mechanisms currently in place are well adapted to meet their needs. However, if there are other expectations, their demands remain to be met. According to a 2019 study by Bank of America, it is essential to offer portfolio investments that incorporate ESG matters, especially for clients considered as 'high revenue, women, or millennials'. This survey, which was published in September 2019, quoted '10 reasons you should care about ESG',[6] one of them being: 'You can do good and do well'. For Bank of

---

[6] www.bofaml.com/content/dam/boamlimages/documents/articles/ID19_1119/esg_matters.pdf.

America, ESG is the 'best signal of earning risks' and 'ESG controversies have cost investors a lot. Major ESG-related controversies during the past six years were accompanied by peak-to-trough market capitalization losses of \$534bn for large US companies. Loss avoidance is key for portfolio returns over time.'

To meet the expectations of individual savers and investors, advisors need to establish links between ESG integration into asset management and major trends like financial crisis, climate emergency and serious social tensions. This means not only to be able to talk about selected companies into the portfolio, to have ESG information about them but also to know quite well the process used by the asset manager.

Depending on the chosen approach, two types of screenings can be adopted: positive and negative ones as shown in Table 12.1.

Savers do not need too many details. They would prefer a global picture with the purpose of their sustainable portfolio being associated with environmental and social metrics. But even that is still a work in progress.[7] Every fund manager has its own definition of sustainable investment, elaborates its own ESG analysis using a wide range of existing sources and establishes its own complex version of sustainable management. The result of this initiative often has a barely visible impact on the final portfolio.

12.4   A LACK OF STRONG ESG DATA

What makes the situation more difficult is that most companies publish virtually no clear information on their 'green' engagements, nor the segment of their activities that produce environmental benefits. Companies also neglect to publish information on the negative externalities of business activities that risk having a multiplying

[7] See, for example Cambridge Institute for Sustainability Leadership, Investment Leaders Group (2019).

Table 12.1 *Screening choices*

	Negative Screening	Positive Screening
Sectorial Approaches *(products and services)*	Sector-based exclusions • Coal • Tobacco, alcohol • Weapons	• Choice of certain sectors that favour sustainable development (taxonomies) • 'Positive impact' approach
General Approaches (ESG practices)	Norm-based exclusions • Human rights • Corruption	ESG scores-based portfolio construction: • Best in class • Best in universe • Best effort

effect on biodiversity. An asset manager is therefore currently incapable of creating a financial product that could select the so-called best listed European companies in respect to biodiversity. Compared to the market for organic food products, whose central engagement is being pesticide-free, offers for sustainable funds are confused on their engagements.

In concrete terms, the objective for asset managers concerned with finding common ground with all their clients on sustainable development often requires a product which does the splits. At the same time, asset managers force themselves to not deviate too much from their benchmark, and therefore, the market economy, while favouring investment in 'eco-friendly' or 'socially responsible' assets as they adapt their management techniques with regulations barely intelligible to a lay audience.

This subtle technique may let large, emblematic companies, such as those in the oil industry, slip through the net, leaving individual clients puzzled and discrediting the entire process at the same time. Jean Laville, vice president of Swiss Sustainable Finance, recently explained during the PRI conference in Paris: 'When a Swiss pension fund received a rough wake-up call from young climate protestors, the following week it adopted a strict coal exclusion policy. Exclusion is at the base of sustainable finance and the most understandable approach to the general public, thus making it the most credible.' Yet if standard exclusions, like assets linked to coal, become widespread practice for controversial companies, relevant sustainable finance portfolios will rarely differ from those that are not.

Theoretically, the time has come for massive development in sustainable finance, especially in Europe since offers for Socially Responsible Investment (SRI) funds have greatly developed. Realistically, the weak visibility of sustainable finance offers, and their lack of readability, serve as a handicap in front of investors who often have very simple requests.

There is a high risk of mis-selling as Morningstar mentioned during a meeting at UK SIF in September 2019. Morningstar offers an ESG rating for more than 20,000 portfolios based on Sustainalytics ratings, a Morningstar subsidiary that performs extra-financial analysis. In November 2019, Morningstar announced that they had changed their methodology, both in terms of ESG risk scoring and ESG rating of funds. The new method for calculating the ESG score of listed companies offers comparability between the various sectors. This score, ranging from 0 to 100 (zero being the best score), thus reflects exposure to companies' ESG risks, but also their ability to respond, or not, to the risks inherent in their business model. The choice of risks and their weighting varies according to the 138 sectors covered, but the score is nevertheless intended to be absolute. This therefore means the end of a best-in-class approach which dominated the SRI market between the first decade of the century (2000–2010).

The best-in-class approach is still prominent on the French market, but it is always difficult to justify it for retail use. To be closer to their benchmarks, asset managers who adopt the best-in-class approach avoid sectorial exclusion and keep larger listed companies with good ESG ratings even if they symbolise environmental contradictions such as oil majors. Customers are often surprised to find a controversial company in a sustainable portfolio. This may happen: it remains at the charge of the advisor to explain that ESG ratings of that company are the best of its sector in spite of the global negative contribution on climate change of the sector itself.

This gap between client demand for traceability and transparency and the sustainable products on offer that are rather ambiguous on these aspects is striking. This is particularly concerning since these are the same clients that want products to provide guarantees on the positive contributions they make to the environmental and social landscape.

12.5 TOO MANY SUSTAINABLE LABELS TO CLARIFY THE MARKET

Sustainable finance labels could be a lighthouse for savers, but the market must progress considerably for this to happen. In June 2019, Novethic published the first overview of sustainable finance standards and labels available in Europe.[8] At a time when the demand for sustainable finance alternatives is growing, we felt it was essential to clarify the promises of the current offer of sustainable finance labels in Europe.

In just over a decade, sustainable finance has led to the creation of eight specialised labels. Designed to provide guarantees on the asset allocation in portfolios, they are used as points of reference by responsible investment practitioners and will have to win a larger audience when they will be distributed in retail banking and insurance.

In its panorama of labels and funds, Novethic reviewed different benchmarks (references, frameworks) and came to the following conclusion: between funds with a 'green' emphasis and funds that concentrate on ESG criteria, not to mention those that incorporate both, we are still far from a clear offer that delivers on its promise to the end customer.

[8] https://www.novethic.com/sustainable-finance-trends/detail/overview-of-european-sustainable-finance-labels.html.

Table 12.2 *Funds with particular ESG labels*[a]

Label	Number of Labelled Funds
FNG (Germany SIF)	101
Greenfin (France)	19
LuxFlag ESG (Luxembourg)	100
LuxFlag Environment (Luxembourg)	10
LuxFlag Climate Finance (Luxembourg)	2
Umweltzeichen (Austria)	116
Nordic Swan (Nordic Countries)	32
SRI label (France)	321
Towards Sustainability (Belgium)	265

[a] https://www.novethic.com/sustainable-finance-trends/detail/overview-of-european-sustainable-finance-labels-2020.html.

The French public label Greenfin[9] is a noticeable exception. It is exclusively attributed to environmental funds that combine investment in green activities related to a set classification system, exclusion of fossil fuels and nuclear energy and exclusion of companies with controversial ESG practices. The situation is so complex that even the marketing is unclear. Analysing labelled funds confirmed the sector's wide-ranging diversity in terms of marketing, as shown in Novethic's study on European sustainable finance labels.

As of 31 December 2019, 808 funds possess at least one of the new European labels listed on our panorama (overview) (Table 12.2).

It is easy to note the large variety of terminology and widespread market coverage. With less than 1,000 funds, the number of funds deemed 'sustainable' is just a drop in the ocean compared to all UCITS funds (less than 5 per cent). Only two labels, the French public SRI label and the Belgian 'Towards Sustainability' label, include more than 200 products and have real weight in their respective markets.

[9] www.novethic.com/greenfin-label-green-finance.html.

Despite the successes, these labels will have to revitalise their level of visibility and readability for individual savers and investors in Europe.

At the end of 2019, promoters of the SRI label launched a promotional campaign on city buses in Paris. Advertisements consisted of simple messages, such as 'your personal savings are making good resolutions' or 'Your personal savings are being used to finance a more responsible world'.

It is too early to measure the impact of these campaigns on individual savers and investors, but we already know the limits. For the past ten years, the French Forum for Responsible Investment has published annual results from a survey on individual investors interested in this type of product. Year after year, the results are essentially the same. Less than 10 per cent of those interviewed knew the concept of SRI (Sustainably Responsible Investment) and a large majority were very interested in integrating ESG dimensions into the management of their savings.

One of the most helpful tools for retail investors could be a website with clear explanations about sustainable products. Towards Sustainability, the last born in the series of labels, launched by the Belgian federation of asset management Febelfin, is a game changer as its website[10] provides with details on management processes of each fund and allows clients to understand its main characteristics on the following topics: sustainability strategies used in the product, **sustainability policies** on weapons, tobacco, fossil fuel extraction and electricity generation.

The Febelfin[11] standard combines three requirements: transparency, ESG analysis on the entire portfolio and exclusions with low thresholds, not only on coal but also on unconventional fossil fuels. This triptych corresponds to the idea of minimum requirements as imagined by the HLEG to harmonise the supply of sustainable funds in Europe.

---

[10] www.towardssustainability.be.
[11] www.febelfin.be/sites/default/files/2019-02/quality_standard_-_sustainable_financial_products.pdf.

As of today, this minimum base is more or less implemented by each of the European labels, but the guarantees are not clearly identifiable by the end customer. Hence, there is a significant difference between supply and demand. If we analyse the labelled funds in detail, they can be better understood. Faced with environmental requirements, products possessing a 'green' label or those considered to be 'green' represent only 65 funds, or 8 per cent of the 808 labelled funds.

If we base our thinking on a semantic analysis of the respective languages behind these labels (French, English, German, Swedish and Danish) using the following keywords: energy/energy transition; renewable; environment; ecological; earth; green; clean; climate/climate change; global warming; carbon; we find less than 100 (97), or 12 per cent of the 808 labelled funds for 2019.

Not only does this represent a mere drop in the ocean, since there are nearly 60,000 funds on the European market, but additionally, it is rare to find products capable of responding to the expectations of clients wishing to mobilise their savings for environmental good, as they do with other consumption habits. The clear guidelines outlined in the November 2019 European regulation should help improve the market, even if there is a significant risk of countries wanting to keep their sustainable finance specificities. This is exactly what occurred during implementation of the EU's green taxonomy. France fought to include nuclear power and eastern European countries, led by Germany, fought for gas to be considered as sustainable energy. The last, but certainly not least, difficulty is extending ESG consideration to all areas of finance with, once again, varying strategies from one asset manager to another.

France will experiment in 2020 with a new way to promote labelled funds in life insurance as initiated by the PACTE law.[12] Indeed, life insurers will have to offer an official labelled product (Greenfin, SRI label or Finansol dedicated to inclusive economy).

---

[12] See: www.legifrance.gouv.fr/affichTexte.do?cidTexte=JORFTEXT000038496102& dateTexte=&categorieLien=id.

This will remain a real challenge as – apart from the Greenfin label which focusses on environmental characteristics – these labels focus more on process than on impact.

Insurers take steps to explain to their customers this new approach. For instance, Aviva launched a campaign in Spring 2019 with a simple message: 'There is a life insurance which respects environment'.

The challenge was then for them to apply this message to their products. And they did with the launch of a thematic fund dedicated to Climate Transition which allows the possibility to invest in solutions to mitigate climate change.[13]

Thematic funds appear to be the best way to help retail investors understand and buy sustainable finance: they have a story to tell. More broadly, ESG integration required more skills on asset management and corporate's analysis. That's why institutional investors are the first target of sustainable finance, but the end user is the citizen. Financing retirement on long term is a core issue and sustainable finance could be the right tool to address these challenges.

12.6 MANAGING PENSIONS WITH SUSTAINABLE FINANCE

In Europe, pensions concern almost a quarter of assets under management (€14trn). This is done on a voluntary basis without a real set of standard practices. France, currently struggling with a major battle over its retirement system, is an interesting case. Indeed, the idea of a funded pension system has resurfaced during anti-retirement reform protests in the country. BlackRock, the largest asset manager in the world, has been targeted by numerous press articles as one of the architects behind this reform. The American multinational company has a keen interest in French retirement savings, as do all asset managers. Nevertheless, the pay-as-you-go retirement system remains preserved under the reform for now.

---

[13] See: www.avivainvestors.com/en-gb/capabilities/equities/climate-transition-european-equity-fund.

Retirement reform has sparked impassioned debate in France. The revelation that BlackRock is suspected of having actively participated in this reform has made the situation even more polarising. Several media outlets have pointed fingers at the asset manager over its interest in French retirement savings and the fact that BlackRock leadership, including CEO Larry Fink, met with Emmanuel Macron and other government representatives.

The risk is having the pay-as-you-go French retirement system, in which every employee contributes to pay for the pensions of retirees, be progressively transformed into a funded retirement system. Under a funded retirement system, employees contribute to funds that distribute pensions at the age of retirement. '[We never] sought to exert an influence on the reform of the Pay-as-you-go pension system underway with public authorities or any other player in the sector', BlackRock claimed in a press release.

12.7   VYING FOR THE PER (FOR PLANS D'ÉPARGNE RETRAITE, RETIREMENT SAVINGS PLAN)

Nevertheless, BlackRock clearly remains interested in French retirement savings. The world's largest asset manager even expressed their interest in a locally written note entitled 'The Covenant Law: The Right Retirement Plan'.[14] France is one of the largest European savings markets, with almost €5,000bn in assets under management which is largely invested in life insurance products (€1,700bn).

Retirement savings, which is a voluntary form of funded retirement, represent only a small part of total savings (around €230bn). It is this part of the French retirement system that is the envy of BlackRock, and all other French asset managers. This is especially true as the government decided to boost retirement savings with the PACTE law.

The PACTE law has simplified the many systems (PERP, PERE, Perco, etc.) in existence since the early 2000s. They have been

---

[14] www.BlackRock.com/corporate/literature/whitepaper/viewpoint-loi-pacte-le-bon-plan-retraite-juin-2019.pdf.

consolidated into a single system, the PER (Plans D'Épargne Retraite), or Retirement Savings Plan, which operates collectively (corporate) or individually. A simpler and more attractive system from a tax perspective, the government's aim is to bring total assets under management to €300bn by 2022. This PER savings plan should particularly benefit from current pension reforms as it plans to cap contributions for high wage earners.

The government is betting on individuals being more encouraged to save through the PER, in part, to preserve their standard of living in retirement. At the same time, sustainable investment is not part of the debate on pension reform, despite its guarantees for long-term financial reserves. The way it is implemented will be crucial in its ability to grow assets and play a buffer role in the event of a demographic or economic shock.

This universal reserve fund must guarantee its sustainability. The reserves serve, in part, to reconcile the divergent trend between the larger number of retired workers and the number of active workers. While the public debate on pension financing does not include sustainable finance at all, all proponents managing French retirement reserves are historic players in responsible investment. The French Pension Reserve Fund, FRR, (Fonds de Réserve pour les Retraites) adopted a responsible investment strategy very early on, enabling it to manage ESG risks. It regularly updates its strategy, dating back to 2005, and integrates climate risk into its management whilst gradually reducing the carbon footprint of its asset portfolio.

The two public retirement investors, the ERAFP[15] and the Ircantec,[16] have adopted very engaged policies on sustainable finance. ERAFP's policy has been in place since its creation in 2005[17] and Ircantec since its charter's adoption in 2009.[18]

---

[15] ERAFP stands for Établissement de Retraite Additionnelle de la Fonction Publique.
[16] Ircantec stands for Institution de Retraite Complémentaire des Agents non Titulaires de l'Etat et des Collectivités.
[17] See: www.rafp.fr/en.
[18] See: www.ircantec.retraites.fr/sites/default/files/public/dpresse_oct18gb.pdf.

All three are international leaders on the subject and were further awarded on 3 December 2019 at the IPE (Investment and Pensions Europe) Awards which recognises the best European pension funds. The FRR received the prize for best risk management and the ERAFP for best equity investment strategy. Additionally, AGIRC-ARRCO[19] adopted its SRI charter in June 2019 and joined the global sustainable finance movement by adhering to the Principles for Responsible Investment (PRI).

The main French retirement organisations have upheld the idea that to finance pensions over a horizon of ten, twenty or thirty years, it is essential to integrate climate, environmental and social criteria into investment strategy. It is a shame that this approach is not more widely integrated into discussions on pension funding.

FRR, ERAFP and Ircantec play a key role to explain to a larger audience why sustainable finance matters for long-term investors. This is even more the case for ERAFP and Ircantec which count a high number of beneficiaries.

FRR Policy presentation states: *'To optimize the risk-return trade-off whilst at the same time reduce the carbon footprint of its equities investment portfolio.* It is within the context of this aim that the FRR has undertaken to convince businesses to adopt the necessary measures to reduce their impact on climate in particular by reducing their carbon footprint and fossil fuel reserves' (*ERAFP Policy*, updated in November 2019).

Since its creation, the French public sector additional pension scheme (ERAFP) implemented a rigorous best-in-class investment policy that incorporates a focus on promoting more sustainable and responsible economic activities. Under this approach, ERAFP is cementing its positioning with a view to ensuring that its investment

---

[19] ARRCO (Association des Régimes de Retraite Complémentaire) is a plan for blue-collar workers and AGIRC (Association Générale des Institutions de Retraite Complémentaire) is a plan for white-collar workers and management staff. See: www.agirc-arrco.fr.

activities are consistent with its commitment to a decarbonised economy.

Limiting a company's exposure to thermal coal-related activities today is a powerful way to limit greenhouse gas emissions, while providing scope for opportunities to contribute to the energy transition.

Based on this observation, ERAFP is adapting its best-in-class policy by requiring companies in sectors with high energy transition stakes to adopt strategies consistent with the objectives of the Paris agreement and by withdrawing from those that fail to do so and whose thermal coal-related activities exceed 10 per cent of their turnover.

ERAFP will also seek to ensure a just transition, considering the social aspects of business restructuring in these sectors and will encourage companies to take initiatives in this direction.

These three investors give examples of responsible practices. FRR adds on its website that 'the responsiveness and dynamism of the FRR encourage the development of sustainable finance'.

The French Law on Energy Transition for Green Growth (LTECV) enacted in 2015 and its article 173 appear as a strong support for them and encourages such market players to explain clearly to citizens their sustainable strategies. Novethic has performed a yearly survey over the past three years[20] called '173 shades of reporting' about ESG integration and climate policy of the 100 main French asset owners. The study clearly demonstrated that there is room for improvement as climate change reports very often remain too technical.

12.8 NGO'S PRESSURE AIMS TO MOBILISE CITIZENS

In 2018, WWF France has analysed climate-related financial disclosures of the top seventeen French insurance companies[21] according to Article 173 (vi) of the French Law on Green transition. This year, the

---

[20] See: www.novethic.com/sustainable-finance-trends/detail/173-shades-of-reporting
.html.

[21] WWF (2018) 'Article 173! Message Not Delivered: Summary of WWF France's Second Report on French Insurer's Climate Reporting under Article 173'. www.wwf
.fr/sites/default/files/doc-2019-02/201811_Insurer_climate_reporting-min.pdf.

second since the new transparency requirements for institutional investors entered into force in 2017, WWF France looked at insurance companies' climate-related financial disclosures from a fresh perspective: over a hundred WWF volunteers conducted 180 interviews with sales representatives in local retail branches of their banks and insurance companies. The result was mixed: while it was noteworthy that disclosures improved and new tools emerged since last year, retail investors still did not have access to clear information about the link between their savings and climate change. The survey recorded that 89 per cent of retail investors considered that their bank or insurance company gives them little or no information about the impact of their savings on climate change. Only 13 per cent of investigators found relevant climate-related information online and understood it.

In a context where climate activists use all possible means to push transition to a low-carbon economy, citizens are also mobilized through demonstrations against banks about fossil fuel energy financing. Examples include *BankTrack* advocating for the signature of its global call on banks to stop financing fossil fuels[22] and Friends of the Earth organising demonstrations in Société Genérale's agencies to protest against shale gas support and Rio Grande LNG Project.[23]

This is just a few examples of harassment strategy adopted by NGOs. Some banks answer with sustainable policies that are updated regularly and announced to be stronger and stronger.

The engagement and embedding of citizens in the Action Plan on Financing Sustainable Growth launched by the EU in 2018 is key. Citizens need to be part of the sustainable transformation that is taking part through their savings, which remain an important lever of action. If not, it would be difficult to trust financial actors – especially banks – on their ability to protect their savings in the long term. Banks need trust of their clients to survive and thrive: if they choose

[22] See: www.banktrack.org/article/banking_on_climate_change_fossil_fuel_finance_report_card_2019.
[23] See: http://foeeurope.org/climate-activists-disrupt-gas-industry-conference.

to put sustainable finance at the heart of their strategies, they will need to give evidence that they are willing to deeply transform their practices. NGOs doubt that strongly, but citizens are the ones who need to be convinced with ESG metrics that are in some way comparable and understandable. This is the great challenge!

13 Individual Impact Investors
The Silenced Majority
Stan Dupré

13.1 THE POLITICAL AMBITION: MOBILISING RETAIL INVESTORS AND BENEFICIARIES

As illustrated in the earlier chapters of this book, the general public and policy makers increasingly expect the finance sector to help address the challenge of climate change and commit to actions beyond their traditional function of risk-adjusted returns optimisation. The Paris Agreement, in its article 2.1.c, recognised the role of finance in enabling the transition to a low-carbon and resilient economy. Several years later, the European Commission's Action Plan (2018b) on Financing Sustainable Growth set the ambitious goal to 'reorient capital flows towards sustainable investment in order to achieve sustainable and inclusive growth'.

More specifically, through shareholder rights and the capacity to allocate capital, financial markets influence the climate trajectory of many capital-intensive sectors, such as energy, power and transport. Europe is expecting the finance sector, including private actors, to use this influence on decisions made in the real economy, in order to support policy goals.

13.1.1 Capital Markets on a 5°C Pathway

Today, our analysis of capital markets and bank loans suggests that they are on a 5°C pathway.[1] Some institutional investors and banks have started to tackle the issue but, in most cases, their mandate – as currently interpreted – limits their ability to integrate climate goals as such. Buying the market or financing the local economy, while

---

[1] See www.transitionmonitor.com.

276

optimising risk-adjusted returns, in a world on a 5°C pathway does not leave much room to actively bet on a 1.5°C scenario. And, unless drastic central planning measures are taken, this sudden 'temperature drop' in investment and lending portfolios will not take place without a clear mandate from the end beneficiaries. Whether they directly invest in securities, buy shares of mutual funds, keep their money on savings accounts or simply benefit from pension plans, 'consumers' are the end clients for many institutional investors and a strategic source of capital for commercial banks. In Europe, households hold €97trn of financial assets (30 per cent of total financial assets), including €30trn of liquid financial assets.

13.1.2 Investors' Views

Recent consumer research across different European countries (2DII, 2020c) clearly indicates that a large majority of individual investors – between 60 per cent and 75 per cent, depending on how the questions are framed – *want* to invest sustainably. Interestingly, consumers declare that they are willing to give up return for environmental outcomes: a recent survey of German and French retail investors suggests that 64 per cent would accept a sacrifice of 5 per cent on their pension benefits (2DII, 2020c). These results are comparable to another study conducted in the United States.[2] In this context, the €97trn question is obviously why most of them still invest in non-sustainable investment products? Behavioural finance research seems to provide a first answer to this question.

13.1.3 Pension Fund Beneficiaries Walk the Talk

In a 2019 study from the Netherlands (Bauer et al., 2018) and conducted on 1,700 pension fund beneficiaries, the University of Maastricht tried to simulate the effect of a 'real choice': 'The pension fund in our study gave its members a real vote for more or less sustainable investments. A comparison group made the same

---

[2] Cambridge Institute for Sustainability Leadership (2019).

decision, but hypothetically'. The results were very similar to the surveys conducted in Germany and France. Maastricht University found 'that 66.7% of the participants favour to invest their pension savings in a sustainable manner'. The researchers also found that 'choice is driven by social preferences' rather than the objective to maximise returns on investments or reduce risks:

- They first assessed consumers' perceptions on the expected returns from more sustainable investments: '13% of participants expect lower returns and 45% "don't know"'.
- Then, they asked participants who expected similar or higher returns 'whether they would be willing to accept lower financial returns in order to expand sustainable investments?' Only a minority (below 40 per cent) refused in the real case.

As the authors stressed: 'Respondents in the real treatment thus were aware of the fact that their choice could have an impact on the investment activities of their pension fund. More importantly, the fund could thus also consider a willingness to accept lower returns as the right to give up financial returns in order to increase the social impact of their investments'. These surprising results might have to do with what behavioural finance researchers call 'hyperbolic discounting'. Behavioural economics tells us that given two similar rewards, animals and humans show a preference for one that arrives sooner rather than later. They are said to 'discount' the value of the later reward. Discounting is called 'hyperbolic' when individuals reveal a strong tendency to become more impatient when rewards are more imminent (Dasgupta and Maskin, 2015). They make choices today that their future self would prefer not to have made, despite knowing the same information. Applied to the case of preferences for sustainable investment, it seems that the psychological rewards related to more sustainable choices (e.g. self-esteem and social status) are immediate and certain, while the downside on financial returns are uncertain and only have consequences in the far future. The application of hyperbolic discount could therefore lead consumers to fully value the psychological rewards and entirely discount the financial downside.

These results seem to indicate that 80 million Europeans (65 per cent of people holding financial assets) would walk the talk and invest all their savings in sustainable products if they have the opportunity to do so. More research is obviously necessary, and underway, to reach definitive conclusions. One thing is certain though: most of them are not offered this opportunity.

13.1.4 A Principal–Agent Problem for 80 Million Europeans

In 2017, a series of 'mystery shopping' visits in retail banks in Europe (2DII, 2017) revealed that financial advisors never ask about the 'non-financial' investment objectives of their clients. They usually rely on 'suitability questionnaires' provided by their employer to define the profile of their clients and automatically recommend one or a couple of preselected products,[3] and these questionnaires happen to be designed on the inaccurate assumption that clients do not have any expectations regarding the social and environmental outcomes of their investments.

13.1.5 Sustainability Investment Objectives Ignored

In a more recent series of visits in French retail banks,[4] three researchers pretended to be potential clients with environmental objectives: the first one did not express them spontaneously, the second gave heavy clues repeatedly and the third explicitly mentioned the objectives. The experiment reveals that only 3 per cent of French financial advisors ask spontaneously about sustainability objectives or explore

---

[3] European Commission (2018c).

[4] Approximately 100 visits were conducted by 2° Investing Initiative, between October 2019 and January 2020, in the following distribution outlets: Banque Populaire, BNP, Caisse D'Epargne, CIC, Crédit Agricole, Crédit du Nord, Crédit Mutuel, HSBC, La Banque Postale, LCL, Societe Generale, Bred, Cooperative Credit. Mystery visitors mimic three typical client profiles: (1) Young, active, thirty years old looking for responsible investments. (2) Risk-averse, forty to fifty years old. (3) Pro-risk, forty to fifty years old. Preliminary gross results prior to quality review by lawyers and behavioural finance experts.

the topic when it is brought by the clients. About a third ignore the topic even after heavy clues or push back on the objective expressed.

Based on these findings, we concluded in 2017 that most distribution channels were breaking the law and still do today.[5] These findings were then integrated in the EC Sustainable Finance action plan, which concluded that the existing regulations[6] 'require investment firms and insurance distributors to offer "suitable" products to meet their clients' needs, when offering advice. For this reason, those firms should ask about their clients' preferences (such as environmental, social and governance factors) and take them into account when assessing the range of financial instruments and insurance products to be recommended'.[7] In application of this plan, the EC decided to modify the legal framework governing financial advice to retail clients.

More mystery shopping visits are planned in France and across Europe to confirm these findings, but preliminary evidence suggest that at least 75 million Europeans might be currently invested in financial products that are considered 'unsuitable' by the existing regulation.

13.2   RETAIL INVESTORS DEPRIVED OF VOTING RIGHTS ON SUSTAINABILITY ISSUES

This issue also has major implications for what appear to be the most straightforward technique (Kölbel et al., 2019) to deliver environmental at scale through the management of retail investors' money: the use of shareholder rights.

Most listed companies operating in sectors relevant from a climate change perspective have a base of assets (e.g. power plants,

---

[5] In a public hearing, the European Securities and Markets Authority (ESMA) confirmed our interpretation. www.youtube.com/watch?v=bnrzpUKMSTY&list=PLG9hYNY83JSY0cdHKJiYMXqy-LdsaTFeg&index=3&t=0s.

[6] *Markets in Financial Instruments Directive* (MiFID II) and the *Insurance Distribution Directive* (IDD).

[7] Action 4 of the EC Action Plan (European Commission, 2018b).

cement plants, oil fields), production plans (e.g. for cars, aircrafts) and related investment plans misaligned with the 1.5°C–2°C pathway.[8] Each year, at their Annual General Meeting, the top management of these companies receive a green light from their shareholders on these Paris-misaligned strategies. A recent analysis of the 500 climate-related resolutions filed since 2006 (2DII, 2019b) concludes that only 3 per cent of climate-related resolutions were successful. The researchers identified 150 resolutions requesting companies to set climate targets, among which only 11 explicitly requested alignment with a 2°C pathway, and only three were successful.

In other words: in a world where it is possible to estimate whether a given company's strategy is aligned or misaligned with the Paris agreement and a growing number of asset managers pay attention to the issue,[9] most shareholders still de facto 'vote against Paris' each year; and to a large extent, this vote is powered by house-holds' savings.

Direct ownership of listed equities only represents 5 per cent of households' financial assets (EFAMA, 2019). Retail investors are now commonly offered packaged financial products as a means of investing in listed equities. The EU financial framework has encour-aged this indirect holding of shares and other securities by retail investors. In the majority of cases the intermediary is therefore the actual owner of the shares, who has the power to exercise voting rights attached to those shares.

Combined with other structural barriers such as unequal voting rights, this principal–agent problem prevents retail investor voting preferences being acted upon. Instead, voting power is concentrated at a tier of the investment chain (asset managers) far removed from retail investors.

---

[8] See www.transitionmonitor.com and https://compass.transitionmonitor.org.
[9] See the Climate Action 100+ Coalition, the Net Zero Asset Owner Alliance and the January 2020 announcements made by BlackRock (e.g. at www.nytimes.com/2020/01/14/business/dealbook/larry-fink-BlackRock-climate-change.html).

In a 2019 survey (2DII, 2020c[10]), French and German retail investors were asked how they would respond to ethical, social or environmental concerns related to their equity investments and offered a list of options. A majority prioritised the use of their (indirect) shareholder rights.

When asked whether financial intermediaries should consult their end clients about the use of shareholder votes on climate resolutions, an overwhelming majority responded positively and thought that their preferences should impose binding constraints on how financial intermediaries exercise voting power on climate resolutions. About 52 per cent of survey respondents also indicated they would spend one to two hours per year, and 35 per cent were prepared to spend more.[11] More critically, a majority of interested investors would push for resolutions explicitly requesting alignment with a 2°C pathway (2DII, 2020a); voting preferences that bear little resemblance to asset managers' exercise of their voting power (Figure 13.1).

As a consequence of this principal–agent problem, the largest group of climate-conscious investors acts as a 'passive-aggressive' force supporting the 5°C status quo, including allocation strategies aligned with 5°C and the use of shareholder rights to support companies with 5°C strategies.

13.2.1   No Suitable Product Offer for 40 Per cent of Individual Investors

As one would expect, a distribution system based on pushing unsuitable products to consumers and ignoring their expectations leads to an

---

[10] Participants were at least eighteen years old and were recruited from the base population of potential retail investors (every participant has €1.000 in savings and/ or a saving rate of at least €100 per month).

[11] These results should be interpreted with caution. Survey respondents' willingness to devote time to considering this information may be highly dependent on the context and the norm. For example, if information is embedded in a daily news reading experience, the response may be very different from when the information is contained in formal company circulars associated with the general meeting.

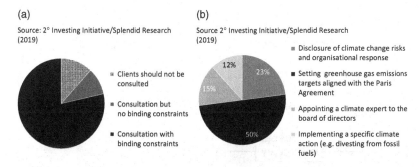

FIGURE 13.1 The preferences of French and German retail investors: consulting clients and AGM resolutions; (a) Should end clients be consulted on voting preferences on climate? Should the preferences be binding for intermediaries?; (b) Preferred categories of climate resolution for retail investors
Source: 2° Investing Initiative (2020a)

innovation gap: there appears to be no product suitable for about 40 per cent of individual investors.

13.2.2 *Defining and Proving the Environmental Impact of a Product*

When considering an investment in a 'sustainable' financial product, consumers tend to apply the same mental framework as for any green *purchase*: the 'claim' that the product is 'green' is associated with a concrete product 'feature', which translates directly into a measurable environmental 'benefit': the gas savings of an hybrid car lead to less pollution, the absence of pesticides in organic farming saves bees and other species and so forth.

The consumers can then 'take credit' for the environmental benefit because there is a causal and linear relationship between the purchasing decision on the one hand, and the environmental benefit on the other end:

- They save fuel when using the car;
- They assume that another organic product is produced for the one consumed. This perfect *elasticity* might not be entirely accurate due to stocks and price effects, but it is overall a reasonable assumption.

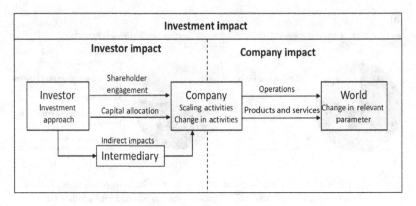

FIGURE 13.2 Investment impact
Source: Kölbel et al. (2018)

In the case of the investment in a 'sustainable' investment product, however, the logic is much more complex: there is no direct relationship between the product 'feature' (e.g. investment process, fund composition, voting policy) and the expected environmental benefits in the real economy: purchasing stocks of a wind farm operator or selling stocks of a coal-fired power plants operator does not add or retire power production capacity.

Besides, the benefit is at best uncertain. Academic literature[12] defines 'investment impact' as a 'change in a specific social or environmental parameter that is caused by the actions of an investor' (see Figure 13.2), and it concludes that, at this stage no evidence supports the general statement that any green, fossil-free, low-carbon or SRI fund generates, by design, an environmental impact.

For instance, from an environmental perspective, the purpose of increasing the exposure of a portfolio to green economic activities is to bridge a financing gap. Being a 'green activity' (as defined by the EU taxonomy for instance) does not necessarily involve being underfinanced, however. The growth of some green activities is capped by other factors, such as a lack of consumer demand, an unfavourable tax

[12] See Kölbel et al. (2018, 2019).

environment, technological obstacles and so forth. The low level of financing observed is in most cases the consequence of these factors rather than their cause. When a financing gap is experienced, it does not necessary take place across the entire capital stack: it usually relates to a specific phase, such as seed capital or the 'Death Valley' (the market gap between venture capital and private equity). Increasing the ownership of corporate bonds to boost an activity that suffers from a lack of venture capital simply misses the point. The same types of caveats apply to underweighting and divestment from polluting activities.

Such obstacles lead researchers to conclude that

> While the impact of capital allocation may seem intuitive at first sight, it touches upon a rather fundamental question, namely to what extent the decisions of investors influence the course of the real economy. We were not able to find studies that relate the capital allocation decisions of sustainable investors to corporate investment activities or operational practices. Hence, direct empirical evidence for the capital allocation impact is lacking. ... Indirect impacts are mostly unproven due to a lack of empirical studies that indicate their effectiveness.

Regarding the use of shareholder rights, the researchers conclude that

> the impact of shareholder engagement is relatively straightforward to trace. An investor requests a company to implement a certain change, and the investee either follows through or not. ... The success probability of any particular shareholder engagement depends on a host of determinants related to characteristics of the engagement request, the engaged company, the engaging investor, and the specific process of engagement.
>
> *(Goranova and Ryan, 2014)*

As described previously, on climate-related objectives, these conditions are not yet met.

As a result, there is no ex ante evidence that a given 'sustainable' financial product, whatever the approach adopted, actually contributes to deliver social and/or environmental outcomes. To make such claims, produce manufacturers, and financial institutions more broadly, therefore need to gather ex post evidence on the effectiveness of their approach, and they are not there yet.

Estimating, at collective level, if certain 'sustainable investment' practices are effective in generating changes in the real economy, and the magnitude of this effect requires observation and modelling. The attribution of the estimated environmental benefits to the actions of a specific fund manager would however require an additional calculation step. A myriad of social science and economics tools can be mobilised in this respect.

However, to date, only a few academic studies have explored the topic, methodological frameworks are still under development[13] and only a handful of consumer-facing financial institutions are starting to pilot test such assessment. At the stage, they mostly acknowledge the challenges.

> The real-world impact of our engagements may not be immediately quantifiable, or comparable across companies in the portfolio. . . . we are committed to reporting both on the progress and outcomes of our engagement efforts. . . . we use narratives to communicate how our corporate engagement has generated real changes within companies. . . . Importantly, the companies will corroborate the narratives after meeting any of the SDG objectives – ensuring integrity and adding credibility to our claims of effective engagement and additionality.
>
> *(Hermès, 2019)*

There is a difference between the outcomes of portfolio climate alignment and the impact of absolute GHG emissions reduction in

---

[13] See for instance the Impact Management Project and related measurement experiment by Hermès IM at https://impactmanagementproject.com.

the real economy. Challenges such as carbon leakage present limitations to how much a bank can control in terms of climate impact, especially when applying capital allocation choices as a tool for steering. . . . Should ING take robust measures to support and engage a client to transition, the client's actions may have been a response to pressure from multiple stakeholders or their own internal decision-making. It would therefore be difficult for ING to claim that impact as a result of our efforts alone.

(ING Group, 2019)

In this context, in order to make its product suitable for environmental impact-oriented clients, a fund manager needs to gather specific evidence that its investment strategy works and measure the related impact. This is not only a logical conclusion, but also a legal obligation.

13.3 DECEPTIVE GREEN MARKETING IS THE NORM RATHER THAN THE EXCEPTION

In order to foster consumers' confidence across Europe, the EU adopted in 2005 a renewed regulatory framework on unfair commercial practices aimed at prohibiting any practice 'that materially distorts or is likely to materially distort the economic behaviour with regard to the product of the average consumer whom it reaches or to whom it is addressed' (European Union (2005): Unfair Commercial Practices Directive (UCPD): art. 5.2.b).

Among those, a misleading practice is one that

contains false information and is therefore untruthful or in any way, including overall presentation, deceives or is likely to deceive the average consumer, even if the information is factually correct, in relation to one or more of the following elements, and in either case causes or is likely to cause him to take a transactional decision that he would not have taken otherwise: . . . the main characteristics of the product.

(UCPD, art. 6)

Regarding more specifically green marketing claims, the European Consumer Agenda adopted by the EU in 2012, acknowledged that 'consumers should be supported in easily identifying the truly sustainable choice' and that 'effective tools are needed to protect them against misleading and unfounded environmental and health claims' (European Commission, 2012, p. 5).

To that effect, the EU gathered a Multi-Stakeholder Dialogue on Environmental Claims (MDEC), which defined a set of compliance criteria aimed at tackling misleading green allegations and greenwashing, in light of the two following principles of interpretation established by the EC:

- 'Based on the general clauses of the UCPD, particularly Articles 6 and 7, traders must present their green claims in a clear, specific, accurate and unambiguous manner, to ensure that consumers are not mislead'.
- 'Based on Article 12 of the UCPD, traders must have the evidence to support their claims and be ready to provide it to competent enforcement authorities in an understandable way if the claim is challenged' (European Commission, 2016, p. 97).
- 'As such, claims should be based on robust, independent, verifiable and generally recognised evidence which takes into account the latest scientific findings and methods' (MDEC, 2016).

Applied to claims made by financial product managers, this framework reveals a pretty problematic situation. In 2019, our legal team reviewed a sample of 230 funds potentially associated with environmental impact claims (2DII, 2020b). The review concludes that almost no fund manager currently performs and discloses such science-based 'impact assessment' measurement (Figure 13.3). Many SRI and green funds (49 per cent of our preliminary sample of 230) are not even explicitly managed to deliver an environmental impact, they therefore make no claim on the topic.

At this point of our review, the researchers identified 118 funds (51 per cent of the sample) that make environmental impact claims, but almost all of them assume – without evidence – that their approach (e.g. increasing the exposure of the portfolio to green

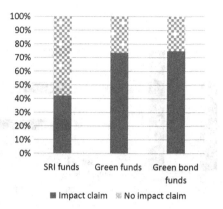

FIGURE 13.3 Frequency of investors' environmental impact claims by sustainable investment products manufacturers
Source: 2° Investing Initiative (2020b)

activities, excluding certain polluting sectors, selecting 'best-in-class' companies) automatically translate into environmental benefits in the real economy, which can then be attributed to the fund and its clients.

On top of being unsubstantiated, most of the claims reviewed appeared to be ambiguous, misleading and sometimes inaccurate (see Figure 13.4). Although the legal team did not find specific case law on financial products' green claims, these practices appear to be incompatible with the general regulatory framework.[14]

The main inaccuracies are based on two confusions, sometimes combined:

- Confuse the impact of certain economic activities of the investee companies with the impact of the investment strategy itself (as defined previously);
- Compare an indicator associated with the companies in the portfolio (usually their carbon footprint) with the market average and present the difference as 'a reduction' in the real economy.

---

[14] Multi-Stakeholder Dialogue on Environmental Claims (MDEC) guidelines are a piece of soft law established without prejudice of the 'national courts and authorities ... case-by-case assessment of whether a claim is misleading either in its content or in the way it is presented to consumers, taking into account its impact on the average consumer's purchasing decisions' (MDEC, 2016).

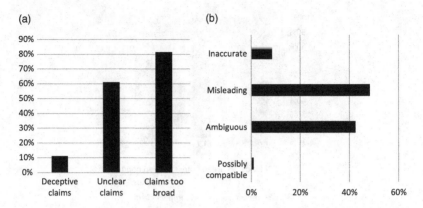

FIGURE 13.4 Compliance of investors' environmental impact claims made by sustainable investment products manufacturers; (a) Frequency of problematic claims per MDEC criteria (in per cent of funds); (b) Funds categorised based on how deceptive the claims are (by per cent of funds)
Source: 2° Investing Initiative (2020b)

In other words, the fund manager takes credit for the impact of the companies in their portfolios, without any evidence that their action influenced their activities in any way.

To go a step further, the researchers tested some of the misleading environmental claims on 2,000 French and Germany retail clients.[15] Figure 13.5 illustrates the results for a false and an ambiguous claim. Overall, based on a limited sample, the conclusion is that most misleading claims are actually misleading consumers on the environmental benefits associated with the products.

13.4   FROM IMPACT-WASHING TO MIS-SELLING

In order to understand if these misleading marketing practices actually lead to mis-selling, the researchers conducted 100 interviews, as a

---

[15] 2DII (2020c). Participants were at least eighteen years old and were recruited from the base population of potential retail investors (every participant has €1,000 in savings and/or a saving rate of at least €100 per month).

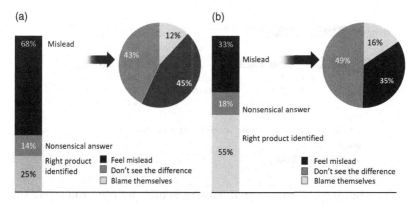

FIGURES 13.5 Interpretation of investor impact claims by German and French consumers; (a) Interpretation of a false claim (green equity fund): The equity fund allows investors to have a real impact on climate change. The design of the fund aims at generating a real impact on the environment and create solutions for climate change: For example, a €5mn investment in the fund for one year would reduce polluting emissions by 4,200 tons of CO_2, which is equivalent to taking 1,900 cars off the road for a year. These figures are reported every year and audited; (b) Interpretation of an accurate but ambiguous claim (thematic equity fund): The fund invests in companies which help to realise the energy transition to a low-carbon economy, having as such a positive impact on CO_2 emissions. Those who invest in the fund invest in companies that contribute to and profit from the transition.
Source: 2DII (2020c)

potential impact-oriented client,[16] with 100 financial advisors in French retail banks. The findings suggest that when the clients express spontaneously and explicitly their environmental impact objective, most advisors first recommend the sale of unsuitable products: standard products (30 per cent), SRI funds (50 per cent) or green-themed funds (5 per cent). Eventually, when the client flags that these products are not associated with any evidence of environmental impact and/or do not even claim that they have an environmental impact, a majority of advisors try to downplay the difference and push the sale.

---

[16] One hundred visits were conducted by 2° Investing Initiative, between October 2019 and January 2020, in France. See details 2DII (2020c).

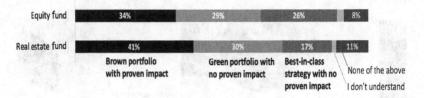

FIGURE 13.6 Sustainability investment preferences of French and German consumers
Source: 2DII (2020c)

The most common argument presented by fund managers or financial advisors to justify the status quo is that the environmental benefit being intangible anyway for the clients, they might be satisfied with a product investing in green economic activities, even if there is no evidence that it changes anything in the real economy.

To test this hypothesis, the research team asked 1,000 French and German retail investors interested in 'sustainable investments' if they would prefer (a) a fund invested in green economic activities, but with no proven environmental impact, or (b) a fund invested in polluting activities but associated with evidence of a positive environmental impact in the real economy[17] (see Figure 13.6).

The survey concludes that about 30–40 per cent of retail clients prioritise investment products delivering actual impacts over products that are simply only associated with environmental features, even if it leads them to invest in polluting activities. These results are consistent with the answers regarding the motivations for investing sustainably, revealed by both this survey (see Figure 13.7) and in the above-mentioned field experiments.

Overall, the research concludes that about 40 per cent of retail investors expect their investment strategy to generate a measurable impact in the real economy, and for them, the evidence matters. Extrapolated to Europe, this group represents about 80 million clients.

---

[17] The questionnaire is based on several hypothetic products from different categories (real estate funds, equity funds, bond funds).

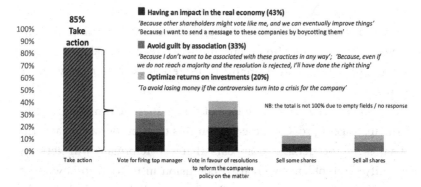

FIGURE 13.7 French and German consumers for taking action on their equity investment
What motivated you to choose this action?
Source: 2DII (2020c)

These findings suggest that, moving forward, the main mis-selling problem regulators will have to deal with is not the blunt ignorance of social and environmental objectives by financial advisors, but their misrepresentation of clients' objectives in order to force the sale of on-shelf 'sustainable' products that are unsuitable to impact-oriented clients.

13.5   A POLICY RESPONSE STUCK IN POST-TRUTH POLITICS

Reacting to our initial findings,[18] the European Commission decided to clarify the requirements and oblige financial advisors to take non-financial preferences into account when recommending investment products.[19] This decision represents a giant leap in the right direction.

More precisely, the regulation aims at clarifying that an investment firm providing financial advice and portfolio management

---

[18] See recommendation four of the High-Level Expert Group on Sustainable Finance (European Commission, 2018a).

[19] See Action seven of the EC Action Plan (European Commission, 2018b), and the Draft Delegated Act.

should carry out a mandatory assessment of client sustainability preferences during the suitability assessment. Additionally, the investment firm's financial product recommendation must satisfy the client's sustainability preferences if these have been expressed.

So far so good – on the face of things these reforms address the principal–agent problem described in this chapter. But as always, the devil is in the details: it appears that the reforms[20] will actually amplify the problem by creating confusion in relation to how green financial products are understood and, above all, how to deal with the expectations of impact-focussed consumers.

In the upcoming reform of financial advisors' duties, social or *environmental investment objectives* are defined as 'a client's or potential client's choice as to whether and which *environmentally sustainable investments* … should be integrated into his or her investment strategy'.[21] The EC then normatively defines that an '"*environmentally sustainable investment*" means an investment that funds one or several economic activities that qualify under this Regulation[22] as environmentally sustainable'. In other words, only the funds exposed to the 'green' economic activities listed in the EC taxonomy are considered suitable to impact investors, irrespective of whether or not the investment strategy has a proven contribution to scaling up these activities or delivering other environmental impacts.

The rationale behind this regulation is summarised by the EC as 'Summarily, financial products or investments in themselves cannot

---

[20] The analysis is based on the latest version of the draft regulations, as of 10 January 2020. The analysis covers the delegated acts of MIDIF and IDD, the Disclosure Regulation, and the Taxonomy.

[21] Draft MIFID/IDD delegated Acts: https://ec.europa.eu/finance/docs/level-2-measures/mifid-delegated-act-2018_en .pdf and https://ec.europa.eu/info/law/insurance-distribution-directive-2016-97-eu/ amending-and-supplementary-acts/implementing-and-delegated-acts_en.

[22] EU Framework to facilitate sustainable investment (Green Taxonomy) at: https://eur-lex.europa.eu/legal-content/EN/TXT/PDF/?uri=CELEX:52018PC0353& from=EN.

be green. Greenness is derived from the uses to which they are being put in underlying assets or activities';[23] an assumption that is factually inaccurate, rejected by most impact-oriented consumers (see above-mentioned surveys) and directly contradict the academic research and the emerging international standards on the topic:

> we refer to investor impact as the change that investor activity achieves in company impact, and we refer to company impact as the change that a company's activities achieve in a social or environmental parameter. This definition is in line with the recently released principles for impact management from the International Finance Corporation (IFC), which stipulate that investors should establish a narrative that outlines how the investor contributed to the achievement of company impact (IFC, 2019).
>
> *(Kölbel et al., 2019)*

Doubling down, the upcoming future EU Ecolabel for financial products also follows this flawed logic and is exclusively defined by the exposure of the underlying portfolio to green economic activities.

Doing so its criteria entirely ignore the actual environmental impact of the investment strategy even though the label is supposed to '(i) allow retail investors concerned with the environmental impact of their investment to make informed choices and contribute to the green transition and (ii) provide incentives to industry to develop financial products with a reduced environmental impact or a positive environmental impact'. More critically, this approach in consistent with the essence and legal framework applicable to all ecolabels, which essentially require it to identify the best products of a category in terms of positive/reduced environmental impact, based on scientific evidence.

As a member of the EC High Level Expert Group (HLEG) that recommended the EC action plan, I have flagged the issues related to

---

[23] Draft EU ecolabel criteria:
https://ec.europa.eu/environment/ecolabel/criteria-development-and-revision
.html.

impact measurement and substantiation of claims through official channels and subsequent meetings. The EC has offered no technical rebuttal, nor did they include these questions in the scope of the TEG.

More recently, this issue has been raised, in response to the EC consultation on the technical criteria of the ecolabel (2DII, 2019a) by my organisation and others, but the latest documents available on the approach of the EC when this book was printed suggest that they have chosen to ignore the science and stay focussed on the political talking points around 'shifting the trillions' and 'greening portfolios'.

It is too soon to tell what the outcome of this process will be when you will read this book, but at this stage the progress on this issue shows that sustainable finance policymaking has not yet broken 'the evidence barrier': this invisible wall that prevents us from determining what works and what doesn't, to go beyond talking points and slogans in order to accelerate the 'reorientation of capital flows towards sustainable investment' without crashing the plane.

For the foreseeable future, the 80 million Europeans willing to contribute to the Paris agreement with their money will continue to invest in products that do not deliver such outcomes.

REFERENCES

2° Investing Initiative (2017), 'Non-Financial Message in a Bottle: How the Environmental Objectives of Retail Investors are Overlooked in MIFID II – PRIIPS Implementation'. https://2degrees-investing.org/non-financial-message.
2° Investing Initiative (2019a), 'Impact-Washing Gets a Free Ride: An Analysis of the Draft EU Ecolabel Criteria for Financial Products'. https://2degrees-investing.org/impact-washing-gets-a-free-ride.
2° Investing Initiative (2019b), 'Passing the Baton: Shareholder Resolutions and Their Contribution to Investor Climate Pledges'. https://2degrees-investing.org/passing-the-baton-shareholder-resolutions-their-contribution-to-investor-climate-pledges.
2° Investing Initiative (2020a), 'Retail Clients Want to Vote for Paris', March. https://2degrees-investing.org/wp-content/uploads/2020/03/Retail-Clients-Want-to-Vote-for-Paris-1.pdf.

2° Investing Initiative (2020b), 'EU Retail Funds' Environmental Impact Claims Do Not Comply with Regulatory Guidance', March. https://2degrees-investing.org/resource/marketing-claims.

2° Investing Initiative (2020c), 'A Large Majority of Retail Clients Want to Invest Sustainably: Survey of French and German Retails Investors' Sustainability Preferences', March. https://2degrees-investing.org/resource/retail-clients-sustainable-investment.

Bauer, R., Ruof, T. and Smeets, P. (2018) 'Get Real! Individuals Prefer More Sustainable Investments', Discussion Paper, University of Maastricht. https://sustainable-finance.nl/upload/researches/Bauer-Ruof-Smeets-2018-Get-real.pdf.

(University of) Cambridge Institute for Sustainability Leadership (2019). 'Walking the Talk: Understanding Consumer Demand for Sustainable Investing'. Cambridge, UK: University of Cambridge Institute for Sustainability Leadership. www.cisl.cam.ac.uk/resources/sustainable-finance-publications/walking-the-talk-understanding-consumer-demand-for-sustainable-investing.

Dasgupta, P. and Maskin, E. (2015), 'Uncertainty and Hyperbolic Discounting'. *American Economic Review* 95(4), 1290–1299. https://scholar.harvard.edu/files/maskin/files/uncertainty_and_hyperbolic_discounting_aer.pdf.

European Commission (2012), 'European Consumer Agenda'. https://eur-lex.europa.eu/legal-content/EN/TXT/PDF/?uri=CELEX:52012DC0225&from=EN.

European Commission (2016), 'Guidance on the Implementation/Application of Directive 2005/29/EC on Unfair Commercial Practices'. https://ec.europa.eu/info/sites/info/files/ucp-guidance-en.pdf.

European Commission (2018a), 'Final Report of the High-Level Expert Group on Sustainable Finance'. https://ec.europa.eu/info/sites/info/files/180131-sustainable-finance-final-report_en.pdf.

European Commission (2018b), 'Action Plan: Financing Sustainable Growth'. https://eur-lex.europa.eu/legal-content/EN/TXT/PDF/?uri=CELEX:52018DC0097&from=EN.

European Commission (2018c), 'Distribution Systems of Retail Investment Products across Europe'. https://ec.europa.eu/info/sites/info/files/180425-retail-investment-products-distribution-systems_en.pdf.

European Fund and Asset Management Association (EFAMA) (2019) 'Ownership of Investment Funds in Europe'. February. www.efama.org/Publications/EFAMA_Ownership_Investment_Funds.pdf.

European Union (2005), 'Directive 2005/29/EC of the European Parliament and of the Council', *Official Journal of the European Union* L149/22–L1 49/39 https://eur-lex.europa.eu/legal-content/EN/TXT/PDF/?uri=CELEX:32005L0029&from=EN.

Goranova, M. and Ryan, L. V. (2014), 'Shareholder Activism: A Multidisciplinary Review', *Journal of Management* 40(5), 1230–1268. https://papers.ssrn.com/sol3/papers.cfm?abstract_id=2384280.

Hermès (2019), 'SDG Engagement Equity: 2018 Annual Report'. www.hermes-investment.com/insight/equities/sdg-engagement-equity-2018-annual-report.

ING Group (2019) 'Terra Progress Report 2019'. www.ing.com/Newsroom/News/Press-releases/ING-publishes-first-Terra-progress-report.htm.

Kölbel, J. F., Heeb, F., Paetzold, F. and Busch, T. (2018), 'Beyond Returns: Investigating the Social and Environmental Impact of Sustainable Investing'. SSRN 3289544, University of Zurich. www.zora.uzh.ch/id/eprint/162661.

Kölbel, J. F., Heeb, F., Paetzold, F. and Busch, T. (2019), 'Can Sustainable Investing Save the World? Reviewing the Mechanisms of Investor Impact'. https://papers.ssrn.com/sol3/papers.cfm?abstract_id=3289544.

Multi-stakeholder Dialogue on Environmental Claims (MDEC) (2016), 'Advice on Compliance Criteria on Environmental Claims'. https://ec.europa.eu/info/sites/info/files/ucp-guidance-en.pdf.

14 Strengthening Green Finance by Better Integrating the Social Dimensions in the European Union's Sustainable Finance Laws

Myriam Vander Stichele

In order to tackle climate change and achieve the commitments of the Paris climate agreement, the European Union (EU) embarked in 2018 on an EU Action Plan on financing sustainable Growth (European Commission, 2018b). In an attempt to ensure that sufficient private investment supports the transition to a climate-friendly economy, the European Commission (EC) launched legislative initiatives that aimed at promoting more clarity about green and climate-related investments and transparency on how the investment industry deals with ESG risks and impacts. This chapter exposes how the EC has focussed in those legislative proposals primarily on climate change mitigation and adaptation objectives, while social aspects have been ignored or have been included in an incoherent way. There are, however, growing political statements and events that indicate that integrating and promoting social progresses can reinforce policies, measures and actions to stop and prevent climate change.

14.1 INTRODUCTION TO THE EU'S INCOHERENCE ON CLIMATE FINANCE INITIATIVES

Since the Rio Declaration on environment and development in 1992,[1] sustainability has been defined as including both social and environmental dimensions, with the understanding that they are reinforcing

[1] United Nations Conference on Environment and Development (1992).

each other. For instance, land grabbing and pollution for oil and gas extraction, which deprived people from their livelihoods, has resulted in CO_2 emissions-related climate change. In turn, CO_2 emissions have affected people's health or, in some cities, prevented children from going to school. The dual social and environmental/climate approach has been integrated for a long time in the many voluntary initiatives by the financial sector,[2] often resulting in specific sectoral guidelines, principles or corporate codes. Also, the Principles for Responsible Banking launched in September 2019 stated that 'only in an inclusive society founded on human dignity, equality and the sustainable use of natural resources, can our clients and customers and, in turn, our businesses thrive'.[3] Financial institutions have, for instance, been taking a leadership role in financing the UN Sustainable Development Goals (SDGs), which combine social and environmental objectives, through the Global Investors for Sustainable Development (GISD) Alliance.[4]

The EU wants to take a leadership role in tackling climate change and achieving the Paris agreement's climate commitments. During her presentation in 2019 as President-elect of the new EC, Ursula von der Leyen called for a European Green Deal as well as 'an economy that works for people'.[5] When defending his designated mandate to implement a European Green Deal, the Executive Vice-President-designate, Frans Timmermans, emphasised that the European Green Deal also means improving social aspects and avoiding negative social impacts of the energy transition as part of the deal; it will not 'leave one region, one person behind'.[6] 'We can only succeed if both prosper, neglect one and both will suffer'.[7] While the discourse promised to raise public spending on social issues, such

---

[2] See for instance Vander Stichele (2015).   [3] UNEP FI (2019).
[4] United Nations (2019).   [5] Von der Leyen (2019).
[6] Frans Timmermans, Zondagbrief – Europa richting een duurzame toekomst, email letter to Dutch voters, 13 October 2019.
[7] European Parliament, Hearing of Frans Timmermans, Executive Vice President-designate, 'European Green Deal: opening statement by Frans Timmermans', soundbite 00:05:11, 8 October 2019, https://multimedia.europarl.europa.eu/en/

as a dedicated 'just transition fund' to support people and communities most affected by the transition, for example closed coal power plants,[8] there were little proposals how exactly the private sector would be involved in improving the social dimensions.

In his hearings to be re-nominated as a Commissioner responsible for the EU's financial sector, Executive Vice-President-designate Valdis Dombrovskis, who has been spearheading sustainable finance in the previous Commission, promised to re-invigorate legal and other initiatives following up from the existing EU Action Plan on financing sustainable growth.[9] So far, the previous Commission and the EU have focussed on the climate change challenge when taking the bold initiative to enact on legislative proposals in order to make the investment industry finance more sustainable activities. For instance, the revised EU law on benchmarks[10] provides investors with two reliable benchmarks for investment funds covering companies or other entities that are (1) in transition towards decarbonisation in a measurable, science-based and time-bound way (to be labelled EU Climate Transition Benchmarks) or (2) aiming to achieve CO_2 reduction and elimination as required by the Paris climate agreement (to be labelled a EU Paris-aligned Benchmarks). The EC's launching of an International Platform on Sustainable Finance on 18 October 2019 was also focussing only on 'environmentally sustainable finance' and aiming at scaling up 'environmental sustainable investments'.[11]

hearing-of-frans-timmermans-executive-vice-president-designate-european-green-deal-opening-statement-by-frans-timmermans_I178173-V_rv.

[8] Dumas (2019).   [9] European Commission (2019f).

[10] European Union, Regulation 2019/2089 of 27 November 2019 amending Regulation (EU) 2016/1011 as regards EU Climate Transition Benchmarks, EU Paris-aligned Benchmarks and sustainability-related disclosures for benchmarks, *Official Journal of the European Union*, 9 December 2019, L 317/17-27. https://eur-lex.europa.eu/legal-content/EN/TXT/?uri=CELEX:32019R2089. (Note that the Technical Expert Group on Sustainable Finance (TEG) published a 'Handbook on Climate Benchmarks and benchmarks' ESG disclosures', 20 December 2019. https://ec .europa.eu/info/sites/info/files/business_economy_euro/banking_and_finance/documents/192020-sustainable-finance-teg-benchmarks-handbook_en_0.pdf: there is no mentioning of the minimum social safeguards.)

[11] European Commission (2019d), see also the related documents.

One way the EC is dealing with social factors in sustainable finance legislation is to avoid unintended consequences from negative social and human rights impacts on the climate-related projects and the value of climate-related investment. Indeed, lack of consideration of social aspects have already led to reputational damage, stranded assets and loss of investors' money, such as wind mill projects on indigenous land without consent of the people whose livelihoods rights were endangered, for example in Kenya[12] and Mexico.[13] The hidden social and human rights costs in mining the minerals for the solar panels, batteries, windmills and other renewable energy techniques are also affecting the viability of CO_2-mitigating products.[14]

14.2   THE EU FRAMEWORK LAW FOR A GREEN TAXONOMY WITH MINIMUM SOCIAL SAFEGUARDS

In its legislative proposal for a taxonomy regulation (European Commission, 2018c), the EC has applied an approach of minimum social safeguards to ensure climate-friendly financing does not endanger the reputation and the value of the investment. This approach was accepted but also broadened by the co-legislators, the European Parliament[15] and the Council of Finance Ministers (ECOFIN),[16] who agreed on a compromise for the final legal text as published on 17 December 2019. The legal framework for an EU taxonomy Regulation and its technical standards have been officially published

---

[12] Obulutsa (2016); Nazalya (2019) the cancellation of a 61 MW wind farm in Kenya in February 2016 due to widespread community opposition, included a court case over the project location and resulted in a shareholder investment loss of US$66 million.

[13] Nazalya (2019); Business and Human Rights Resource Centre, 'Mexico: Oaxaca Wind Farms impact indigenous peoples in Oaxaca', web page: www.business-humanrights.org/en/mexico-oaxaca-wind-farms-impact-indigenous-peoples-in-oaxaca.

[14] See for example Hodal (2019); ActionAid (2018) and Business and Human Rights Resource Centre (2018).

[15] European Parliament (2019).   [16] Council of the European Union (2019a).

on 18 June 2020, including important changes made in December 2019 (integrated in this chapter).[17]

The EC's proposal for a framework law to establish and regulate an officially accepted EU 'taxonomy' focussed on a uniform EU definition and classification of climate and environmentally sustainable economic activities to be financed. The Taxonomy Regulation covers six categories of sustainable economic activities with environmental objectives for:

   i. Climate change mitigation.
   ii. Climate change adaptation.
   iii. Sustainable use and protection of water and marine resources.
   iv. Transition to a circular economy.
   v. Pollution prevention and control.
   vi. Protection and restoration of biodiversity and ecosystems.

To be compliant with the taxonomy, the economic activity does not only have to apply the specifications in the Regulation's articles but also the environmental screening criteria, environmental technical standards and benchmarks specific to each activity.[18] In addition, each of the environmentally sustainable activities have to be carried out in compliance with minimum social safeguards, that is an environmentally sustainable economic activity needs to be in alignment with:

(a) the OECD Guidelines for Multinational Enterprises,
(b) the UN Guiding Principles on Business and Human Rights,
(c) the eight core labour rights conventions identified by the Declaration of the International Labour Organization (ILO) on Fundamental Rights and Principles at work, and
(d) the International Bill of Human Rights.

In its legislative proposal, the EC had limited the application of the minimum social safeguards (Article 18) to respecting the eight ILO

---

[17] Council of the European Union (2019b). European Union, Regulation 2020/852 of 18 June 2020 on the establishment of a framework to facilitate sustainable investment, and amending Regulation 2019/2088, *Official Journal of the European Union*, 22 June 2020, L 198/13-43, https://eur-lex.europa.eu/legal-content/EN/TXT/PDF/?uri=CELEX:32020R0852&from=EN.

[18] For more explanation, see for example: Vander Stichele (2019).

core labour rights conventions. As a result, in June 2019 the preliminary advice of the Technical Expert Group (TEG)[19] to elaborate the details of the taxonomy (the 'TEG report') described the implementation of minimum social safeguards in very general terms, that is in less than a page,[20] and not in detail for each climate change mitigation or climate change adaptation activity. Until the end of 2019, the TEG had a mandate only to complement the missing details of some identified environmentally sustainable economic activities and incorporate the feedback of the public consultation on its preliminary advice.

How all the minimum social safeguards will be elaborated, including those added by the European Parliament and by the Ministers of Finance (ECOFIN) (see (a), (b) and (d) discussed previously), has not been clarified. The EC will need to undertake specific efforts to provide all the minimum social standards with sufficient details before the time the taxonomy comes into effect. Article 18 on the minimum safeguards in the final Taxonomy Regulation text of 18 June 2020 does not provide a mandate to the EC to develop and decide on a Delegated Act that outlines how investors must ensure that the minimum social safeguards are being respected. Such an amendment was not inserted during the final decision-making of the legislative process (the 'trialogue'). Since the EC cannot develop a Delegated Act, the EC can use its own and EU member state expertise to develop guidelines and standards, supported by well-resourced advisory groups with experts and representatives from labour, the social sector and civil society, and monitored by the Platform on

[19] European Commission (2018a), 'Technical expert group on sustainable finance – Overview', web page at: https://ec.europa.eu/info/publications/sustainable-finance-technical-expert-group_en. (Note that on 20 December 2019, the TEG published a *Handbook on Climate Transition Benchmarks, Paris-aligned Benchmark and Benchmarks' ESG Disclosures*. The minimum social safeguards were not mentioned. https://ec.europa.eu/info/sites/info/files/business_economy_euro/banking_and_finance/documents/192020-sustainable-finance-teg-benchmarks-handbook_en_0.pdf.)
[20] European Commission (2019b), pp. 64–65.

Sustainable Finance that is to be created according to the taxonomy law (Article 20).

To be effective, details to elaborate the minimum social standards should include: how due diligence requirements have to be applied in an adequate way and adapted for each identified environmental economic activity, to assess the respect of, and prevent and repair breaches of ILO core labour rights conventions (and beyond), the International Bill of Human Rights, the OECD Guidelines for Multinational Enterprises and the UN Guiding Principles on Business and Human Rights. Each of these minimum social safeguards need clearly predefined and standardised procedures for screening criteria and benchmarks that will ensure a harmonised and verifiable application for all taxonomy-based activities by the investors and other financial actors in the EU. These should not only be management box-ticking exercises but also be monitored and adjusted to social progress, such as more equitable distribution of benefits of economic activities throughout the supply chain that result in living wages, health safety and access to health care, and sustainable housing and protection of livelihoods of local or indigenous communities (see also Section 14.5).

Strict and high detailed standards for minimum social safeguards are needed since the EC has been unwilling to develop a taxonomy of socially sustainable economic activities, or activities that are both environmentally and socially sustainable, and in accordance with good governance. The Taxonomy Regulation does not foresee a legislative process of such socially sustainable activities before 2022, that is after a report describing provisions to extend the scope of the application of the taxonomy law is being published by 31 December 2021. This is not coherent with the new EC commitment to advance climate, environmental as well as social goals, and to achieve the UN Sustainable Development Goals. Also, the reality of the problems on the ground of climate- and environmental-associated activities need to integrate a strong social and human rights component, and vice versa, to be effective (see for instance Choidas et al., 2019).

An important obstacle for the actual application of the minimum social safeguards is that the EU taxonomy is not compulsory but only has to be adhered to by investment products, investors and financiers who claim, or are certified, to use the taxonomy's standards. Many renewable energy companies have little to no human rights safeguard and remedy policies,[21] so how can financiers guarantee minimum financial safeguards for climate-mitigating economic activities? Also, the full supervisory mechanisms to enforce the taxonomy's implementation are not yet fully clarified. Given the financial industry's record on lobbying[22] to water down and delay the taxonomy's legislation and related climate implementation standards, screening criteria and benchmarks, the effective implementation of the social minimum requirements might be a challenge. The legal amendment of the Disclosure of Sustainability Regulation, agreed in the final Taxonomy Regulation text of 18 June 2020, should however provide some clarity and incentive. Financial products that do not invest in activities that are compliant with the Taxonomy Regulation will need to include a statement that the underlying investments 'do not take into account the EU criteria for environmentally sustainable economic activities'.[23]

14.2.1   Green Bonds

The EU taxonomy law is an important basis for identifying the environmental activities that can be financed according to an EU Green Bond Standard (GBS). Green bonds have been popular for climate sustainable investments while social bonds and impact bonds have not attracted so much investment. The issuance of green bonds based

---

[21] Business and Human Rights Resource Centre (2018).

[22] As experienced by CSO monitoring of the decision-making process at the European Parliament and the EU Council of Ministers, as well as exposed by oral public statements by European Parliamentarians, for example by Bas Eickhout and Pervenche Perez at: EC, High-level conference: A global approach to sustainable finance, Brussels, 21 March 2019, https://ec.europa.eu/info/events/finance-190321-sustainable-finance_en (attended by the author).

[23] European Union, Regulation 2020/852 of 18 June 2020, Article 7.

on voluntary principles has been increasing in 2018 to US$168bn.[24] In 2017, such green bond issuance was US$162.1bn,[25] which was not 1 per cent of the total long-term global bond issuance in 2017 estimated at US$21.1trn.[26] In comparison, estimations of issuance of social bonds in 2017 and 2018 was US$10bn and US$13bn, and sustainability bonds US$9bn and US$18bn, respectively.[27]

The EC plans to develop an EU GBS for which it has asked advice from the TEG. In June 2019, the TEG's advisory report (European Commission, 2019c) proposed that the green bond issuers that want to apply the EU GBS[28] should:

- define the financed or re-financed activities according to the EU taxonomy, apply the taxonomy's do-no-harm screening criteria and comply with the minimum social safeguards;
- publish upfront a 'Green Bond Framework' that explains all key aspects of the proposed use of funds paid by the bond holders, the processes and reporting, and how the issuer's strategy aligns with environmental objectives;
- report (1) regularly on how the money is allocated and (2) on the environmental impact;
- require an external verifier to review the 'Green Bond Framework' and the final report on the financial allocation.

The emphasis of the TEG advice is evidently on the environmental and climate-related aspects of the EU GBS. However, the implementation and verification instruments proposed by the TEG have little ways to verify whether the minimum social safeguards have been applied.[29] Even the environmental impact reports are not subject to compulsory external verification, independent verification is only encouraged.

---

[24] IMF (2019), figure 6.5. Developments in Global Sustainable Debt Markets, p. 88 and Climate Bonds Initiative (2019).
[25] Climate Bonds Initiative (2019).   [26] SIFMA (2018).   [27] IMF (2019).
[28] For more details, see European Commission (2019c), pp. 57–61.
[29] European Commission (2019c), annexes 1, 2, 3.

According to the TEG advice, the EU GBS should be voluntary and non-legislative, that is not all green bond issuers are obliged to adhere to the EU standard, nor is the EU standard to be set by law. The EC, however, has the power to take the final decision. It can make the EU GBS compulsory for all issuers of green bonds sold in the EU, which would support the application of the broad minimum social safeguards as defined in the taxonomy law and avoid unintended social consequences. Given the growing interest in green bonds, strict standards would be able to guarantee their long-term value and prevent financial and reputational damage from unexpected social (and governance) risks and impacts. Due to COVID-19, the interest in social bonds standards has also increased.

14.2.2   Non-financial Disclosure by Companies

A huge challenge for investors, lenders and other financial services to fully implement the new taxonomy is the dependence on information from companies to be financed. So far, standardisation and verification of company reports on ESG issues are not yet fully in place. The EU's Non-Financial Reporting Directive (NFRD) has voluntary guidelines on reporting requirements for large listed companies, banks and insurance companies (European Commission, 2014, p. L330/1 onwards). The guidelines and related examples of key performance indicators (KPIs) related to social issues cover social and employee matters, respect for human rights, gender issues, labour issues in supply chains, and the principles set out in the European Pillar of Social Rights (European Commission (2017), p. C215/15 onwards).

The EC so far failed to propose clear legally binding reporting standards. It could have done so according to Article 3 of the NFRD after submitting a review report by 6 December 2018. Rather than submitting a report with legislative proposals, the EC opted for only strengthening the guidelines related to the climate aspects. It proposed in June 2019 new non-binding NFRD guidelines on reporting climate-related information, based on the recommendations (FSB, 2017) of the industry-led Task Force on Climate-related

Financial Disclosures (TCFD),[30] supported by the Financial Stability Board (FSB).[31] The TCFD has not provided processes on how to take account of unintended social consequences or minimum social safeguards. Rather than only strengthening the climate-related guidelines, the EC could also have strengthened those on the social aspects, not least because the EU has introduced another law that requires investors to report on not only climate or environmental risks, but also social risks and governance aspects, as explained further subsequently.

The European Parliament and ECOFIN decided to improve the corporate disclosures and require that all large financial and non-financial companies should provide more information about how their activities are environmentally sustainable as defined and regulated according to the taxonomy law. Article 8 of the final Taxonomy Regulation text of 18 June 2020 requires[32] those companies to disclose:

1. the proportion of their turnover derived from environmentally sustainable economic activities
2. the proportion of their total capital and/or operating expenditures related to environmentally sustainable economic activities.

14.3   THE INTEGRATED APPROACH

There are many arguments for going beyond the EU's minimal approach of doing no harm to social aspects when incentivising and clarifying the private financial sector's contribution in reversing climate change. Citizens need to have the means and be empowered to adapt their energy, consumption and lifestyle patterns to sustainable

---

[30] FSB, About the Task Force, web page at: www.fsb-tcfd.org/about.

[31] FSB, Climate-related Financial Disclosures, web page at: www.fsb.org/work-of-the-fsb/policy-development/additional-policy-areas/climate-related-financial-disclosures.

[32] European Union, Regulation 2020/852 of 18 June 2020, Article 8: amending NFRD through the related Directive 2013/34/EU of 26 June 2013 on the annual financial statements, consolidated financial statements and related reports of certain types of undertakings.

levels. Official climate change mitigation policies will need to take into account that integrating climate and environmental externalities might well result in higher costs. The arguments for a 'just transition' aim at ensuring that the transition towards climate-friendly (energy) production and consumption are not too burdensome on people who have not caused climate change and do not have the means to bear the costs of an energy transition, for example in their housing and transport. The nation-wide protest of the 'yellow vests' in France and in Ecuador[33] against the increase of petrol and energy prices, for instance, show how poverty, growing inequality and neglect of remote regions can halt measures against climate change.

Accelerating the financing of activities and companies with improved positive social impacts are likely to result in more popular support for climate change mitigating corporate strategies, government policies and innovative citizens' initiatives. Protests and popular or populist movements around the world against rising inequality, poverty, poor wages, basic human rights violations, gender and race discrimination, corruption and related migration, derail efforts and political will to tackle climate change. They are often symptoms of structural social problems that need to be addressed and integrated in a just transition strategy. Ensuring that developing countries can finance measures that prevent climate change and adapt to new climate circumstances are imperative for a global approach against climate change. In the private sector, this could include high social standards and equitable distribution of profits and benefits throughout the value chains of products from developing countries. For instance, the low salaries, exploitative social practices, land grabbing and corruption by palm oil companies in Indonesia has resulted in palm oil being so cheap and included in so many consumption products. In turn, more and more forest and peatland are slashed and

---

[33] See Borja Cornejo (2019): Rural poverty rates increased from 38.2 per cent in December 2016 to 43.8 per cent in June 2019, and poverty in the capital increased from 7.9 per cent in June 2016 to 11.9 per cent in 2019.

burned for palm cultivation, which increases CO_2 emissions and deforestation. The shares of large palm oil-growing companies are being included in many investment funds around the world (Vander Stichele, 2018). However, the 'No Deforestation, No Peat, No Exploitation (NDPE)' sourcing policies by major palm oil refiners and processors has led to the suspension of supply by large palm oil-growing companies, whose annual profits and equity value have declined since (see Chain Reaction Research, 2019).

The private financial sector can play an important role to better integrate both social and environmental, and governance, issues. In general, the primacy of shareholder value and the importance of short-term corporate profitability for the investment fund industry has resulted in high pressure to reduce labour costs throughout the value chains, including flex labour and jobs without social security or living wages. Indeed, a company that cuts its labour force costs often sees its share value going up. Banks and investors who want to ensure that living wages and respect for human rights are guaranteed in all the climate-friendly activities they are financing will face challenges because such information is not readily available and has not been requested or received from all borrowers or investees. Moreover, information received from companies might be costly to check on the ground. The EU's Regulation on disclosure of ESG risk assessment by investors might incentivise the investment industry to integrate social aspects in 'green' investments.

14.4 AN ESG DISCLOSURE REGULATION: WHAT ABOUT THE 'S'?

Despite the fact that the EC proposed that the taxonomy and the benchmark laws should focus on climate and environmental matters, it proposed also a law that requires that the investment industry be transparent about not only the environmental but also social and governance (ESG) risks and impacts. This means that green investment products based on the taxonomy and the climate-related benchmarks will have to report on the environmental as well as the social and governance issues.

The European Parliament and the Council agreed on 18 April 2019[34] to introduce the new EU Regulation on 'disclosures relating to sustainable investment and sustainability risks' (DSR).[35] The Regulation requires extensive transparency on ESG issues. It covers all institutional investors, fund managers and investment advisors, with a few exceptions, and their investment products: insurance companies and insurance-based investment product, investment managers and investment fund managers, pension funds and pension products, alternative investors such as hedge funds, venture capital funds, social entrepreneurship funds and banks that provide portfolio investment and advise.[36] They have to disclose amongst others:

- Policies and the manner in which sustainability risks are being integrated into investment decision-making or advice, and if not, why not; the result of the ESG risk assessment must be described to potential investors (Articles 3 and 6). The 'sustainability risk' means an 'actual or potential material negative impact on the value of the investment' due to an ESG event or condition (Article 2.(22)).

---

[34] European Parliament Legislative resolution of 18 April 2019 on the proposal for a regulation on disclosures relating to sustainable investments and sustainability risks and amending Directive (EU) 2016/2341 (COM(2018)0354 – C8–0208/2018 – 2018/0179(COD)). www.europarl.europa.eu/doceo/document/TA-8-2019-0435_EN.html.

[35] The text of the DSR was agreed on 18 April 2019. The legally 'scrubbed' text was released on 23 October 2019 and is used for this article: The European Parliament and the Council, Regulation on disclosures relating to sustainable investments and sustainability risks and amending Directive (EU) 2016/2341, 23 October 2019, https://eur-lex.europa.eu/legal-content/EN/TXT/PDF/?uri=CONSIL:PE_87_2019_INIT&qid=1572004855709&from=EN. The final legal text was officially published in December 2019: European Union, Regulation 2019/2088 of 27 November 2019 on sustainability-related disclosures in the financial services sector, *Official Journal of the European Union*, 9 December 2019, L 317/1-26, https://eur-lex.europa.eu/legal-content/EN/TXT/PDF/?uri=CELEX:32019R2088&from=EN. The DSR has been amended by the Taxonomy Regulation as agreed on 17 December 2019 (Council of the European Union, 2019b), which has been integrated in this chapter.

[36] For the legal definitions and the EU laws by which the investors are covered, see: DSR, Preamble (4) and footnotes 1–14, Article 2.(1)–(16), 2.(18–21), and 2.(23).

- Whether or not they consider negative impacts of investment decisions on sustainability factors (Article 4). If they consider negative impacts, they must state their policies, including on due diligence and any actions taken related to the described adverse sustainability impacts. If the investment companies and advisors do not consider adverse impacts on sustainability factors, they must state why and whether they intend to consider them in the future. 'Sustainable factors' are defined as 'environmental, social and employee matters, respect for human rights, anti-corruption and bribery matters' (Articles 2.(24) and 7).

Each investment product 'with sustainability characteristics or objectives' has additional transparency obligations. The DSR distinguishes somewhat between the requirements for investment products that promote environmental or social characteristics and 'sustainable investment' products that have as an objective a positive impact on the environment and society.[37] All those ESG investment products need to disclose information as to what the environmental or social characteristics or sustainable investment objectives are, and how they are (to be) measured and attained (details on methodology, screening criteria and indicators), including when an index is used as a reference benchmark (Articles 8 and 10). Also, periodic reports are to be made available by all the institutional investors offering sustainable investment products, according to these investors' own legal reporting obligations (Article 11.2).[38]

'Sustainable investment' refers to what the Regulation defines in Article 2.(17) as an investment in an economic activity that contributes to an environmental objective or a social objective[39] and does not significantly harm any of those objectives provided that the

---

[37] DSR, Preamble, Paragraph. (17), (21).

[38] The laws referred to are: AIFM Directive 2011/61/EU, Solvency II Directive 2009/ 138/EC, IORPs II Directive (EU)2016/2341 and national private pension funds, European venture capital funds Regulation (EU) No 345/2013, European social entrepreneurship funds Regulation (EU) No 346/2013, UCITS Directive 2009/65/ EC, the MiFID II Directive 2014/65/EU and PEPP Regulation (EU)2019/1238.

[39] The mentioning of 'or a combination of any of the following' has been left out of the final legal text after 'legal scrubbing' as opposed to what was written in the text agreed by the European Parliament after the trialogue.

314 MYRIAM VANDER STICHELE

investee companies follow good governance practices, in particular with respect to sound management structures, employee relations and remuneration of staff and tax compliance. The related definition of social objectives is in particular described as contributing 'to tackling inequality', fostering 'social cohesion, social integration and labour relations' or investing in 'human capital or economically or socially disadvantaged communities'.

The definitions of DSR do not provide details of what is an ESG risk, namely an 'environmental, social or governance event or condition' that can have actual or potentially negative impact on the value of the investment (Article 2.(22)). For investment products that are short term, such ESG risks might not be substantial. Adverse negative ESG 'impacts' refers to longer-term impact on the environment and society, beyond the interest of the investor. The preamble of DSR, paragraph (18),[40] indicates that procedures for considering negative sustainability impacts might be guided by due diligence policies as developed by the OECD Due Diligence Guidance for Responsible Business Conduct (2018) and the related sectoral guidance reports (OECD, 2018) and the UN-supported Principles for Responsible Investment.[41] It does not refer to the UN Guiding Principles on Business and Human Rights (UNGP) that operationalise the UN 'protect, respect and remedy' framework for human rights. The OECD Due Diligence Guidance for Responsible Business Conduct, however, aligns with the UNGP and does cover human rights as well as employment and industrial relations, and consumer interests as regards social aspects.

---

[40] DSR, Preamble, Paragraph. (18): 'financial market participants and financial advisers should consider the due diligence guidance for responsible business conduct developed by the Organisation for Economic Co-operation and Development (OECD) and the United Nations-supported Principles for Responsible Investment.'

[41] PRI, What Are the Principles for Responsible Investment?, web page at: www.unpri .org/pri/an-introduction-to-responsible-investment/what-are-the-principles-for-responsible-investment.

The co-legislators of the Taxonomy Regulation have ensured consistency between the DSR and taxonomy laws by amending the DSR so that disclosures have to mention whether the environmental sustainability claims are according to the Taxonomy Regulation or not.[42]

Many of the details for implementing the law – the 'level 2' technical standards – have to be elaborated by the ESAs, twelve months after the DSR being into force, and ultimately decided by the EC. The DSR came into force after being officially published on 9 December 2019.[43] Note that in case negative ESG risks or impacts are disclosed, this still does not prevent institutional investors from offering, or invest in, that particular investment. Nevertheless, the whole of the mainstream financial industry has been lobbying for a delay for the full application of the DSR, because of what they argue is a too short time frame for implementing the technical standards (AFME et al., 2019; Tang, 2019). This contrasts with for instance the banks' new voluntary commitment at the same time to 'be transparent about and accountable for our positive and negative impacts and our contribution to society's goals' (Principle 6, Principles for Responsible Banking, UNEP FI, 2019).

The financial industry will have an even higher challenge if the EC implements its intention to introduce technical standards in each of the investment laws, which will require that all institutional investors actually apply, and not only disclose, ESG risk and ESG impact assessments.

14.5 CONCLUDING RECOMMENDATIONS

By promoting and legislating an improved social impact by the financial sector, the EU should be able to enhance the support for, and the capacity of, the EU to achieve its commitments to the Paris climate

---

[42] European Union, Regulation 2020/852 of 18 June 2020, Articles 5, 6, 7, 8 and 25.

[43] European Union, Regulation 2019/2088 of 27 November 2019 on sustainability-related disclosures in the financial services sector, *Official Journal of the European Union*, 9 December 2019, L317/1-16. https://eur-lex.europa.eu/legal-content/EN/TXT/PDF/?uri=CELEX:32019R2088&from=EN.

agreements as well as the UN's Sustainable Development Goals. The aim is to include all citizens, workers and employees, managers and entrepreneurs, and authorities to implement climate, environmental and social sustainable production and consumption transitions, innovations, corporate strategies and structural changes.

First, the EU should avoid an imbalance between the sustainability obligations on the investment industry and the banking sector. For instance, the EC should ask the European Banking Authority (EBA) to speed up (1) ESG disclosure requirements for all the activities of the banks, (2) the development of a uniform definition of ESG risks, to be implemented by the banking institutions for identifying, assessing and managing ESG risks as well as by supervisors including for stress testing and scenario analysis, before 28 June 2021[44] and (3) encourage the EBA to report on prudential ESG risk-weighting for capital requirements long before the legal deadline of 28 June 2025.[45]

Second, if the current cabinet of the EC wants to apply its promises that both reversing climate change and poor social conditions have to go hand in hand, it has to develop as soon as possible a taxonomy of 'socially sustainable activities'. In combination with the taxonomy on environmentally sustainable economic activities, it would also be applied to investments, lending and other financial products that are socially and environmentally sustainable and have such positive sustainable impacts, based on good governance.

---

[44] European Union Directive 2019/878 of 20 May 2019 [CRD V] amending Directive 2013/36/EU [CRD IV] as regards exempted entities, financial holding companies, mixed financial holding companies, remuneration, supervisory measures and powers and capital conservation measures, *Official Journal of the European Union*, 7 June 2019, L 150/274, Article 1 (29): related to CRD IV Article 98. (d). 8. https://eur-lex.europa.eu/legal-content/EN/TXT/PDF/?uri=CELEX:32019L0878&from=EN.

[45] European Union Regulation (EU) 2019/876 of 20 May 2019 [CRR II] amending Regulation (EU) No 575/2013 as regards the leverage ratio, the net stable funding ratio, requirements for own funds and eligible liabilities, counterparty credit risk, market risk, exposures to central counterparties, exposures to collective investment undertakings, large exposures, reporting and disclosure requirements, and Regulation (EU) No 648/2012, *Official Journal of the European Union*, 7 June 2019, L 150/216, Article 1 (135): related to Article 501c. https://eur-lex.europa.eu/legal-content/EN/TXT/PDF/?uri=CELEX:32019R0876&from=EN.

Third, to be effective, the EC will have to improve and accelerate the coherence, uniformity and the quality of the social standards and definitions in the EU's sustainable finance laws, standards, guidelines, KPIs and other regulatory or voluntary financial instruments, including related to climate and environmental financing.

There are basic minimum uniform standards and definitions that the EU should adhere to in all its sustainable legislation and initiatives, related to the financial sector and otherwise. For many of these standards, there exists already implementing instruments[46] which could inspire the development of EU social sustainability mechanisms. The basic social and human requirements should be the application of the following.

14.5.1 *The Bill of Human Rights*

Implementation should at least be based on:

- the UN International Covenant on Economic, Social and Cultural Rights;[47]
- the European Pillar of Social Rights;[48]
- the UN Guiding Principles on Business and Human Rights (UNGP);[49]
- the OECD Due Diligence Guidance for Responsible Business Conduct and its sectoral guidance for institutional investors, lending and securities underwriting.[50]

The respect for human rights should be applied by companies and their supply chains financed by banks and investors, and by the financial sector towards their customers, stakeholders and societies in which they operate.

In order to meet their responsibility to respect human rights, companies (including the financial sector) should have in place,

---

[46] See for instance: ShareAction and ACCA (2018).

[47] Office of the United Nations High Commissioner for Human Rights (1966).

[48] European Commission (2019e).

[49] Office of the United Nations High Commissioner for Human Rights (2011).

[50] For these sectoral OECD reports, see OECD, Responsible business conduct in the financial sector web page, https://mneguidelines.oecd.org/rbc-financial-sector.htm.

according to UNGP principle 15,[51] policies and processes appropriate
to their size and circumstances, including:

1. a policy commitment to meet their responsibility to respect human rights;
2. a human rights due diligence process to (i) identify and assess; (ii) prevent
   and mitigate; (iii) track implementation and results; and (iv) communicate
   about how they address their impacts on human rights;
3. processes to enable the remediation of any adverse human rights impacts
   they cause or to which they contribute.

The UN Guiding Principles on Business and Human Rights, OECD
Due Diligence Guidance for Responsible Business Conduct recognise
that it is not possible to focus on all aspects of the material impact and
risks of human rights breaches at the same time. They promote due
diligence practices and the prioritisation based on the severity (scale,
scope and inability to restore) of the negative impacts on human
rights, even if the probability is low.[52]

The application should not be limited to solely corporate management tools and KPIs, but also involve for instance engagement and an
approach that identified the causes of the human right breaches. There
should be particular attention that these policies and processes result in
concrete impact on tackling poverty and inequality, labour issues (see
below), removing (gender and race based) discrimination, protecting the
rights and inclusion of indigenous people and economically or socially
disadvantaged communities, and engagement with civil society.

14.5.2   The Eight Core ILO Labour Standards

The ILO core labour standards should be the minimum labour standards and the basis for applying labour rights, 'employee relations' and
'remuneration of staff', namely:[53]

---

[51] Office of the United Nations High Commissioner for Human Rights (2011).
[52] See Office of the United Nations High Commissioner for Human Rights (2019),
pp. 5, 32.
[53] For more explanation, see: International Labour Organization, Conventions and
Recommendations, www.ilo.org/global/standards/introduction-to-international-
labour-standards/conventions-and-recommendations/lang–en/index.htm.

1. Freedom of Association and Protection of the Right to Organise Convention, 1948 (No. 87);
2. Right to Organise and Collective Bargaining Convention, 1949 (No. 98);
3. Forced Labour Convention, 1930 (No. 29) (and its 2014 Protocol);
4. Abolition of Forced Labour Convention, 1957 (No. 105);
5. Minimum Age Convention, 1973 (No. 138);
6. Worst Forms of Child Labour Convention, 1999 (No. 182);
7. Equal Remuneration Convention, 1951 (No. 100);
8. Discrimination (Employment and Occupation) Convention, 1958 (No. 111).

Particular attention should be paid that the implementing of these ILO labour standards and all benchmarks, screening criteria, KPIs and so forth result in all workers having at least living wages, social security and decent work opportunities (which is for instance not the case for flex workers and the working poor throughout supply chains, as compared to the high remuneration of top management and the profit distribution with shareholders), protection of their health and safety, and their continued capacity to participate in the work force and in society.

14.5.3 Protection of Consumers

The protection of consumer rights should include at least matters related to:

- product safety and sustainable quality;
- advertisement, advice and labelling ethics;
- data protection, cyber security and data privacy;
- the use and impact of artificial intelligence;
- financial inclusion and avoidance of excessive indebtedness.

The consumer protection related to data, the internet of things and artificial intelligence are becoming more urgent issues whose assessment will need further development.

14.5.4 Governance Issues

Some corporate behaviour and governance issues also have important social and societal impacts, such as:

- tax evasion and avoidance strategies since they deprive governments to support, promote and subsidise activities to tackle climate change and promote sustainability;
- lobbying against regulation that strengthen ESG issues, including against sustainable finance laws, which can have long-term negative consequences for societies;
- corporate strategies of excessive competitive behaviour and abusive buying power that squeezes profit margins throughout the supply and distribution chain ('unfair trading practices');
- corruption and bribery by corporations.

14.5.5 Recommendations for Long-Term Solutions

Social standards described previously should make it easier for the EC to identify what are activities that are socially unacceptable (a 'red taxonomy'?) alongside activities that are environmentally unacceptable (a 'brown taxonomy'). The current lack of prohibition to finance activities that are clearly identified as being non-sustainable and creating climate change have resulted in a situation whereby 'green' financial products are more expensive, due to verification costs, than those that result in climate change or environmental destruction. This situation does not sufficiently discourage the continuing externalisation of ESG damage and costs, even though investment products have now to mention whether they do not align with the Taxonomy Regulation. Nor does it encourage the creation of much more 'bankable' and 'investable' sustainable and climate change mitigation and socially responsible activities, which could fill the current gap in such activities to be financed. So far, sustainable finance has remained a niche.

Respecting labour, social and human rights can be a challenge for the financial industry, given that many problems are not reported on by companies (European Commission, 2019b, pp. 73–74) and can be difficult and costly to detect on the ground, although many reports of official bodies, academics, local and international civil society organisations are publicly available. Reporting on social and human rights can involve qualitative reporting that is not easily integrated in existing computerised quantitative data-driven management and reporting processes.[54]

There are however many instruments and initiatives that include respect for human rights, such as the Dutch Banking Sector Agreement on Human Rights[55] and the Investor Alliance for Human Rights,[56] which is a voluntary endeavour to concretely contribute to respect of human rights up to remedial action. A few investors even created a 'Platform Living Wage Financials' (Braaksma, 2019).

The business models of banks and the investment industry might not be accommodative to apply instruments that prevent harm to environmental and social sustainability as well as prevent bad governance, let alone in promoting sustainable long-term impacts. For instance, the investment industry prefers large-scale investments to reduce costs, or creates investment funds with shares of hundreds or more companies in order to spread the risks and enhance profitability. Such approach makes it difficult to know what is actually happening on the ground and in companies all over the world. Nor is it conducive to finance original innovative sustainability initiatives that are often small, by non-listed companies or might need experimentation that is financially risky. Schoenmaker and Schramade (2018) therefore advise that investors should concentrate on much fewer companies, whose activities and managements they closely monitor and with whom they actively engage to assess and improve their transition to and impact on ESG factors.

The EU can improve the quality of the standards being applied throughout the financial industry by ensuring that sustainability ratings, and all providers of sustainability or ESG ratings, are clearly

---

[54] See for instance the new sustainable business accounting standards by the Sustainability Accounting Standards Board (SASB, 2019), the social capital and human capital dimensions are quite weak.

[55] See, Dutch Banking Sector Agreement at www.imvoconvenanten.nl/en/banking.

[56] See https://investorsforhumanrights.org/what-we-do.

regulated by legally binding sustainability standards, need to be registered and are duly supervised.

The financial industry's lack of will to reorient much more financing and financial products towards environmentally and socially sustainable activities also results from fears that the costs of detailed ESG impact assessment processes and the internalisation of environmental and previously described social factors might result in the EU financial industry becoming less competitive towards its competitors, at least in the short term and during the transition period. This relates to a structural problem that the EU could deal with by introducing clear and coherent sustainability standards and laws to be applied by all financial actors operating in the EU, as well as incorporating these binding standards in services trade and investment treaties that the EU negotiates around the world. This would create the enabling environment for changing the business models of the banking and investment industry so that they have positive impacts on the climate, and the environmental and social challenges of society. The European Commission could integrate the above recommendations in its renewed sustainable finance strategy (2020-2024).

REFERENCES

ActionAid (2018), 'Human Rights in Wind Turbine Supply Chains – Towards a Truly Sustainable Energy Transition', January. www.somo.nl/nl/wp-content/uploads/sites/2/2018/01/Final-ActionAid_Report-Human-Rights-in-Wind-Turbine-Supply-Chains.pdf.

(The) Association for Financial Markets in Europe (AFME), the Alternative Investment Management Association (AIMA), the Association of Mutual Insurers and Insurance Cooperatives in Europe (AMICE), the European Association of Cooperative Banks (EACB), the European Banking Federation (EBF), the European Fund and Asset Management Association (EFAMA), Insurance Europe and Pensions Europe (2019), 'Application Date of the Regulation on Sustainability Disclosures', Letter to O. Guersant, Director General to DG FISMA, European Commission, 19 September. https://insuranceeurope.eu/sites/default/files/attachments/Joint%20letter%20on%20regulation%20on%20sustainability%20disclosures.pdf.

Borja Cornejo, D. (2019), 'Ecuador: Brutal Economic Decisions ("paquetazo")', 11 October. www.cadtm.org/Ecuador-Brutal-economic-decisions-paquetazo.

Braaksma, J. (2019), 'Financiële sector zet leefbaar loon op agenda van bedrijven', Het Financiële Dagblad, 10 October.

Business and Human Rights Resource Centre (2016), 'Towards Responsible Renewable Energy – With Rising Allegations of Abuse, Are 50 Wind and Hydropower Companies' Human Rights Policies Fit for Purpose?', Briefing Note, November. www.business-humanrights.org/sites/default/files/Towards %20Responsible%20Renewable%20Energy%20Briefing%20-%20Final_1.pdf.

Chain Reaction Research (2019), 'Palm Oil Growers Suspended over Deforestation Lose US$1.1bn in Equity Value', 30 August. https://chainreactionresearch.com/ report/palm-oil-growers-suspended-over-deforestation-lose-usd-usd-1-1b-in-equity-value.

Choidas, E., Cunha, L. and Owens, R. (2019), 'Human Rights and Green Finance: Friends or Foes?', Euractiv, 22 August. www.euractiv.com/section/energy-envir onment/opinion/human-rights-and-green-finance-friends-or-foes.

Climate Bonds Initiative (2019), 'Green Bonds: The State of the Market 2018', March. www.climatebonds.net/resources/reports/green-bonds-state-market-2018.

Council of the European Union (2019a), 'Proposal for a Regulation on the Establishment of a Framework to Facilitate Sustainable Investment – Mandate for Negotiations with the European Parliament', 23 September. https://data .consilium.europa.eu/doc/document/ST-12360-2019-ADD-1/en/pdf.

Council of the European Union (2019b), 'Proposal for a Regulation on the Establishment of a Framework to Facilitate Sustainable Investment – Approval of the Final Compromise Text', 17 December. https://data.consilium .europa.eu/doc/document/ST-14970-2019-ADD-1/en/pdf.

Dumas, A. (2019), 'Leaving Carbon Behind: Ursula von der Leyen Wants to Create a Just Energy Transition Fund for the EU', 13 August, published by Novetic. www.novethic.com/sustainable-finance/isr-rse/leaving-carbon-behind-ursula-von-der-leyen-wants-to-create-a-just-energy-transition-fund-for-the-eu-147592.html.

European Commission (2014), 'Directive 2014/95/EU of 22 October 2014 Amending Directive 2013/34/EU as Regards Disclosure of Non-financial and Diversity Information by Certain Large Undertakings and Groups', *Official Journal of the European Union*, 15 November. https://eur-lex.europa.eu/legal-content/EN/TXT/?uri=CELEX%3A32014L0095.

European Commission (2017), 'Guidelines on Non-financial Reporting (Methodology for Reporting Non-financial Information)', (2017/C 215/01),

Official Journal of the European Union, 5 July. https://eur-lex.europa.eu/legal-content/EN/TXT/?uri=CELEX%3A52017XC0705(01).

European Commission (2018a), 'Technical expert group on sustainable finance – Overview', web page at: https://ec.europa.eu/info/publications/sustainable-financetechnical-expert-group_en.

European Commission (2018b), 'Commission Action Plan on Financing Sustainable Growth', March. https://ec.europa.eu/info/publications/180308-action-plan-sustainable-growth_en.

European Commission (2018c), 'Proposal for a Regulation on the Establishment of a Framework to Facilitate Sustainable Investment', May. https://eur-lex.europa.eu/legal-content/EN/TXT/PDF/?uri=CELEX:52018PC0353&from=EN.

European Commission (2019b), 'EU Technical Expert Group on Sustainable Finance: Taxonomy Technical Report', June. https://ec.europa.eu/info/sites/info/files/business_economy_euro/banking_and_finance/documents/190618-sustainable-finance-teg-report-taxonomy_en.pdf.

European Commission (2019c) 'Technical Expert Group on EU Green Bond Standard', June. https://ec.europa.eu/info/files/190618-sustainable-finance-teg-report-green-bond-standard_en.

European Commission (2019d), 'International Platform on Sustainable Finance', October. https://ec.europa.eu/info/business-economy-euro/banking-and-finance/sustainable-finance/international-platform-sustainable-finance_en.

European Commission (2019e), 'European Pillar of Social Rights, Proclamation', November. https://ec.europa.eu/commission/priorities/deeper-and-fairer-economic-and-monetary-union/european-pillar-social-rights_en.

European Commission (2019f), 'Answers to the European Parliament Questionnaire to the Commissioner-Designate Valdis Dombrovskis'. https://ec.europa.eu/commission/commissioners/sites/comm-cwt2019/files/commissioner_ep_hearings/answers-ep-questionnaire-dombrovskis.pdf.

European Parliament (2019), 'Legislative Resolution of 28 March 2019 on the Proposal for a Regulation of the European Parliament and of the Council on the Establishment of a Framework to Facilitate Sustainable Investment'. www.europarl.europa.eu/doceo/document/TA-8-2019-0325_EN.html?redirect.

Financial Stability Board Task Force on Climate-related Financial Disclosures (2017), 'Final Report: Recommendations of the Task Force on Climate-related Financial Disclosures', June. www.fsb-tcfd.org/publications/final-recommendations-report.

Hodal, K. (2019), '"Most Renewable Energy Companies" Linked with Claims of Abuses in Mines', *The Guardian*, 5 September 2019. www.theguardian.com/global-development/2019/sep/05/most-renewable-energy-companies-claims-mines.

IMF (2019), 'Global Financial Stability Report', October. www.imf.org/en/Publications/ GFSR/Issues/2019/10/01/global-financial-stability-report-october-2019.

Nazalya, S. (2019), 'Human Rights Cast Shadow over Green Energy's Clean Image', 14 October. Verisk Maplecroft. www.maplecroft.com/insights/analysis/human-rights-cast-shadow-over-green-energys-clean-image.

Obulutsa, G. (2016), 'Kenyan Wind Power Project Cancelled due to Land Disputes', Reuters, 23 February. www.reuters.com/article/kenya-electricity/kenyan-wind-power-project-cancelled-due-to-land-disputes-idUSL8N1620QG.

OECD (2018), 'Due Diligence Guidance for Responsible Business Conduct'. http:// mneguidelines.oecd.org/OECD-Due-Diligence-Guidance-for-Responsible-Business-Conduct.pdf.

Office of the United Nations High Commissioner for Human Rights (1966), 'International Covenant on Economic, Social and Cultural Rights', 16 December. www.ohchr.org/en/professionalinterest/pages/cescr.aspx.

Office of the United Nations High Commissioner for Human Rights (2011), 'UN Guiding Principles on Business and Human Rights'. www.ohchr.org/docu ments/publications/GuidingprinciplesBusinesshr_eN.pdf.

Office of the United Nations High Commissioner for Human Rights (2019), 'Benchmarking Study of Development Finance Institutions' Safeguards and Due Diligence Frameworks Against the UN Guiding Principles on Business and Human Rights', Published Draft, September 2019. www.ohchr.org/Documents/ Issues/Development/DFI/OHCHR_Benchmarking Study_HRDD.pdf.

Schoenmaker, D. and Schramade, W. (2018) *Principles of Sustainable Finance*, Oxford University Press.

ShareAction and Association of Chartered Certified Accountants (2018), 'Human Rights Metrics: Reaching Scale through the Sustainable Finance Agenda', September. https:// shareaction.org/wp-content/uploads/2018/10/18.09.25-EuropeanEventReport.pdf.

SIFMA (2018), 'SIFMA Fact Book 2018'. www.sifma.org/wp-content/uploads/2017/ 08/US-Fact-Book-2018-SIFMA.pdf.

Sustainability Accounting Standards Board (2019), 'Materiality Map'. https:// materiality.sasb.org.

Tang, P. (2019), 'Practise What You Preach: Banks Should Endorse the Sustainability Practices They Publicly Support', Euractiv, 7 October. https:// www.euractiv.com/section/economy-jobs/opinion/practise-what-you-preach-banks-should-endorse-the-sustainability-practices-they-publicly-support/.

United Nations Conference on Environment and Development (1992), 'The Rio Declaration on Environment and Development', June. www.unesco.org/educa tion/pdf/RIO_E.pdf.

United Nations (2019), '30 Business Titans Join UN Push to Scale Up Private Sector Investment for Sustainable Development', Press release, 16 October. www.un.org/sustainabledevelopment/blog/2019/10/gisd-alliance.

United Nations Environmental Programme Finance Initiative (2019), 'Principles for Responsible Banking', September. www.unepfi.org/banking/bankingprinciples.

Vander Stichele, M. (2015), 'Mobilising the Financial Sector for a Sustainable Future', SOMO, October. https://www.somo.nl/mobilising-the-financial-sector-for-a-sustainable-future/.

Vander Stichele, M. (2018), 'Investment Funds – The Untold Story about the Link between Dutch Banks and Industrial Palm Oil Companies', October. www.somo.nl/wp-content/uploads/2018/10/Rapport-Palmolie-web.pdf.

Vander Stichele, M. (2019), 'A Legal Framework for an EU definition', SOMO Newsletter – EU Financial Reforms, 27 September (updated version). www.somo.nl/an-eu-definition-of-green-finance-in-the-making.

Von der Leyen, U. (2019), 'A Union That Strives for More – My Agenda for Europe – Political Guidelines for the Next European Commission 2019–2024'. https://ec.europa.eu/commission/sites/beta-political/files/political-guidelines-next-commission_en.pdf.

Index

AAK case study 201
Active fund 214–215, 220
Alecta 196, 211
Asian Development Bank 37
Asian Infrastructure Investment Bank 37

Bank notes 52, 57
Bank of England 7, 52, 56–57, 62–63, 70, 98, 122, 125, 137
Basel 59, 65–67, 76, 79, 81, 83, 88, 99, 124
Basel Committee on Banking Supervision 78, 84
BlackRock 80, 197, 269–270
Bogel, 'Jack' 216–217
Brown Penalising Factor 77, 98–99

Cambridge Centre for Risk Studies 125
Cambridge Institute for Sustainability Leadership 4
Capital Asset Pricing Model 215
Capital Requirements Directive/Regulation 77, 79
Carbon bubble 6
Carbon Disclosure Project 23
Carbon pricing 6, 22
Carbon Trust (The) 57
Carney, Mark 7, 54, 98
Climate Bonds Initiative 4
Climate Governance Principles 151
Conference of the Parties (COP) 21, Paris, 2015 6, 26, 42–44, 46–47, 84, 88, 91, 105, 118, 181, 183, 186, 229, 234–235, 237–239, 241, 247, 249, 251, 263, 267, 273, 281, 299–301, 315

Disclosure 46, 63, 66, 76, 81, 85, 87, 90–91, 93, 98, 114, 127, 140, 151, 160, 175, 185, 191, 203, 209–210, 212, 229, 240, 254, 259, 311, 316
Discount factor 2
Dombrovskis, Valdis 301

Ecolabel 116, 120, 295
EIB 36, 43, 253
Electrolux case study 200
Ellen MacArthur Foundation 27
ESG indexes 222, 232–233
EU Action Plan on Financing Sustainable Growth 28, 66, 89, 105, 110, 116, 118, 153, 155, 161, 209–211, 229, 253, 258, 274, 276, 299, 301
EU Economic and Financial Affairs Council (ECOFIN) 93, 302, 304, 309
EU green taxonomy 45–46, 66, 85, 89–91, 94, 115, 229, 253, 259, 268, 302–309, 311, 315–316, 320
EU Observatory on Sustainable Finance 44–45
Europe's Climate Bank 43
European Bank for Reconstruction and Development 39
European Banking Authority 88–89, 99, 316
European Banking Federation 66, 91–92
European Central Bank 7, 52, 58–59, 149, 254
European Insurance and Occupational Pensions Authority 7, 89–90, 92
European Investment Advisory Hub 39
European Investment Bank 39, 43, 252
European Political Strategy Centre 29
European Securities and Markets Authority 119
European Sustainable Investment Forum (Eurosif) 108, 111–112, 115
Expert Support Facility 36
Extinction Rebellion 8, 238

Facebook 203
Fiduciary duty 7, 10, 16, 18, 68, 90, 94, 119, 168, 172–173, 175, 180, 188–190, 193, 197, 201–203, 210, 230, 249
Financial Conduct Authority 68
Financial literacy 104, 106–107
Financial stability 7, 22, 46, 50–52, 54–55, 58, 61–63, 66, 69, 71, 85, 125, 128, 141, 148, 168, 309

Financial Stability Board 7, 98, 141, 148–149, 308
Fonds de Réserve pour les Retraites (FRR) 271–273
French Law on Energy Transition for Green Growth 140, 184, 273
French retirement system 270
FTSE4Good Global Index 222, 227

G20 Green Finance Study Group 122, 142
Governance 3, 10, 16, 37, 45, 61, 63, 67–68, 89, 91–92, 95, 108, 133, 145–146, 148–149, 151–152, 154–156, 159, 161, 164, 166, 168, 172–174, 177–178, 189, 199, 203, 206, 209, 219, 222, 224, 239, 247, 258–260, 267, 299, 305, 308–309, 311–312, 314, 316, 319, 321
Great Financial Crisis 2, 49
Green Bond Standard 116, 307
Green bonds 3, 37, 116, 184, 306, 308
Green Deal for Europe 43
Green Economy Financing Facility 39
Green Finance Taskforce 29
Green Investment Bank 35, 37, 44
Green Supporting Factor 66, 100

High-Level Expert Group on Sustainable Finance 28–29, 38, 44–45, 68, 88, 107, 116, 118, 174, 229, 239, 259, 267
High-Level Political Forum 21
HSBC UK Pension Fund case study 231

Independent Financial Advisors 68
Inside-out data 224
Institutions for Occupational Retirement Provision Directive 77, 79, 94
Insurance Supervision 63, 85
Internal Capital Adequacy Assessment Process 77, 98
International Association of Insurance Supervisors 79, 86–87
International Capital Standard 79
International Corporate Governance Network 148, 154–157, 159–161
International Development Finance Club 40–42, 44
International Labour Organization 241, 243, 303, 305, 318–319
International Organisation of Pension Supervisors 79, 87–88, 185

International Organisation of Securities Commissions 23, 185
International Panel on Climate Change 50
Investment gap 26, 28

Just Transition 10, 237–242, 244, 246–254, 258, 301, 310

The Kay Review 218

Labels 111–113, 117, 258, 265–269
Legal risk 133, 137
Leyen, Ursula von der 43, 252, 300
Liquidity risk 59, 76

Macron, Emmanuel 270
Market failure 7, 15, 18–19, 54
Markets in Financial Instruments Directive 17, 68, 119, 153, 183
Mizuno, Hiro 232
Model Mandate 154
Monetary policy 55
Monetary stability 52, 56–57
MSCI data 186, 188, 203, 221–222, 227
Multi-stakeholder Dialogue on environmental Claims 288, 290, 298
Mystery shopping 279–280

De Nederlandsche Bank 127, 130, 137, 147, 150
Network for Greening the Financial System 7, 70, 84, 142, 184, 254
New Climate Economy 10, 26, 243
Novethic 112, 265–266, 273

Ofgem 29
One Planet Summit 40, 44, 84
Organisation for Economic Co-operation and Development 79, 155–156, 202, 240, 243, 303, 305, 314, 317–318
Outside-in data 225
Own Risk and Solvency Assessment 77, 91–93, 98

Pacte law (France) 270
Passive fund 215
Pension Funds 87, 90, 177
Pension supervision 87, 89
PensionsEurope 94
People's Bank of China 57, 122, 184

Performance benchmark 218, 220
Physical risk 132
Pope Francis 8, 237
Principal–agent problems 198
Principles for Responsible Investment 7, 51,
    148, 168, 170, 172–173, 175–176,
    186–191, 193, 223, 247, 263, 272
Private Finance for Energy Efficiency
    Initiative 36
Private Finance Initiative 38
Project Bond Credit Enhancement 36–37
Prudential Regulation Authority (UK) 7, 53,
    63, 67, 125, 133, 150–151
Prudential supervision 54, 63, 75, 77, 85, 88,
    98

Quantitative easing 53, 58–60

Renewable energy 34
Retail investors 68, 70, 110, 116, 154, 267,
    269, 274, 277, 280–282, 292, 295
Rio Declaration 299
Risk management 3, 60, 66–67, 76–77, 81–82,
    87–88, 90–93, 95, 97–99, 123,
    126–127, 129, 131, 133, 138, 140, 142,
    150, 188, 204, 209, 224, 230, 254, 272

Senior Managers Regime 67, 150
Smart beta 214, 221–222, 230–231
Smart sustainability 214, 229, 232
Solvency II 77, 79, 83, 90–93, 183
Sovereign Wealth Funds 22, 61
Spain – photovoltaic energy 32
Stern, Nick
    The Stern Review 19, 35, 54, 240–241,
    244
Stewardship 145, 148, 154, 156, 158–160, 176,
    191, 198, 232–233, 246
Stranded assets 62
Stress testing 90–91, 98, 128, 130, 134, 211,
    316
Super Storm Sandy, New York 64

Supervisory Review and Evaluation Process
    88
Sustainable and Responsible Investment
    104–105, 108–114, 117, 264, 266–268,
    272, 284
Sustainable Insurance Forum 7, 86–87, 264,
    266

Task Force on Climate-related Financial
    Disclosures 7, 23–24, 46, 60, 63, 70,
    86, 91, 141, 161, 209–210, 240, 251,
    309
Technical Expert Group 89–90
Three lines of defence 82
Thunberg, Greta 238
Tilted indexes 228, 233
Tragedy of the Horizon 54, 98
Transition Pathway Initiative 234
Transition risk 3, 91, 135
Transparency Code 112
Trump, President Donald 238

UK Committee on Climate Change
    9, 246
UN Secretary General 27
UN Sustainable Development Goals 3, 7,
    20–21, 26, 46, 164, 183, 186, 249, 300,
    305, 316
Unfair Commercial Practices Dir,
    ective 287–288
United Nations 3, 6, 27, 51, 169, 172, 238
United Nations Environmental Programme
    Finance Initiative 51, 169, 172–173,
    189, 193, 315
US dust bowls 50

Valley of death 30, 33
Value-at-Risk 19, 83

Wildfires 8
World Economic Forum 51–52, 151
World Wildlife Fund 273–274

Printed in the United States
By Bookmasters